Uncle John's
TRUE
CRIME

By the
Bathroom Readers'
Institute

Bathroom Readers' Press
Ashland, Oregon

UNCLE JOHN'S TRUE CRIME

Articles in this edition have been included from the following books: *Uncle John's Ultimate
Bathroom Reader* © 1996; *Uncle John's Giant 10th Anniversary Bathroom Reader* © 1997;
Uncle John's Great Big Bathroom Reader © 1998; *Uncle John's Absolutely Absorbing Bathroom
Reader* © 1999; *Uncle John's All-Purpose Extra Strength Bathroom Reader* © 2000; *Uncle John's
Supremely Satisfying Bathroom Reader* © 2001; *Uncle John's Ahh-Inspiring Bathroom Reader*
© 2002; *Uncle John's Unstoppable Bathroom Reader* © 2003; *Uncle John's Bathroom Reader
Plunges Into Great Lives* © 2003; *Uncle John's Bathroom Reader Plunges Into the Presidency*
© 2004; *Uncle John's Bathroom Reader Plunges Into Texas* © 2004; *Uncle John's Slightly
Irregular Bathroom Reader* © 2004; *Uncle John's Bathroom Reader Plunges Into History Again*
© 2004; *Uncle John's Fast-Acting Long-Lasting Bathroom Reader* © 2005; *Uncle John's
Curiously Compelling Bathroom Reader* © 2006; *Uncle John's Bathroom Reader Wonderful
World of Odd* © 2006; *Uncle John's Bathroom Reader Plunges Into Minnesota* © 2006; *Uncle
John's Tales to Inspire* © 2006; *Uncle John's Bathroom Reader Plunges Into Music* © 2007;
Uncle John's Triumphant 20th Anniversary Bathroom Reader © 2007; *Uncle John's Bathroom
Reader Plunges Into Ohio* © 2007; *Uncle John's Bathroom Reader Takes a Swing at Baseball*
© 2008; *Uncle John's Unsinkable Bathroom Reader* © 2008; *Uncle John's Certified Organic
Bathroom Reader* © 2009; *Uncle John's Endlessly Engrossing Bathroom Reader* © 2009;
Uncle John's Heavy Duty Bathroom Reader © 2010; *Uncle John's Bathroom Reader Plunges Into
Canada* © 2010; *Uncle John's Bathroom Reader History's Lists* © 2010; *Uncle John's Bathroom
Reader The World's Gone Crazy* © 2010; *Uncle John's Bathroom Reader Plunges Into New York*
© 2011. *Uncle John's Bathroom Reader Tunes Into TV* © 2011.

For information, write:
The Bathroom Readers' Institute, P.O. Box 1117, Ashland, OR 97520
www.bathroomreader.com • 888-488-4642

Cover design by Michael Brunsfeld, San Rafael, CA (*Brunsfeldo@comcast.net*)

ISBN-13: 978-1-60710-178-9 / ISBN-10: 1-60710-178-5

Library of Congress Cataloging-in-Publication Data

Uncle John's true crime.
    p. cm.
ISBN 978-1-60710-318-9 (pbk.)
1. Crime—Miscellanea. 2. Criminals—Miscellanea. I. Bathroom Readers' Institute
(Ashland, Or.)
 HV6251.U53 2011
 364.1092'2—dc23

2011029580

Printed in the United States of America
First Printing: October 2011
1 2 3 4 5 15 14 13 12 11

THANK YOU!

*The Bathroom Readers' Institute sincerely thanks
the people whose advice and assistance
made this book possible.*

Gordon Javna

Jay Newman

Amy Miller

Brian Boone

Kim Griswell

John Dollison

Thom Little

Michael Brunsfeld

Angela Kern

James Greene, Jr.

Dan Mansfield

JoAnn Padgett

Melinda Allman

Sydney Stanley

Monica Maestas

Annie Lam

Lilian Nordland

Ginger Winters

David Cully

Mustard Press

Erin Corbin

Publishers Group West

Raincoast Books

Felix the Crime Dog

Thomas Crapper

*...and the many writers,
editors, and other contributors
who have helped make
Uncle John the bathroom
fixture he is today.*

CONTENTS

Because the BRI understands your reading needs, we've divided the contents by length as well as subject.

Short—a quick read
Medium—2 to 3 pages, but still brief
Long—for those extended visits, when something a little more involved is required
*Extended—for those leg-numbing experiences

INTRODUCTION

GREETINGS TO OUR PARTNERS IN CRIME
Here at the Bathroom Readers' Institute, we consider ourselves first and foremost to be storytellers. And few types of stories pack a punch like those in the "true crime" genre: There are villains, victims, and heroes, and the stakes are always high—often a matter of life and death. To that end, we scoured our entire *Bathroom Reader* catalog—more than 100 books spanning 25 years—to bring you the very best "Law and Order" stories that have ever graced our pages.

Some are short, like this odd headline: "Crack Found in Man's Buttocks." Some are long, like the story of the mysterious disappearance of Judge Joseph Crater in 1930. And since we first wrote about the judge more than a decade ago, new details have emerged that may finally solve the mystery. We've added that update, as well as a few others. Plus you'll find some new articles—including how to join the Japanese Mafia (a.k.a the Yakuza), and a chilling page of quotations by serial killers.

And this being a *Bathroom Reader*, you know you're also going to find a rogues' gallery of weird and blunderful stories to laugh at. (Our favorite: one about the toothless man who stole a toothbrush.) So let the perp walk commence. Here's what's in store for you in *Uncle John's True Crime*:

• **Masterminds:** New York City's "Mad Bomber," Britain's "Unabashed Bandit" Ronnie Biggs, and the "Terror of La Porte" Belle Gunness

• **Not-so-Masterminds:** Bungling bank robbers, stupid smugglers, 9-1-1 numbskulls, and the dumb crook who tried to shoplift some CDs from a Walmart…while he was dressed up as Superman

• **It's a Mob, Mob, Mob, Mob World:** Wiseguys who ain't so wise, how to talk like a mobster, where's Jimmy Hoffa, and beware the Godmother

• **Crime and History:** How stealing the *Mona Lisa* turned it into the world's most famous painting, how a botched bank robbery marked the beginning of the end of Jesse James, and how the schizophrenic notions of a house painter led to America's first presidential assassination attempt

• **The Long Arm:** A crime-fighting ape, the story of the TV show *Cops*, the origin of Canada's Mounties, and the D.C. police officer who brought a gun to a snowball fight

• **Prison Life:** The "Queen of the Jail" who helped the Biddle Boys escape, the "Lady of the Lockup" who helped countless convicts change their ways, strange prison food, and some too-weird-to-be-true (but they are) prisoner lawsuits

• **International Intrigue:** Canadian ganglands, the Beijing Tea Scam, Somali pirates, and a murderous Norwegian "death metal" band

• **Lifestyles of the Rich and Infamous:** The celebrity murder that rocked Hollywood…in 1921, Johnny Cash's captive audience, the story behind the rap song "Cop Killer," and the hard-boiled tale of a P.I.-turned-writer named Dashiell Hammett—whose razor-sharp prose pierced the dreary city like a thousand daggers waiting inside a thousand dark closets for a thousand dames to hang up a thousand coats (or something like that).

While you let that last sentence sink in, we'll make a quick getaway. But first, Uncle John would like to put out an APB on our gallant gang of writers, editors, researchers, and designers—including G-man Javna, AmyK-47, Ain't-no-Angel Angie, Boom-Boom Brunsfeld, and Noodles Newman.

So whether you're a cop on a bathroom break, a convict doing hard time, or just a regular "crumb" (see page 54) who likes a good yarn, get ready for some pulpy *non*fiction fun.

And as always…

Go with the Flow!

—**Uncle John, Felix the Crime Dog,
and the BRI Staff**

TOYS ABOVE THE LAW

Proof that it's never too early to start learning about True Crime.

UZI WATER GUN. "The look! The feel! The sound! So real!" Banned in 1990, this line of squirt guns—which included RPGs, AK-47s, and Berettas—looked so much like the real things that police officials throughout the U.S. lobbied to have them discontinued.

TAMAHONAM. This toy from Hong Kong has Mob connections. Instead of "feeding" this digital pet like you would a virtual dog or cat, you provide Tamahonam with cigarettes, booze, and weapons so he can, says the packaging, "go out and wage turf wars."

ROGER CLEMENS PRISON ACTION FIGURE. The former major league pitcher is posed in his windup, but instead of a baseball uniform, the indicted steroid user and perjury committer is dressed in an orange prison jumpsuit. Says the packaging: "Once he was destined for Cooperstown. Because of Clemens's false bravado and obsession with his image, though, he now seems headed for jail instead. Get yours today!"

"LETTER BOMB." Sold in the Philippines, this game lets kids "have fun and become a terrorist!" Each kid gets his or her own "airmail envelope." They write their "victim's" name on it, clap on the envelope, and then give it to the victim. In seven seconds, one of the envelopes "explodes." That player is the loser.

THE SWEENEY TODD RAZOR. "Your friends will think you're really sharp when you flash this authentic prop replica of the murderous singing barber's straight razor! Fashioned from real metal, the realistic reproduction is intricately detailed and arrives in a red-velour, drawstring pouch, ready for more musical mayhem in your hands!"

BRASS KNUCKLE TEETHING TOY. For the "edgy" parent. This limited-edition, handmade teething toy looks like a set of brass knuckles, but is made of finely sanded maple. So it's safe for your baby, but not for the "lil bullies buggin' him!"

The LAPD's motto, "To Serve and Protect," was coined in 1955 by Officer Joe Dorobek.

COURT TRANSQUIPS

These were actually said, word for word, in a court of law.

Clerk: Please state your name and spell your last name.
Judge: She's already been sworn.
Clerk: I'm sorry, Your Honor. She looks different.
Witness: I ate.

Q: What happened then?
A: He says, "I have to kill you because you can identify me."
Q: Did he kill you?
A: No.

Q: Have you lived in this town all your life?
A: Not yet.

"So when he woke up the next morning, he was dead?"

Q: So you were unconscious, and they pulled you from the bucket. What happened then?
A: Mr. S. gave me artificial insemination, you know, mouth-to-mouth.

A: You know, I don't know, but I mean, you know—you don't know, but you know. You know what I'm saying?
Q: Do I? No. Do I know? No.

Q: To the charge of driving wile intoxicated, how do you plead?
A: Drunk.

Plaintiff's attorney: Why do you think your home developed cracks in the walls?
Defendant's attorney: I object! The witness has no expertise in this area, there is an obvious lack of foundation.

Q: Did he pick up the dog by the ears?
A: No.
Q: What was he doing with the dog's ears?
A: Picking them up in the air.
Q: Where was the dog at this time?
A: Attached to the ears.

"Do you have any children or anything of that kind?"

Q: Well, sir, judging from your answer on how you reacted to the emergency call, it sounds like you are a man of intelligence and good judgment.
A: Thank you, and if I weren't under oath, I would return the compliment.

In cop lingo, a "muppet" is an acronym of the "most useless police person ever trained."

IS THIS BRAIN LOADED?

*Before they allow some people to buy guns, maybe
police should skip the background check and give
the applicants an IQ test. Here's why.*

• A Washington man became frustrated trying to untangle Christmas lights in his driveway and became even more frustrated when his daughter came home and drove over them. So he went inside, got his .45-caliber pistol, took it into his backyard, and fired several shots into the ground, after which he was arrested.

• A man at Dallas–Fort Worth Airport damaged a window and caused panic among passengers when he accidentally fired his hunting rifle at a security checkpoint. The gun went off while he was demonstrating to guards that it wasn't loaded.

• A 32-year-old man was treated for a gunshot wound in his thigh in a Kentucky hospital. He had accidentally shot himself, he explained, while practicing his quick draw…with a snowman.

• Daniel Carson Lewis was charged with criminal mischief, driving while intoxicated, weapons misconduct, and assault after shooting a hole in the Alaskan Pipeline north of Fairbanks. Result: 280,000 gallons of crude oil were spilled over two acres of tundra before crews could stop the leak, the worst in about 20 years. Cleanup costs were estimated at $7 million. He did it, said his brother, "just to see if he could." He faces up to 10 years in prison.

• Chaddrick Dickson, 25, was treated for wounds received while trying to get the gunpowder out of a .22-caliber bullet by holding it with pliers and smashing it on the floor. The bullet exploded, hitting him in the leg. Dickson needed the gunpowder, he said, to put in his dog's food "to make him meaner."

• To get the attention of officers in a passing police car after getting a flat tire, a man in Pretoria, South Africa, shot his gun at it. The officers didn't help him with the flat, but they did charge him with attempted murder.

"We hang the petty thieves, but appoint the great ones to public office." —Aesop

LOONEY LAWS

Believe it or not, these laws are real.

In Kentucky, it's against the law to throw eggs at a public speaker.

In Shawnee, Oklahoma, it's illegal for three or more dogs to "meet" on private property without the consent of the owner.

In Hartford, Connecticut, transporting a cadaver by taxi is punishable by a $5 fine.

In Michigan, it's illegal for a woman to cut her own hair without her husband's permission.

You can ride your bike on main streets in Forgan, Oklahoma, but it's against the law to ride it backwards.

If you tie an elephant to a parking meter in Orlando, Florida, you have to feed the meter just as if the elephant were a car.

California law forbids sleeping in the kitchen…but allows cooking in the bedroom.

It's a felony in Montana for a wife to open a telegram addressed to her husband. (It's not a crime for the husband to open telegrams addressed to his wife.)

You can gargle in Louisiana if you want to, but it's against the law to do it in public.

In Maryland it's against the law for grandchildren to marry their grandparents.

It's against the law to anchor your boat to the train tracks in Jefferson City, Missouri.

In Columbus, Montana, it's a misdemeanor to pass the mayor on the street without tipping your hat.

It's illegal to throw an onion in Princeton, Texas.

Kentucky law requires that every person in the state take a bath at least once a year.

It's against the law to pawn your wooden leg in Delaware.

TASERS debilitate people by temporarily overriding their entire nervous system.

AMERICAN CANNIBAL

In 1977 U.S. Dept. of Agriculture officials named a new dining hall after 19th-century pioneer Alferd G. Packer. The hall was renamed a few months later. Why? The officials discovered that Packer did more than just explore.

A DUBIOUS DISTINCTION

Alferd G. Packer holds a unique spot in American jurisprudence. He is the only U.S. citizen ever charged, tried, and convicted for the crime of murder and cannibalism.

Born in rural Colorado in 1847, Packer drifted into the Utah Territory, supporting himself as a small-time con artist, claiming to be an experienced "mountain man." In the fall of 1873, he persuaded 20 greenhorns in Salt Lake City to grubstake an expedition to the headwaters of the Gunnison River in Colorado Territory. He swore that the stream was full of gold and promised to lead them to it if they would finance the operation.

GOLD FEVER

With Packer leading, they plunged into the San Juan Mountains and promptly got lost. The party was near starvation when they stumbled into the winter quarters of the friendly Ute tribe. The Indians nursed them back to health, but the leader, Chief Ouray, advised them to turn back. Winter snows had blocked all trails. Ten of the party listened and returned to Utah. The other 10, still believing Packer's tales of gold-filled creeks, stayed with him.

Ouray gave them supplies and advised them to follow the river upstream for safety, but Packer ingored this counsel and plunged back into the mountains. The party split up again. Five turned back and made their way to the Los Pinos Indian Agency. Fired up with gold fever, the others continued on with their con man guide. Days later, exhausted, half frozen, and out of food, they found refuge in a deserted cabin. Most of them were now ready to give up and go back to Salt Lake City.

The exception was Alferd Packer. He was broke, and returning to Salt Lake City would cost him his grubstake. When the others fell asleep, Packer shot four of them in the head. The fifth woke and tried to defend himself, but Packer cracked his skull with the barrel of his rifle. Then, he robbed them....He also used them for food.

Three most common U.S. cop cars: Ford Crown Victoria, Chevy Impala, and Dodge Charger.

When his strength returned, he packed enough "human jerky" to get back to the Los Pinos Agency. Several miles from the agency, he emptied his pack to conceal his crime. He was welcomed by General Adams, commander of the agency, but shocked everyone by asking for whiskey instead of food. When he flashed a huge bankroll, they started asking questions.

WELL, YOU SEE, OFFICER...

Packer's explanations were vague and contradictory. First, he claimed he was attacked by natives, then he claimed that some of his party had gone mad and attacked him. On April 4, 1874, two of Chief Ouray's braves found the human remains Packer had discarded. General Adams locked him up and dispatched a lawman named Lauter to the cabin to investigate. But while Lauter was away, Packer managed to escape.

He made his way back to Utah and lived quietly for 10 years as "John Schwartze," until a member of the original party recognized him. Packer was arrested on March 12, 1884 and returned to Lake City, Colorado, for trial.

Packer claimed innocence but as the evidence against him mounted, he finally confessed. Apparently, he reveled in the attention his trial gave him and even lectured on the merits of human flesh. The best "human jerky," he said, was the meat on the chest ribs. The judge was not impressed.

"Alferd G. Packer, you no good sonofabitch, there wasn't but seven Democrats in Hinsdale County, and you done et five of 'um," he thundered. "You're gonna hang by the neck until dead!"

SAVED BY A TECHNICALITY

His lawyer appealed the decision, citing a legal loophole. The crime was committed in 1873, in the *territory* of Colorado. The trial began in 1884, in the new *state* of Colorado. The state constitution, adopted in 1876, did not address such a heinous crime, so the charge was reduced to manslaughter and Packer was sentenced to 40 years in prison. He was a model prisoner and was paroled after 16 years. Freed in 1901, he found work as a wrangler on a ranch near Denver.

On April 21, 1907, Alferd G. Packer, horse wrangler and cannibal, died quietly in his sleep.

Murders claimed more American lives during the 20th century than wars did.

THE BLACK PANTIES BANDIT STRIKES AGAIN

When it comes to disguises, crooks can be very creative. We once read about a guy who smeared his face with Vaseline before he robbed a bank, figuring the security cameras couldn't photograph him through the hazy goop (they could; he was arrested). Yes, there are some odd and outlandish thieves out there. Like the ones dressed up…

…AS UTILITY WORKERS: In 2005 the Associated Press reported that in Baltimore a group of thieves disguised as city utility workers had stolen more than 120 street light poles. They said the thieves put up orange traffic cones around their "work area" while they dismantled and made away with the 30-foot-tall, 250-pound aluminum poles. (Why would anyone steal a light pole? Police theorize that they were stealing them to sell as scrap metal.)

…AS PRIESTS: Police in Serbia said three men disguised as Orthodox Christian priests, complete with fake beards and ankle-length cossacks, entered a bank in Serbia, gave the traditional "Christ is born" greeting, then pulled shotguns out of their robes. Within minutes they had made off with more than $300,000.

…AS A CHIMPANZEE: A man walked into an EZ Mart in Garland, Texas, with a gun in his hand and a chimpanzee mask over his face. He fired one shot, took the money from the register, and fled. TV news programs in the area tried to help police by airing the surveillance video of the robbery, which clearly shows… a man in a chimpanzee mask robbing the store.

…AS SUPERHEROES: A group of young "activists" in Hamburg, Germany, showed up at a high-priced food store in April 2006. They were dressed as comic book superheroes, and they made off with several cartloads of expensive food. Police said similar robberies had taken place at other high-end supermarkets over the years, and believed they were intended as protests against inequitable income distribution. Police also

---

Originally, the Italian word *mafioso* had no criminal ties. It simply meant "suspicious of authority."

reported that the superhero robbers gave the cashier a bouquet of flowers and posed for a photograph before fleeing. Although 14 police cars and a helicopter were involved in the search, the bandits got away.

...AS COPS: At 1:30 a.m. on the night of March 18, 1990, two men disguised as cops knocked on the door of the prestigious Isabella Stewart Gardner Museum in Boston. The security guards on duty let them in and were immediately overpowered by the thieves. The not-cops made off with several paintings—a Vermeer, a Manet, and three Rembrandts, among other masterpieces—worth about $300 million. It still ranks as the largest art theft in U.S. history and has never been solved.

...AS A PAIR OF UNDERWEAR: Police in Calgary, Alberta, announced in June 2004 that they had finally caught the "Black Panties Bandit," who had robbed at least five convenience stores while wearing a black pair of women's underwear over his face as a disguise.

MORE MASKED ADVENTURERS

• In February 2006, a man in a tiger suit climbed to the top of the St. Augustine Lighthouse in Florida. Frank Feldmann, 35, an author of children's books, was protesting against child pornography on the Internet. But police couldn't understand him—the tiger suit muffled his voice. He eventually came down and was arrested.

• In December 2004, Lionel Arias, 47, of San Jose, Costa Rica, was "playing a practical joke" by wearing an Osama bin Laden mask, carrying a pellet rifle in his hand, and jumping out and scaring drivers on a narrow street near his home. He was shot twice in the stomach by a startled taxi driver. Arias recovered from his wounds; the taxi driver was not charged.

*　　*　　*

MYTH-CONCEPTION

Myth: If you think someone is an undercover cop, ask them. If they are, they have to tell you.

Truth: It's a common scene in movies: The criminal asks a suspicious character if he's a cop and avoids entrapment. No such law exists. Undercover cops are allowed to lie to protect themselves.

FILM NOIR

*Here's our tribute to some classic (and
not so classic) Hollywood movies.*

Burt Lancaster: "Why did you bolt your cabin door last night?"

Eva Bartok: "If you knew it was bolted, you must have tried it. If you tried it, you know why it was bolted."

—*The Crimson Pirate* (1952)

"My first wife was the second cook at a third-rate joint on Fourth Street."

—**Eddie Marr,**
The Glass Key (1942)

"When I have nothing to do at night and can't think, I always iron my money."

—**Robert Mitchum,**
His Kind of Woman (1951)

Guy Pearce: "All I ever wanted was to measure up to my father."

Russell Crowe: "Now's your chance. He died in the line of duty, didn't he?"

—*L.A. Confidential* (1997)

"I used to live in a sewer. Now I live in a swamp. I've come up in the world."

—**Linda Darnell,**
No Way Out (1950)

"He was so crooked he could eat soup with a corkscrew."

—**Annette Bening,**
The Grifters (1990)

"It looks like I'll spend the rest of my life dead."

—**Humphrey Bogart,**
The Petrified Forest (1936)

Rhonda Fleming: "You drinkin' that stuff so early?"

Bill Conrad: "Listen, doll girl, when you drink as much as I do, you gotta start early."

—*Cry Danger* (1951)

"You're like a leaf that the wind blows from one gutter to another."

—**Robert Mitchum,**
Out of the Past (1947)

"I've got an honest man's conscience…in a murderer's body."

—**DeForest Kelley,**
Fear in the Night (1947)

"I'd hate to take a bite out of you. You're a cookie full of arsenic."

—**Burt Lancaster,** *Sweet Smell of Success* (1957)

Fewer than 10% of criminals commit about 67% of all crimes.

TWO-TIMING

We recently read a newspaper story about an identical twin who switched places with his brother so that the brother could escape from prison. That got us wondering—how often does this happen? Answer: More often than you might think.

TWINS: Bernic Lee and Breon Alston-Currie, 19, of Durham, North Carolina

BACKGROUND: In May 2002, both brothers were being held at the Durham County jail. Bernic Lee was awaiting trial for murder, and Breon was being held on an unrelated robbery charge.

TWO-TIMING: On the day that Breon was scheduled for release, the jail's computer crashed. The guards, working from a handwritten list of inmates to be released, went to Bernic Lee's cell and asked him if he was Breon. Bernic Lee said yes. His face matched the photo on the release form (they're twins, remember) and he gave the right home address, but he didn't know Breon's Social Security number. No problem. It's not uncommon for inmates to not know their own Social Security numbers, so the jailers released him anyway.

OUTCOME: Bernic Lee spent about seven hours on the outside, then turned himself back in. He later pled guilty to second-degree murder and was sentenced to 9 to 12 years in prison. County officials never figured out whether Breon played any part in the snafu. "I have no information to believe that," says the jail's director, Lt. Col. George Naylor. "I have no information not to believe it, either."

TWINS: Carey and David Moore, 27

BACKGROUND: Both brothers were serving time in the Nebraska State Penitentiary in October 1984.

OUTCOME: One afternoon they met up in a conference room in the prison and switched clothes when nobody was looking. Afterward Carey, posing as David, was released into the prison yard. David, posing as Carey, was escorted back to Carey's cell. The ruse was exposed when Carey reported for David's kitchen duty. The kitchen supervisor realized that "David" wasn't really David and reported the incident to the guards.

Gaston Glock, who invented the Glock 17 handgun in 1982, wasn't...

WHAT HAPPENED: When confronted, the twins admitted the switch. It's doubtful that it was anything more than a prank, though, and even less likely that the brothers would have kept it up much longer—David was serving 4 to 6 years for burglary; Carey was awaiting execution on death row.

TWINS: Two 18-year-old twins living in Sweden in December 2004 (Their names were not released to the public.)

BACKGROUND: One of the brothers was serving a 10-month sentence in the Kronoberg jail for assault and robbery. Then one day the other brother came to visit. The two were indistinguishable, except for a birthmark on the incarcerated twin's body.

TWO-TIMING: The brothers were allowed a 45-minute, *unsupervised* visit. Guess what happened! They switched clothes and the one without a birthmark used an ink pen to make a fake one. When the visit ended, the brother who was serving time walked out of the jail and disappeared.

OUTCOME: For all we know, the innocent twin might have served the entire 10-month sentence for his brother, were it not for one thing: that night, he panicked at the thought of having to spend a night in jail, called for a guard, and confessed the deception. As of late December, the guilty brother was still loose, and the "innocent" one, temporarily out on bail, was facing the prospect of doing some time of his own. "He thinks he's going to walk," Warden Lars Aake Pettersson told reporters. "But that's probably not going to happen."

TWINS: Tony and Terry Litton, 19, of Cardiff, Wales

BACKGROUND: Tony was about a year into a two-year sentence for burglary when Terry came to visit him at the Cardiff prison in March 1990.

TWO-TIMING: Somehow, the brothers managed to strip down to their underwear and switch clothes in the middle of a bustling visitors room without attracting the notice of the guards. When the visit was up, Terry went back to Tony's cell and Tony walked out of the prison with the rest of the visitors.

A word of advice to identical twins: if you and your sibling plan to trade places, don't have your names tattooed to the backs of your necks. Tony and Terry did; when an inmate noticed that Tony's now read

---

…a gun expert—he was an expert in synthetic polymers.

"Terry," he alerted a guard. The twins' dad, Ken Litton, couldn't figure out why they pulled the stunt, especially since Tony was about to come up for parole anyway. "This time they've gone too far," he told reporters. "The police won't see the funny side of it."

OUTCOME: Tony was caught three days later and returned to jail to serve out his *full* sentence (no parole this time), plus extra time for the escape. Terry served some time of his own for helping him. (No word on whether they were allowed to visit each other in prison.)

TWINS: Ronald and Donald Anderson, 43, of Oxnard, California

BACKGROUND: In July 1993, "Ronald" checked himself into the county jail and began serving a six-month sentence for assaulting his estranged wife. Four days later he was arrested again, for assaulting his wife a second time. But how could he have done it if he was still in jail?

TWO-TIMING: Police checked the fingerprints of the man who'd checked himself into jail as Ronald; sure enough, it was Donald. When asked why he was serving his brother's sentence for him, Donald explained that he was better suited for jail time than Ronald was.

Donald was speaking from experience—it was the *third* time he'd gone to jail for his brother. Years earlier he had served a two-month jail sentence for Ronald in Philadelphia, and when he moved to California he did time in the Ventura County Jail for traffic tickets that Ronald had run up using Donald's driver's license. In the 1970s, Donald even shipped off to Korea for Ronald after Ronald joined the Army, and then decided he didn't want to go.

OUTCOME: For the second assault on his wife, Ronald was convicted of spousal battery, attempted murder, and robbery (he stole his wife's purse) and given the maximum sentence of 14 years in prison. He is now serving time for both of his convictions. Donald got off scot-free—apparently it's not a crime in Oxnard to do someone else's time. Today he lives in an apartment across the street from the jail. "If I could take my twin's place now, I would do it," he said.

*   *   *

"The best car safety device is a rearview mirror with a cop in it."

—**Dudley Moore**

Odds of winning if you challenge a traffic ticket in court: about 1 in 3.

POLICE BLOTTERS

Don't have a lot of time but still want to read interesting little stories?
Just check out the police blotter of your local paper.

• "A man reported a burglary around 10 p.m. Thursday after he returned home and found his 36-inch Samsung TV missing. It had been replaced with an RCA TV. Decorative items were placed around the new TV in an apparent attempt to fool him."

• "A green and gold colored bird on Southwood Drive appeared injured. It ran into the bushes when questioned by police."

• "A male was yelling and screaming obscenities in his Randolph Avenue driveway. Police reported he actually was trying to rap."

• "The glass to a snack machine in the Knott Hall commuter lounge was reported to be broken. Campus Police responded and removed all remaining snacks."

• "A 22-year-old man was arrested after allegedly ordering a stranger to fix his truck at gunpoint."

• "The mother of an adult man called police, concerned he was running with the wrong crowd."

• "Clinton Police responded quickly to an accident in the parking lot of a Dunkin' Donuts. The prompt response time is accredited to there being a squad car waiting in line at the drive-up window."

• "A woman reported that someone entered her condo, tied her shoelaces together, tilted pictures on the walls, and removed the snaps from her clothing."

• "At 11:50 p.m. police talked to four nude people seen running down Lincoln Street, and advised them not to be nude in public again."

• "A woman said she suspected someone had sabotaged her washing machine. A police investigation concluded that an unbalanced laundry load had caused the shaking."

• "Teens who dialed 9-1-1 to report that 'everything is fine' were checked on and found to be in possession of alcohol."

• "A resident called police after finding a 12-pack of toilet paper on her doorstep on Greenridge Drive, not for the first time."

The song "Midnight Rambler" by the Rolling Stones was inspired by the Boston Strangler.

THE LUDDITES: RAGE AGAINST THE MACHINE

If someone hates technology, we call him or her a Luddite. Why?
Because of a 19th-century group of machine-smashing rebels.

OH, WHAT A TANGLED WEB

The weavers and lace makers of Nottingham, England, were once some of the most respected artisans in the world. But the invention of the power loom in the late 1700s—which produced fabric much more quickly and cheaply than the hand-weavers—threatened to put them out of business. In order to survive, most of the weavers started working for miserly wages at the factories that were producing the inferior cloth that was making them obsolete. Day after day, the former weavers simmered with rage at the factory owners who appropriated their life's work…and at the machines that had helped them do it.

All of a sudden, factory looms started to mysteriously break down. At first, just a couple here and there. Then a few more. When asked what had happened, the workers would just shrug and say, "Ned Ludd did it."

BETTER OFF NED

Who was Ned Ludd? Not much is known for certain about him because most of his deeds were stretched beyond belief, but records prove that he was a real weaver who (if the accounts are true) became so angry after he received a whipping that he smashed up two knitting frames. Word spread of his revolt and before too long, other weavers followed suit.

And then the disgruntled workers got organized—they gathered late at night in private to *really* start plotting their revenge. In early 1811, they began sending menacing letters to Nottingham factory owners— signed by "General Ned Ludd"—warning of dire consequences if factory conditions and wages didn't improve. Some of the bolder Luddites, as they came to be called, even showed up in person to make their demands. Intimidated, most factory owners complied and raised wages. Those who didn't found their expensive machines smashed, by the dozens, in after-hours Luddite attacks.

APRIL SHOWERS

As the growing rebellion leaked to nearby British regions, it grew more intense. The first Luddites had been strictly nonviolent, only venting their anger on the hated machines. But in Yorkshire, the owner of Rawfolds Mill, aware of worker unrest at his factory, feared for his life. Hearing rumors about a planned attack on April 11, 1812, he hired a team of private guards. Two former weavers were killed in the clash. Seven days later, the Luddites did kill a mill owner in the region, William Horsfall.

Then it was all-out war: On April 20, an angry mob of thousands attacked Burton's Mill in Manchester. Like the Rawfolds mill owner, Burton knew trouble was coming and hired guards. They fired on the crowd and killed three men. The furious Luddites dispersed. But the next day, they returned and burned down Burton's house. In clashes with Burton's guards and the military (who rushed into the fray) at least 10 men were killed.

SQUASHED

A police crackdown ensued. Scores of leaders and rank-and-file Luddites were arrested and tried for their crimes. Many men were hanged; others were imprisoned or exiled to Australia. And with that, the uprising was over. There were sporadic outbreaks of violence, but by 1817 the Luddite movement ceased to be active in Britain. (Of course, the Luddites were right all along: The hated machines *were* making their jobs obsolete. These days, only a tiny fraction of the world's cloth is made by hand.)

*   *   *

SITTING PRETTY

Menelik II was the emperor of Ethiopia from 1889 until 1913. During his reign, he got excited by news of an invention being used in New York: Criminals were being executed with a device called an "electric chair." Eager to modernize, Menelik ordered three electric chairs. However, it wasn't until the devices arrived and were unpacked that the emperor realized they were useless for killing anyone. Why? Because at the time, Ethiopia lacked electricity. Menelik tossed two of the chairs, but frugally recycled the third by converting it into his throne.

Bipolar: Nevada is the only state that allows casino gambling...but has outlawed lotteries.

DUMB CROOKS
OF THE OLD WEST

Here's proof that stupidity is timeless (and sometimes deadly).

THE DALTON BROTHERS

In the little town of Coffeyville, Kansas, in 1890, Bob, Emmett, and Gratton Dalton, along with two other men, formed a gang of outlaws. Inspired by the exploits of their cousins the Younger Brothers—who 15 years earlier had stolen nearly half a million dollars from trains and banks with the James Gang—the Daltons pulled a few small-time robberies. But they wanted a big payoff and the fame that goes with it—and that could only come from a legendary bank heist. So they planned it all out...all wrong:

1. The Daltons aimed to rob two banks at once: Two men would rob the First National Bank, while the other three hit Condon & Co. across the street. They thought they'd get double the loot, but they only doubled their chances of getting caught.

2. Instead of traveling to another town where no one knew them, they chose Coffeyville—where everyone knew them.

3. The street in front of the banks was being repaired the day of the heist. They could have postponed it, but went ahead anyway. Now they had to hitch their horses a block away, making a clean getaway that much more difficult.

4. *Smart:* They wore disguises. *Dumb:* The disguises were wispy stage mustaches and goatees. Locals saw right through them.

The bank robberies were a disaster. The townsfolk saw the Dalton boys coming and armed themselves. The Daltons did get $20,000 from First National, but came up empty at the other bank when a teller said she couldn't open the safe. When they emerged from the banks, an angry mob was waiting for them in the street. A hail of bullets followed, killing every member except Emmett Dalton, who spent the next 15 years in prison. He emerged from the penitentiary to discover that the Dalton Gang's story had indeed been immortalized, but not as legendary outlaws...only as hapless screwups.

In 1978 the state of Florida ran classified ads in newspapers for the position of "executioner."

URBAN LEGENDS

If you're a crime buff, you've no doubt come across an urban legend or two. Here are three of the best ones we've found over the years. Are they true? Uncle John's best friend's little sister's teacher's neighbor swears they are.

THE STORY: A traveler visiting New York City meets an attractive woman in a bar and takes her back to his hotel room. That's all he remembers—the next thing he knows, he's lying in a bathtub filled with ice; and surgical tubing is coming out of two freshly stitched wounds on his lower chest. There's a note by the tub that says, "Call 911. We've removed your left kidney." (Sometimes both are removed). The doctors in the emergency room tell him he's the victim of thieves who steal organs for use in transplants. (According to one version of the story, medical students perform the surgeries, then use the money to pay off student loans.)

NOTE: Uncle John actually heard this from a friend, Karen Pinsky, who sells real estate. She said it was a warning given by a real estate firm to agents headed to big cities for conventions.

HOW IT SPREAD: French folklorist Veronique Campion-Vincent has traced the story to Honduras and Guatemala, where rumors began circulating in 1987 that babies were being kidnapped and murdered for their organs. The alleged culprits: wealthy Americans needing transplants. From there the story spread to South America, then all over the world. Wherever such stories surfaced—including the U.S— newspapers reported them as fact. The New York version surfaced in the winter of 1991, and in February 1992, the *New York Times* "verified" it. Scriptwriter Joe Morgenstern, thinking it was true, even made it the subject of an episode of the NBC- TV series *Law & Order*.

THE TRUTH: National and international agencies have investigated the claims, but haven't been able to substantiate even a single case of organ theft anywhere in the world. The agencies say the stories aren't just groundless, but also implausible. "These incredible stories ignored the complexity of organ transplant operations," Jan Brunvald writes in *The Baby Train and Other Lusty Urban Legends*, "which would preclude any such quick removal and long-distance shipment of body parts."

THE STORY: One of the most potent forms of marijuana in the world is "Manhattan White" (also known as "New York Albino"). The strain evolved in the dark sewers of New York City as a direct result of thousands of drug dealers flushing their drugs down the toilet during drug busts. The absence of light in the sewers turns the marijuana plants white; raw sewage, acting as a fertilizer, makes it extremely potent.

THE TRUTH: Most likely an updated version of the classic urban myth that alligators live in the New York sewers.

THE STORY: A young woman finishes shopping at the mall and walks out to her car to go home. But there's an old lady sitting in the car. "I'm sorry ma'am, but this isn't your car," the woman says.

"I know," the old lady replies, "but I had to sit down." Then she asks the young woman for a ride home.

The young woman agrees, but then remembers she locked the car when she arrived at the mall. She pretends to go back into the mall to get her sister, and returns with a security guard. The guard and the old lady get into a fight, and in the struggle the old lady's wig falls off, revealing that she's actually a man. The police take the man away, and under the car seat, they find an axe. (The story is kept alive by claims that the mall has bribed reporters and police to keep the story quiet.)

THE TRUTH: The modern form of the tale comes from the early 1980s and places the action at numerous malls...New York, Las Vegas, Milwaukee, Chicago, and even Fresno, California, depending on who's telling the story. Folklorists speculate the tale may date all the way back to an 1834 English newspaper account of "a gentleman in his carriage, who on opening the supposed female's reticule [handbag] finds to his horror a pair of loaded pistols inside."

*　　　*　　　*

OOPS!

"A Dutch man from Maarssen whose stolen car was returned to him by police was greatly surprised to find that the cops had accidentally left the thief's wallet, identity card, crack pipe, and heroin supply in the car."

—The Metro **(The Netherlands)**

Fewer than 1% of people call the police when they hear a car alarm.

LEGALLY SPEAKING

So you're watching Law & Order *on TV, or maybe you find yourself in court (we won't ask why), and you suddenly realize you have no idea what the judge and lawyers are talking about. Ta-da! Here's a handy legal-phrase guide.*

Litigant. A participant in the trial or hearing.

Plaintiff. The side that filed the lawsuit.

Defendant. The person on trial (or being sued).

Prosecutor. The lawyer who represents the state (or city) in a criminal case.

Defense attorney. The lawyer who represents the defendant.

Brief. A document written by each side that outlines and supports their arguments.

Deposition. Testimony of a witness taken outside the courtroom, usually in a lawyer's office.

Arraignment. The first court appearance of a person accused of a crime, usually when a plea is entered.

Writ. A legal paper filed to start various types of civil suits.

Affidavit. A written statement made under oath.

Bail. Also called "bond." Money accepted by the court for the temporary release of a defendant, given as a guarantee they will show up for trial.

Statute of limitations. The window of time during which someone can be charged with a crime.

Bench warrant. If a defendant out on bail doesn't show up for trial, the judge issues this to order that person's immediate arrest.

Cross-examination. Questioning by the other side's attorney.

Contempt of court. Being disrespectful in court or disobeying a judge's order. It often comes with a punishment of a night in jail.

Felony. A criminal offense carrying a sentence of more than one year in prison.

Misdemeanor. A minor crime with a maximum penalty of a year in jail or a fine of no more than $2,000.

Subpoena. An order to appear in court to testify.

Infraction. A minor offense, like a speeding ticket. It doesn't require a court case.

Criminal case. A lawsuit in which the government charges a person with a crime.

Civil action. When one party sues another, not involving the government, such as a divorce or child-support suit.

Testimony. A witness's oral account, presented as evidence.

Jury trial. A group of citizens hear testimony and evidence presented by both sides, and decide the winner of a lawsuit, or whether a criminal act was committed.

Bench trial. Trial by a judge, not by a jury.

Grievance. A complaint filed by litigants against an attorney or judge.

Habeas corpus. A court order used to bring a person physically to court.

Continuance. The postponement of a case to a date in the near future.

Voir dire. The process of questioning prospective jurors or witnesses. It's Latin for "to speak the truth."

Tort. A civil injury or wrong to a person or their property.

No contest. A plea in a criminal case that allows the defendant to be convicted without an admission of guilt.

Plea bargain. An agreement the defendant makes to avoid a trial, usually involving pleading guilty to lesser charges in exchange for a lighter sentence.

Hung jury. When a jury cannot agree and reaches no verdict.

Capital crime. A crime punishable by death.

Damages. Monetary compensation paid for a legal wrong.

Injunction. A court order to do (or not do) something, like pay child support or attend drug counseling.

Appeal. Asking a higher court to review a previous court's decision (or sentence).

Trial de novo. A new trial or retrial.

In college, serial killer Ted Bundy was an honors student studying psychology.

A FAMOUS PHONY

The story of one of history's boldest—and funniest— imposters.

BACKGROUND: In 1906 shoemaker and career criminal Wilhelm Voigt was released from a German prison after a 15-year sentence for robbery. His identity card and passport had been taken away, he was nearly broke, and his prospects weren't good. He was desperate. Then he remembered how he had learned to mimic the speech and mannerisms of the self-important Prussian officers whose boots he had mended when he was young. It gave him an idea.

MOMENT OF "TRUTH": He bought a secondhand army uniform, went to a local army barracks, and waited for the right opportunity. When a corporal and five privates came marching by, he stepped in, started barking orders, and instantly became the leader of a tiny army. Their mission: To take over the town of Kopenick on the outskirts of Berlin.

They marched down the road, got five more men along the way, and commandeered a bus. Once in Kopenick, Voigt marched his men into the town hall. There, after pretending to inspect the accounts, he had the mayor arrested, took over the telegraph and telephone lines, and helped himself to 4,000 marks from the treasury. The mayor was sent in custody to military headquarters in Berlin, and "Captain" Voigt quietly disappeared.

UNMASKED: Nine days later, Voigt was captured and arrested. But the story made headlines around the world and unintentionally brought world attention to the abuses of the German prison system. Whether it was because of this, or as some believe, simply because he thought the ruse was funny, Kaiser Wilhelm pardoned the lifelong crook—who had already spent 27 of his 57 years in prison for petty crimes—and sent him on his way.

IMMORTALITY ACHIEVED: The story inspired a 1932 German movie, *Der Hauptmann von Köpenick* (*The Captain of Köpenick*), which wickedly lampooned the bumbling Prussian officers. A 1956 remake won the 1957 Academy Award for the Best Foreign Language Film.

Only one out of every 700 identity theft cases is solved.

BEHIND THE (MOB) HITS

*A fancy hotel, a homey Italian restaurant, a local bar and grill.
What do these seemingly innocent places have in common? Each
was the scene of the assassination of a ruthless gangster.*

ARNOLD "THE BRAIN" ROTHSTEIN

Background: Rothstein was one of the earliest leaders of American organized crime. He wasn't a gun-toting mobster, though—he was a planner, bankroller, and political fixer. Instead of muscle, he used brains to forge alliances among underworld factions and crooked politicians. He kept a low profile as he financed the bootlegging activities of Dutch Schultz and other gangsters. But Rothstein was also a compulsive gambler. In September 1928, he bought into a high-stakes poker game run by a man named George McManus. The game lasted two days; Rothstein lost $320,000. Claiming the game was fixed, he refused to pay up.

The Place: On November 4, Rothstein received an urgent phone call from McManus to meet him at the Park Central Hotel. The Park Central was (and still is) located across the street from Carnegie Hall. Opened in 1927, this ritzy hotel quickly became one of Manhattan's most popular spots. Ben Pollack's orchestra (featuring Benny Goodman) packed them in nightly at the hotel's Florentine Grill. It was a public place with lots of people around—a place where Rothstein would have felt safe.

The Hit: Hotel employees later found him in the stairwell holding his abdomen—he'd been shot. Was it because of the debt, or had one of his rivals simply found a viable excuse to eliminate him? No one knows for sure, because in the one day that Rothstein lived, every time police asked him who shot him, he answered, "Me mudder did it."

"JOE THE BOSS" MASSERIA

Background: Masseria was an old-line Sicilian mob boss whose ultimate goal was to become head of the Mafia in New York. Not sharing Masseria's dream, though, were younger "family" members Lucky Luciano and Vito Genovese. They wanted him out of the picture, as did powerful mobsters Lepke Buchalter and Owney Madden. When another rival mafioso, Salvatore Maranzano, began to encroach on Masseria's businesses, Joe the Boss fought back. That was the beginning a power struggle that came to be known as the Castellammarese War, during which more than 60 men (on both sides) were killed. Luciano and Genovese secretly contacted Maranzano and offered him a deal: If he'd end the bloodshed, they'd whack Masseria. Maranzano agreed.

The Place: On April 15, 1931, Luciano invited Joe the Boss to a meeting at the Nuova Villa Tammaro Restaurant, a cheap "spaghetti house" in the Coney Island section of Brooklyn. They ate, played some cards, and then Luciano went to the bathroom.

The Hit: According to eyewitnesses, while Luciano was in the bathroom, two unknown men strolled into the restaurant, fired 20 shots at Masseria, and strolled out again. Luciano took over Masseria's crime family. The Nuova Villa Tammaro's owner, an Italian immigrant named Gerardo Scarpato, shut down the restaurant and moved back to Italy. Six months later he returned to New York and was murdered. No one was ever convicted.

JOSEPH "CRAZY JOEY" GALLO

Background: After Gallo and his two brothers split off from the Profaci Family in 1950s, they were involved in several high-profile mafia battles in New York City. The wars were put on hold in 1961 when Gallo was convicted of extortion and sent up the river. (In prison, he reportedly amused himself by trying to poison his fellow convicts with strychnine-laced Italian food.) When he got out in 1971, Gallo resumed his war against Joe Colombo, whom he had never forgiven for murdering one of his men. After Colombo was gunned down that June as he was walking to the podium to deliver a speech at the Italian-American Civil Rights League's Italian Unity Day, the heads of the Five Families surmised that it was Gallo who had ordered the hit, even though they had no proof. They put out a contract on Gallo's life.

The Place: In the wee hours of the morning of April 7, 1972, Gallo was winding down after celebrating his 43rd birthday at the Copa Cabana (Don Rickles was performing). He and his friends wanted something to eat. They went to Chinatown, but everything was closed, so they went to nearby Little Italy. The only place that was open: Umberto's Clam House—the newest restaurant in the "old neighborhood," owned by

---

FBI chemical explosives dogs can detect more than 19,000 different combinations of explosives.

another mobster, "Matty the Horse" Ianniello.

The Hit: Two (or possibly more) gunmen were waiting at Umberto's. They opened fire. Gallo was hit five times and still managed to stagger out into the street, where he collapsed and died. No one was ever charged with Crazy Joey's murder.

ARTHUR "DUTCH SCHULTZ" FLEGENHEIMER

Background: Only 33 when he died, Schultz was the FBI's Public Enemy #1, and one of the best-known criminals of his day. During Prohibition, "The Dutchman" bootlegged beer, ran an illegal saloon in the Bronx, and forced rival saloons to buy beer from him...and *only* from him. He was an extortionist who also ran illegal gambling and slot machines, and didn't hesitate to murder anyone who interfered with "business."

Schultz's activities got a lot of attention from the Feds. In 1933 he was indicted on charges of income tax evasion, but he beat the rap. New York Mayor Fiorello LaGuardia was furious. He banned Schultz from New York City and ordered special prosecutor Thomas E. Dewey to investigate the Dutchman's rackets. Now Schultz was furious—he asked the "National Crime Syndicate" for permission to take Dewey out. They said no (it would have brought the full force of the Feds down on all of them). After Schultz stormed out, the other bosses decided that *he* needed to go.

The Place: The Palace Chophouse on E. 12th Street in Newark, New Jersey, was no palace—just a dark, narrow bar and diner. But since Schultz was no longer allowed to operate in New York, he used a room in the back of the Newark restaurant as his office. And that's where he was on the night of October 23, 1935.

The Hit: At 10:15 p.m., two gunmen walked into the Palace. They gunned down three of Schultz's cronies in the restaurant's back room and then found Schultz in the men's room. What happened next? Go to page 259 for one of the strangest deathbed "confessions" in the history of organized crime.

*　　　*　　　*

"Justice may be blind, but she has very sophisticated listening devices."

—**Edgar Argo**

The term "criminology" was coined by Italian law professor Raffaele Garofalo in 1885.

BAD GRANNY

Why, Grandma, what big teeth you've got!

GRANNY'S GOT A GUN

"A bored granny has been given a suspended prison sentence after staging a fake bank robbery as a practical joke. The 80-year-old, identified only as 'Elfriede,' threatened a cashier at a bank in Austria with a toy pistol and hissed, 'This is a stickup.' Then she started to laugh. 'My heart stopped for a second,' the terrified bank employee said later. 'But when she started laughing, I realized that it was just a joke.'

"When the pensioner told the court that she'd done it 'for a laugh,' the judge warned her that she wouldn't be let off so lightly if she does it again within the next three years.

"Elfriede replied, 'If I live that long. But thanks.'"

—Ananova

BLACK MARKET BABA

"Russian police have arrested a gun-smuggling granny who kept mobsters supplied with everything from artillery to assault rifles.

"The newspaper *Komsomolskaya Pravda* said Tuesday that 'Baba Nina' (Grandma Nina) and her eight-person gang had been bringing in weapons from the Baltics for more than a year. The report described the woman as a Robin Hoodish figure who supported a large number of relatives and a handicapped son while she and her husband lived in a modest apartment with only a black-and-white TV. But it added that the pensioner ran her gang with 'an iron hand' and knew most of the mobsters in the region.

"Disguising herself as one of the millions of 'shuttle traders'—small-time entrepreneurs who buy goods cheap abroad, then sell them at a profit back home—Baba Nina flew to Lithuania twice a month, returning with black-market weapons hidden in her bags among cheap T-shirts and trousers. On the telephone, she spoke in code to gang members, calling machine guns 'big trousers' and handguns 'small trousers.' The newspaper said she is now in jail, but has settled in nicely. 'Other prisoners pay her respect.'"

—Associated Press

In the United States it's a federal crime to imitate Smokey Bear or Woodsy Owl.

GANJA GRANNY

"Meet Molly Williams. The 78-year-old West Virginia woman may have the distinction of being America's oldest pot dealer. She was nabbed last week on felony drug charges after state police investigators executed a search warrant on the woman's home and discovered two pounds of marijuana (divided for distribution in plastic baggies) stashed in a grocery bag at the 'bottom of a deep freeze.' Williams's boyfriend, 72-year-old Jack White, told cops that the pot was his old lady's. She now faces 15 years in prison."

—The Smoking Gun

ORGAN-IZED CRIME

"The boy thought his grandmother was taking him to Disneyland, but Russian police say she had other plans: to sell her grandson so his organs could be used for transplants. Police in Ryazan, 125 miles southeast of Moscow, said Saturday that they arrested a woman after they were tipped that she was trying to sell her grandson to a man who was going to take him to the West. There his organs were to be removed and sold, a Ryazan police officer said. After a surveillance operation, police moved in to arrest the woman, who was being aided in the scheme by the boy's uncle. They expected to get about $70,000. When asked how he could sell his nephew, the uncle replied: 'My mother said that it is none of my business, he is her grandson.'"

—Washington Post

GRANDMADAM

"Lindenwold, New Jersey, police made a surprising discovery when they busted the alleged madam of a prostitution ring. The woman running the show was an 80-year-old grandmother.

"Authorities arrested Vera Tursi last month during a sting operation to crack down on prostitution rings posing as legal escort services. Tursi admitted her role in the business, saying she took it over a few years ago from her daughter, who had died. Tursi said she needed money to subsidize her Social Security checks.

"Undercover police first began to wonder about the age of their suspect when they called the escort service as part of their sting operation. They said she seemed to have difficulty breathing."

—CNN

Technically, the words "insane" and "insanity" are legal definitions, not medical terms.

EPA'S MOST WANTED

*Like the FBI, the Environmental Protection Agency
has its own list of most-wanted fugitives…only
these are environmental criminals.*

C**RIMINAL:** William Morgan
COMPANY: Hydromet Environmental
STORY: Morgan was CEO of this Illinois-based hazardous-waste management and disposal company. Other companies—attempting to responsibly dispose of their own toxic and chemical waste—paid Morgan's company to do it for them. One problem: Hydromet wasn't always equipped to safely or legally handle the waste. The EPA alleges that between 1995 and '98, Morgan allowed his company to accept more than 3.8 million pounds of cyanide, arsenic, and lead. Instead of doing what they were hired to do, Morgan ordered his workers to either store the stuff in warehouses or dump it in municipal landfills, potentially exposing thousands of people to hazardous materials. After the waste was traced back to Hydromet, Morgan denied any involvement. He was indicted in 2006 for making false statements to the Illinois state EPA, illegal transportation of hazardous waste, and conspiracy. He fled to Canada, where he lived until his death in 2008.

CRIMINAL: John Karyannides
COMPANY: Sabine Transportation
STORY: Karyannides, a Sabine VP, received an urgent call in 1999 from the crew of one of the company's cargo ships. They were in the middle of the South China Sea carrying about a million pounds of wheat to aid in humanitarian efforts in Bangladesh, but a diesel fuel leak had contaminated their cargo, rendering it useless. What should they do? Karyannides's answer: Dump all of the tainted wheat into the ocean. The company's lawyers later claimed that the crew cleaned the wheat before dumping it overboard, which investigators ruled was "impossible," given the limited equipment on board. Sabine was ordered to pay a $2 million fine; Karyannides, however, disappeared and is still at large. Among other charges he faces are illegal oil dumping and conspiracy. His last known whereabouts: Athens, Greece.

While in prison, serial killer John Wayne Gacy made over $100,000 from sales of his artwork.

CRIMINAL: Bhavesh Kamdar
COMPANY: Industrial Site Services
STORY: In 2001 Kamdar won a $12 million contract with the state of New York to replace underground storage tanks for oil and gasoline at police stations, prisons, and other public buildings. But by 2004 it had become all too evident to state officials that Kamdar's tanks were prone to leaks. As a result, an unknown amount of groundwater in upstate New York had been contaminated. In addition, Kamdar overbilled the state by $1.1 million for contractual expenses that actually totalled only $59,000. With the investigation heating up, Kamdar fled to his home country of India but was arrested by an Interpol agent in 2006. If he's ever extradited to the United States, he'll stand trial on more than 30 charges, for which he could receive prison time and as much as $5.9 million in fines.

CRIMINAL: Denis Feron
COMPANY: Chemetco
STORY: Illinois-based Chemetco, one of the nation's largest copper processors, produced a *lot* of toxic industrial waste in its day-to-day operations of refining lead, zinc, and cadmium—which, in high concentrations, are deadly to humans and animals. Rather than dispose of it responsibly (or legally), Chemetco CEO Denis Feron ordered a secret pipe be built from the company's smelting plant to Long Lake in Illinois. For a decade, from 1986 to '96, that pipe dumped potentially fatal concentrations of waste into the lake. After the pipe was discovered, Feron was indicted for conspiring to violate the Clean Water Act but fled (reportedly) to Belgium before his trial began. If captured, Feron faces a five-year prison sentence and a $250,000 fine. Chemetco, meanwhile, went bankrupt, and the facility is likely to become an EPA Superfund toxic cleanup site, meaning it's one of the most polluted places in the United States. Feron remains at large.

*   *   *

"The biggest corporation, like the humblest private citizen, must be held to strict compliance with the will of the people."

—Theodore Roosevelt

After Japan's biggest bank heist ($5.4 million), the bank got a thank-you note from the robbers.

THE DISAPPEARANCE OF JUDGE CRATER

We first ran this mysterious story in our 1999 edition, Uncle John's Absolutely Absorbing Bathroom. In subsequent years, a new piece of evidence has been uncovered that may finally reveal the culprits responsible for one of the most-talked-about unsolved disappearances in American history.

JUDGE JOSEPH CRATER

Claim to Fame: Newly appointed justice of the New York Supreme Court—a shoo-in to win reelection in November, and a potential appointee to the U.S. Supreme Court

Disappearance: Crater and his wife were vacationing in Maine on August 3, 1930, when he received a phone call from New York City. Clearly disturbed, he announced to her that he had to go "straighten those fellows out." Then he left for New York.

Crater was apparently taking a break from business when, on the evening of August 6, he bought a ticket for a show and arranged to pick it up at the box office. Then he went to Billy Haas's restaurant, where he ran into friends and joined them for dinner. Later, he took a cab to the theater, waving from the taxi as it disappeared. Someone *did* pick up the theater ticket…but no one knows if it was Crater—he was never seen again. Nine days later, his wife notified the police, and a massive manhunt began.

What Happened: Police searched Crater's apartment and found nothing suspicious. They offered rewards for information…but not even the taxi driver came forward. Even after interviewing 300 people—resulting in 2,000 pages of testimony—they still had no clues to his whereabouts.

But as the investigation continued, police—and the public— were astonished to see Crater's carefully constructed facade unravel. It turned out, for example, that he'd kept a number of mistresses and had often been seen on the town with showgirls. More surprising however, was his involvement in graft, fraud, and political payoffs. Crater was a player in two major scandals, which came to light after he vanished. It also seemed

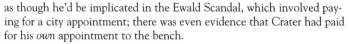
as though he'd be implicated in the Ewald Scandal, which involved paying for a city appointment; there was even evidence that Crater had paid for his *own* appointment to the bench.

Crater's fate was hotly debated by the public. Some were sure he was murdered by gangster associates. Others—noting that the judge had removed files containing potentially incriminating evidence from his office just before he disappeared—speculated that political cronies had killed him to shut him up. Or maybe a mistress who'd been blackmailing him had done it. Then again, perhaps the judge had committed suicide rather than watch his career crumble because of scandal. Whoever was responsible, and whatever happened to the body, it was assumed Crater was dead.

Postmortem: Crater's wife suffered a nervous breakdown and didn't return to their New York apartment until January 1931. There, she found an envelope in the top drawer of her dresser. It contained $6,690 in cash, the judge's will, written five years before (leaving his entire estate to her), and a three-page penciled note that listed everyone who owed the judge money. It closed with the words, "Am very weary. Love, Joe." The police department had searched the apartment thoroughly, and had kept a 24-hour guard on it since the disappearance—so no one could imagine how or when the envelope had gotten there. But it gave rise to another possibility: Crater had intentionally disappeared.

Nothing more came of it. In July 1937, Judge Joseph Force Crater was declared legally dead, and his wife collected on his life insurance. By then, New York's police commissioner believed that "Crater's disappearance was premeditated." The famous file 13595 remains open to this day—no trace of Crater or his body have ever been found.

Update: In 2005, after 91-year-old Stella Ferrucci-Good died in Queens, her daughter found an envelope marked "Do not open until my death." Inside was a letter that implicated the cabbie who picked up Crater as well as his brother, a crooked cop. The letter claimed that they merely wanted to "rough him up," but Crater fought back and was killed. He was buried underneath the boardwalk on Coney Island, where the New York Aquarium is now located. Five skeletons *were* found there in the 1950s, but then they were piled on top of others in unmarked mass graves on Hart Island. Because it would be nearly impossible to test all of the bones to get a match for Judge Crater, the case remains open.

John Dillinger once escaped from prison using a piece of wood shaped like a gun.

NO CAN(ADA) DO

Many of our Canadian readers have sent us items about life in the Great White North…including some strange Canadian laws. Here are a few examples.

In Canada, it's illegal to jump from a flying airplane without a parachute.

In Nova Scotia, you're not allowed to water the lawn when it is raining.

In Toronto, it's illegal to drag a dead horse along Yonge Street on Sunday.

A maritime law in Canada specifies that two vessels cannot occupy the same space at the same time.

In Quebec, margarine must be a different color from butter.

The city of Guelph, Ontario, is classified as a "no-pee zone."

In Montreal, you may not park a car in such a way that it is blocking your own driveway.

It's illegal to ride a Toronto streetcar on Sunday if you've been eating garlic.

In Alberta, wooden logs may not be painted.

It is illegal to kill a Sasquatch in British Columbia.

An Etobicoke, Ontario, by-law states that no more than 3.5 inches of water is allowed in a bathtub.

In Charlottetown, Prince Edward Island, you can only buy liquor with a doctor's prescription.

Burnaby, B.C., has a 10 p.m. curfew—for dogs.

An anti-noise ordinance in Ottawa makes it illegal for bees to buzz.

Pedestrians on Toronto sidewalks must give a hand signal before turning.

In Vancouver, BC, it's illegal to ride a tricycle over 10 mph.

It is illegal to sell antifreeze to Indians in Quebec.

Tightrope walking over the main streets of Halifax is prohibited. (Side streets are okay.)

According to one study, if Sherlock Holmes were real, his IQ would be about 190.

MONKEY SEE, MONKEY DO

*Sure, committing crimes looks all glamorous and fun on the screen,
but try it in real life and the result is often two thumbs down.*

MONKEY SEE: In the 1971 film *The Godfather*, Corleone family henchmen intimidate a Hollywood mogul by killing his prize racehorse and sticking the horse's head in his bed.

MONKEY DO: In 1997 two New York crooks decided to use a similar method to intimidate a witness scheduled to testify against them. On the morning of the trial, the witness found an unwelcome surprise on his doorstep. "We wanted to leave a cow's head," admitted one of the crooks, "because his wife is from India, and they consider cows sacred." Unable to find a cow's head in Brooklyn, they went to butcher and got a goat head. "We figured it was close enough." It wasn't. They both went to prison.

MONKEY SEE: On an episode of *MacGyver*, MacGyver rubs his nose on some buttons so he can later determine which ones were pressed (because the oils from his nose were smudged). He figures out the secret code.

MONKEY DO: An employee at a Bangkok hotel tried the same tactic with guests' safety deposit boxes. He was caught and sent to prison.

MONKEY SEE: In 1996, 17-year-old Steve Barone of Royal Palm Beach, Florida, was *really* into *Pulp Fiction*, *Reservoir Dogs*, and *Goodfellas*.

MONKEY DO: After he was caught while trying to rob a gun store, Barone claimed at his trial that he'd been taken over by another personality—a combination of the "wise guys" from those three crime movies. The judge rejected the "*Pulp Fiction* defense," as the press called it, and sentenced "Mr. Vincent Vega Henry Hill White" to four years in prison.

MONKEY SEE: The *Nancy Drew* books chronicle the adventures of a teenage detective who must often think quickly to get out of danger.

MONKEY DO: An 11-year-old Michigan girl was kidnapped and thrown into the trunk of her car. Instead of panicking, she asked herself, "What would Nancy Drew do?" She then found a toolbox, pried the trunk open, ran to a phone booth, and called the cops. The kidnappers were arrested.

A human body decomposes four times faster in water than on land.

WORD ORIGINS

*Don't be a swindler and cheat your way out of these
crime word origins. It would be downright taboo.*

CHEAT

Meaning: A dishonest person; the act of deceiving for gain

Origin: "Comes from *escheat*—a medieval legal term for 'the reversion of property to the state in the absence of legal heirs, and of the state's right to such confiscation.' The officer who looked after the king's *escheats* was known as the *cheater*. The word's dishonest connotations evolved among thieves in the 16th century." (From *Wicked Words*, by Hugh Rawson)

TABOO

Meaning: A behavior or activity that is prohibited

Origin: "Originally a Tongan word, *tabu*, meaning 'marked as holy.' The first taboos were prohibitions against the use or even the mention of certain things because of religious belief that to do so would invoke the wrath of the gods. The word gradually was extended in use to cover all sorts of prohibitions or bans based upon social convention." (From *Dictionary of Word and Phrase Origins, Vol. III*, by William and Mary Morris)

CRIME

Meaning: An action that is forbidden by a predetermined set of laws

Origin: "Derived from the Latin word *crimen*, which meant 'charge' or 'cry of distress.' The ancient Greek word *krima*, from which the Latin cognate was derived, typically referred to an intellectual mistake or an offense against the community, rather than a private or moral wrong." (From *Klein's Comprehensive Etymological Dictionary of the English Language*, by Ernest Klein)

ADULTERY

Meaning: Having sexual relations with someone other than a spouse

Origin: "You may be surprised to hear that there's no 'adult' in 'adultery.' That's because the word goes back to the Latin term *adulterare*, 'to pol-

Early 1800s female pirate Cheng I Sao beheaded any pirate who disobeyed orders.

lute, corrupt, or defile.' (This in turn comes from *alterare*, 'to alter.') Having extramarital relations was seen as defiling—or adulterating—the marriage vows, and the verb eventually turned into the noun 'adultery.' 'Adult' traces back to the Latin *adultus*, a form of the verb *adolescere*, 'to grow up,' which was the source of the word 'adolescent.'" (From *The Complete Idiot's Guide to Weird Word Origins*, by Paul McFedries)

BLACKMAIL

Meaning: To extort money by threatening to expose a hurtful truth

Origin: "*Blackmail* has nothing whatsoever to do with the post office. *Black* is used in the figurative sense of 'evil' or 'wicked.' *Mail* is a Scots word meaning 'rent' or 'tribute.' The term *blackmail* originated in Scotland, where Highland chiefs at one time extorted tribute from Lowlanders and Englishmen on the Scottish border in return for protection from being plundered." (From *Word Mysteries & Histories*, by the Editors of American Heritage Dictionary)

BANDIT

Meaning: A robber belonging to a gang, operating in a lawless area

Origin: "A man who ventured outside a city could depend upon little or no protection from police. Italians discovered that banishing lawbreakers constituted a severe punishment. Crooks were brought before a crowd, proclaimed a public enemy, and banished. Originally from Latin *bandire* ('to proclaim'), the subject of such a proclamation was called a *bandito*. Finding it difficult to survive alone, the bandito joined other outcasts. Bands of them lurked in the mountains of southern Europe. Forbidden to follow normal trades, they lived by robbery and murder. English visitors to Italy listened to *Bandito* tales." (From *Why You Say It*, by Webb Garrison)

SWINDLER

Meaning: One who cheats or defrauds someone else out of their money

Origin: "It entered English circa 1762. From the Old High German word *swintan*, meaning 'diminish, vanish, or lose consciousness.' This gave rise to the verb *schwindeln*, first used to mean 'to be dizzy' or 'giddy.' Because such a person is often given to flights of fancy, the Germans applied the word as well to a 'fantastic schemer,' or 'a participant in shady business deals.'" (From *The Merriam-Webster New Book of Word Histories*)

Since 2005, New York City has had the lowest crime rate of the 25 largest U.S. cities.

AMERICA'S FIRST PRIVATE EYE

If you're a fan of detective stories—which include everything from
The Maltese Falcon *to* The Pink Panther *to* CSI—*then you*
might be interested in this man: He was the real thing.

WHERE THERE'S SMOKE...

One day in June 1846, Allan Pinkerton, a 27-year-old barrel maker from Dundee, Illinois, climbed onto his raft and floated down the Fox River looking for trees that he could use for lumber. He found a lot more than that—when he went to chop down some trees on an island in the middle of the river, he discovered a smoldering fire pit hidden among them.

If someone found a fire pit in such a beautiful spot today, they probably wouldn't suspect anything unusual. But as Pinkerton explained in his memoirs, life was different in the 1840s: "There was no picnicking in those days; people had more serious matters to attend to and it required no great keenness to conclude that no honest men were in the habit of occupying the place."

GOTCHA!

Pinkerton went back to the island a few more times during daylight, but no one was ever there. So a few days later, he snuck back in the middle of the night and waited to see if anyone would show up. After about an hour he heard a rowboat approaching the island. He waited a while and then crept close to the fire pit to see several shady-looking characters sitting around the campfire.

The next morning he went to the sheriff. After a few nights they went back to the island with a small posse and caught the men by surprise. Pinkerton's suspicions were correct—the men were a gang of counterfeiters, and the posse caught them red-handed with "a bag of bogus dimes and the tools used in their manufacture."

Counterfeiting was rampant in the 1840s: In those days each bank issued its own bills, and with so many different kinds of paper floating

It's against the law to run out of gas in Youngstown, Ohio.

around, fakes were easy to make and difficult to detect. Less than a month after the dime bust, somebody passed fake $10 bills to two shopkeepers in Dundee. The shopkeepers were pretty sure that a farmer named John Craig had something to do with it, but they had no proof. Pinkerton had done a good job catching the last bunch of counterfeiters, so they asked him to look into it.

Pinkerton set up a sting: He met Craig, struck up a conversation, and convinced him that he was looking to make some dishonest money on the side. Craig sold him $500 worth of the fake bills, but rather than have the sheriff arrest him right there, Pinkerton decided to bide his time. He got Craig to reveal the location of his headquarters (a hotel in Chicago) then made an appointment to buy more counterfeit bills. A few days later, Pinkerton met Craig in the hotel bar. Then, just as Craig was passing him $4,000 worth of fake bills, two plainclothes police officers stepped out of the shadows and arrested him.

CAREER CHANGE

Had Pinkerton been left alone, he might have remained a barrel maker, but the Craig bust changed everything. "The affair was in everybody's mouth," Pinkerton later wrote, "and I suddenly found myself called upon from every quarter to undertake matters of detective skill." He quit making barrels and worked a number of different law-enforcement jobs over the next few years: deputy sheriff, Chicago police detective (the city's first), and finally as a U.S. Post Office investigator.

Then in 1850, he decided to go to work for himself—he and a lawyer named Edward Rucker formed what would become the Pinkerton National Detective Agency. Rucker dropped out after a year or two, but Pinkerton stayed with it for the rest of his life.

THE EYE HAS IT

For his company motto, Pinkerton chose "We Never Sleep." For his logo, he chose a large, unblinking eye. His agency wasn't the world's first private detective agency—a Frenchman named Eugène François Vidocq beat him by 17 years when he founded the Bureau des Renseignements (Office of Intelligence) in 1833. But it was Pinkerton who gave private detectives their famous nickname. Thanks to his choice of logo, they've been known as "private eyes" ever since.

TRAIN OF THOUGHT

Pinkerton's timing was perfect. Railroads were beginning to transform the American way of life—in both good ways and bad. As rails began to link major American cities, people could travel greater distances in less time and at less cost than ever before. But criminals could, too: a bank robber could knock over a bank in one state, then hop a train and by the next morning be hundreds of miles away in another state.

Have you ever seen a movie where the sheriff chases a bad guy and has to stop at the county line? That really was the way things worked back then—law-enforcement agencies were organized locally, and a police officer's or sheriff's powers ended as soon as he crossed the city or the county line. There were few if any state police in those days, and no national police to speak of, either. The Bureau of Investigation, predecessor to the FBI, wouldn't come into existence until 1908. Pinkerton's *private* detectives had no formal police powers, but they were free to chase criminals across county and state lines and then work with local law enforcers to arrest criminals and bring them to justice.

With no one else to turn to protect their interests, the railroads went to Pinkerton. By 1854 the agency was earning $10,000 a year (about $200,000 today) on railroad company retainers alone.

UNDERCOVER

Pinkerton's agency achieved its greatest successes by sticking to the principle that Pinkerton himself had used to catch the counterfeiter John Craig back in 1846: The best way to catch a thief was by pretending to *be* a thief—a detective had to win the bad guy's confidence, then get him to spill the beans. The agents infiltrated organized gangs of all types: Confederate spy rings, unions, even the Mafia.

The Pinkerton agency was ahead of their time in many areas. They pioneered the use of the mug shot and by the 1870s had the largest collection in the world. Their centralized criminal filing system has since been emulated by the FBI and other law enforcement organizations worldwide. The agency hired a female detective, a 23-year-old widow named Kate Warne, in 1856; by comparison, the New York City Police Department did not hire its first female investigator until 1903.

After the Civil War, the Pinkerton Detective Agency helped bring the Wild West era to a close by sending manhunters into the field to hunt down infamous train and bank robbers: Jesse James, the Missouri Kid, the Reno brothers, and the Cole Younger gang. Why did Butch Cassidy and the Sundance Kid abandon their life of crime and flee to Argentina in 1901? Because Pinkerton detectives were hot on their trail. With the agency's "wanted" posters and mug shots circulating throughout the United States, there was no place in the country left for them to hide.

END OF AN ERA

After suffering a stroke in 1869, Pinkerton began turning more and more of his responsibilities over to his sons, Robert and William. But he never retired, and he was still working at the agency in June 1884 when he tripped and bit his tongue while taking a walk. In the days before antibiotics, such injuries were very serious—a few days later gangrene set in, followed by blood poisoning, and on July 1, Pinkerton died.

The world of law enforcement has changed a great deal since the Pinkerton National Detective Agency opened its doors in 1850, and if anything, the pace accelerated following Allan Pinkerton's death. The biggest change of all: in 1908 the Bureau of Investigation opened for business. The Pinkerton agency's detective services became increasingly redundant—why pay good money to hire private detectives when the FBI, backed by the resources of the federal government, would investigate crimes for free? As the crime detection side of the business dried up, the agency's security guard division, founded in 1858, came to assume a larger share. By the late 1930s, only a fraction of the company's revenue came from its original detective services. In 1965 Allan Pinkerton's great-grandson, Robert Allan Pinkerton II, acknowledged the inevitable by dropping the word "Detective" altogether and renamed the company Pinkerton's, Inc. He was the last Pinkerton to head the Pinkerton Agency.

So can you still hire a Pinkerton agent today, at least as a security guard? No—in 1999 an international security company headquartered in Sweden, Securitas A.B., bought the firm and stopped doing business under the Pinkerton name.

*   *   *

He who holds the ladder is as bad as the thief. —**German proverb**

Quick! Log off! Someone is a victim of a cybercrime every 10 seconds.

CRIMINAL HEADLINES

*Calling the grammar cops: It's these headline writers
who should have been brought up on charges.*

*Juvenile Court To Try
Shooting Defendant*

MAN ROBS, THEN
KILLS HIMSELF

NJ Judge to Rule on Nude Beach

Mayor Says D.C. is Safe
Except for Murders

*Man, Shot Twice in Head,
Gets Mad*

*Deadline Passes
for Striking Police*

COCKROACH SLAIN,
HUSBAND BADLY HURT

MAN SHOOTS NEIGHBOR
WITH MACHETE

**32 Ignorant Enough
to Serve on North Jury**

**Hostage Taker Kills Self;
Police Shoot Each Other**

Potential Witness to Murder Drunk

Prosecutor Releases Probe
Into Undersheriff

BOMB HIT BY LIBRARY

***ROBBER HOLDS UP
ALBERT'S HOSIERY***

**Multiple Personality Rapist
Sentenced to Two Life Terms**

Stolen Painting Found By Tree

MAN STRUCK BY LIGHTNING
FACES BATTERY CHARGES

**Man Found Dead
in Cemetery**

BAR TRYING TO HELP
ALCOHOLIC LAWYERS

Defendant's Speech
Ends In Long Sentence

*42 Percent of All Murdered Women
Are Killed by the Same Man*

**Silent Teamster Gets Cruel
Punishment: Lawyer**

*CRACK FOUND IN
MAN'S BUTTOCKS*

Two Convicts Evade Noose,
Jury Hung

What is CODIS? The "Combined DNA Index System"—the world's largest DNA data bank.

KOOKY CROOKS

*Over the years, we've written about all kinds of criminals:
dumb ones, nice ones, even clever ones. But some law
breakers can make it difficult for us to classify them.
That's why we created a "Kooky Crooks" page.*

WHEN ART REALLY BOMBS

In 2002 Luke Helder, a University of Wisconsin art student, was arrested for planting 18 pipe bombs in mailboxes in half a dozen states. It was all part of a bizarre "art" project: When plotted on a map, the bomb sites formed a "smiley face," with the "eyes" in Nebraska and Iowa and the left side of the "mouth" in Colorado and Texas. The right side remained unfinished because police caught Helder after his father turned him in. (Nobody died.)

SLEEPY CRIME

Two women approached a man in a park in Sibu, Romania, and struck up a friendly conversation with him. In the course of conversation they asked him to let them hypnotize him. The man agreed, thinking it might be fun. A half hour later the man woke up from his trance. The women were gone, and so was his wallet.

STRESSLING

Simon Andrews of Osbaldwick, England, was sentenced to six months house arrest in 2003. The crime: Andrews had attacked four random men on the street, wrestling them to the ground and taking off—but not stealing—their shoes and socks. Why'd he do it? Andrews, an accountant, says he was "stressed out."

LIFE ON MARS

Dusco Stuppar, 32, of France was able to con an old childhood friend, known only as "Christophe H." into giving him 650,000 francs (about $62,000) to help fund the construction of a city to be built under a secret river on the planet Mars. Stuppar informed Christophe that he was part of a secret society of ultra-intelligent people who had the

In Hong Kong, a wife may legally kill her adulterous husband (but only with her bare hands).

technology possible to make the underwater space city possible. Even more bizarre: Stuppar claimed his evil clone (also part of the Mars project) had injected him with explosives. If Christophe didn't hand over the money, he said, the clone would blow up Stuppar. Christophe later told the story to a psychiatrist, leading to Stuppar's arrest and an 18-month jail term.

HE JUST WANTED TO WATCH TV

A couple living in Dorset, England, called the police in 2001 when they realized their home had been broken into while they were out. An investigation revealed that the thief hadn't actually stolen anything, but had left behind a new television and an unopened bottle of Zima.

CRIME PLAGUE

A biological terror alert went out in January 2003 when Dr. Thomas Butler, an infectious disease researcher at Texas Tech University, informed police that 30 vials of bubonic plague were missing from his lab. Police feared the vials were stolen by terrorists who could convert the samples into a chemical weapon. Even President George W. Bush was briefed about the incident. A day later, Dr. Butler was arrested when it was discovered he'd accidentally destroyed the plague vials himself, and had lied to cover up the error.

IT'S ELECTRIC

In fall 2005, a strange crime wave hit Baltimore, Maryland: Over the course of six weeks, 130 light poles were stolen. Each pole measured 30 feet tall, weighed 250 pounds, and cost $1,200. There were no witnesses and police were baffled. More baffling is why the thieves were so neat—when they stole the poles, they left all the high voltage wiring cleanly wrapped in black electric tape.

OH, *THAT'S* WHERE I LEFT THEM

In 2003 a 23-year-old woman from Tyrol, Austria, went to a police station to report that her expensive pair of ski pants had been stolen. Officers quickly solved the case—they pointed out to the woman that she was *wearing* the pants. "I was so nervous that I forgot to take them off," she said.

Of the 14 escape attempts from Alcatraz, none were known to be successful.

THE MONA LISA CAPER

*How one small act of thievery turned a
picture into a worldwide sensation.*

NOW YOU SEE HER...
August 21, 1911. Louis Beroud, a painter, was setting up his easel
in the Salon Carré, one of the Louvre's more than 200 rooms,
directly facing the spot where the *Mona Lisa* smiled out at her admirers.
Beroud was going to paint her as he had done many times before, but
there was an empty space where the painting should have been.

When he asked a guard about it, he was told that it was in the pho-
tography room, where copies were made. Beroud waited three hours for
the painting's return, but eventually, his patience gave out. He asked the
guard what was taking so long. The guard checked again. When he came
back, he sheepishly admitted that the *Mona Lisa* was...gone.

A STAR IS BORN

The most famous painting in the world today wasn't quite *that* famous at
the turn of the 20th century—she was certainly revered among art afi-
cionados. But news of the mysterious theft of the mysterious woman
caught the public's collective imagination, transforming Da Vinci's mas-
terpiece from mere painting to cultural icon. All of a sudden, the *Mona
Lisa* was a cottage industry: Her likeness showed up on posters, postcards,
mugs...in nightclubs, silent movies, magazines...she was *everywhere*. Perhaps strangest of all: Record crowds showed up at the Louvre just to view
the empty space where the painting had been hanging.

But where was the actual *Mona Lisa*? Theories abounded in France.
Some thought it was an elaborate practical joke; others, a political ploy
by the Germans to humiliate the French. Rumors even flew that it was
the work of local Paris artists—Pablo Picasso among them. They were
rounded up and brought in for questioning.

It took a week for the entire museum to be searched thoroughly. All
that turned up was the painting's empty frame, found at the top of a staircase that must have been the thief's escape route. Months passed. Then
two years. There was still no sign of her.

THE DA VINCI CODE

The big question: What would an art thief do with the painting? At the time, it was worth about $5 million—today, it's priceless. To whom would the thief sell it? Even if a buyer were willing to spend that much, the painting was too high-profile to be passed along the art-theft network. It was too easy to trace. The crook would be caught.

The answer came on November 29, 1913. A wealthy Italian art dealer, Alfredo Geri, received a letter from a man who called himself Leonard Vincenzo. He offered to return the *Mona Lisa* to France…for a fee. Geri figured it was a hoax, but was intrigued enough to set up a meeting at a hotel in Florence, Italy. Geri took along Giovanni Poggi, the director of Florence's Uffizi Gallery. The two men walked into the hotel room to find Vincenzo, a short, mustachioed Italian man who told them he'd been working in Paris at the time of the theft. Vincenzo reached underneath the bed and retrieved an object wrapped in red silk. Geri unrolled it, and Poggi verified its authenticity: It was the *Mona Lisa*.

THE PATRIOT

Leonard Vincenzo didn't receive his ransom. Instead, he was taken to the police station, where he admitted his real name was Vincenzo Peruggia… and it was he who stole the *Mona Lisa*. On the morning of the theft, he explained, he entered the Louvre dressed in a painter's smock and went straight for the *Mona Lisa*. No one else was in the Salon Carré that morning, so Peruggia simply removed the painting from the four wall hooks and hid it under his smock—frame and all. When he reached the staircase, he removed the painting from the frame and walked out. The entire heist took about 20 minutes.

So why did Peruggia do it? "For the love of country," he said in court. "She belongs in Italy, where Leonardo painted her." (Peruggia also said he was upset with Napoleon for his various Italian conquests.) But his past criminal record of burglaries, along with a list of art dealers that police found (including Geri), convinced the judge that his motivations were less than patriotic. Peruggia spent seven months in jail. He went to his grave in 1927 *still* believing he was one of Italy's greatest patriots.

As for the *Mona Lisa*, she made a triumphant return to the Louvre. Today, she smiles out—from her nearly impregnable, climate-controlled, bulletproof glass case—at more than five million admirers each year.

Panda car: British slang for a police car (because it's black and white).

UNCLE ZU'S DICTIONARY

Want to talk like a mobster? These underworld terms will get you started.
(But don't you go tellin' no one where you got it from, crumb!)

Zu. Translates as "uncle," a term of endearment for a senior member of the underworld.

Oobatz. Crazy.

Ace of Spades: The wealthy widow of a dead mobster.

Babbo. An underling who has been deemed useless.

Shy. Short for "shylock," a mobster who lends money at an extremely high rate of interest.

Left-handed wife. A mobster's mistress, also called a *comare*.

Candy brains. A mobster who also partakes of the drugs he sells.

Bubble gum machine. Police car.

Government securities. A set of handcuffs.

Fortune teller. The sentencing judge, who knows your future.

Guest of the state. A mobster serving time in prison.

Do a dime. Ten years in prison.

Chased. Banished from the Mafia (a merciful punishment considering the alternative).

Turban. To give a man a turban is to crack his head open.

Serious headache. A bullet to the head.

Dracula. The guy who has to clean blood from a crime scene.

Buttlegging. Bootlegging untaxed cigarettes.

Crumb. A "regular Joe" who is not a member of the Mob.

On the pad. A cop who receives payment to ignore Mob crimes.

Stugots: From *stu cazzo*, it means "testicles." (It's also the name of Tony Soprano's yacht.)

Cowboy. High-ranking mobster who carries out his own hits.

Omertà. The "code of silence" that prohibits cooperating with the government.

Flip. To abandon the omertà and squeal to the authorities. Do that and you'll likely be…

Whacked. Murdered. Also "hit," "popped," "rubbed out," "bumped off," "iced," "gone for a ride," and "sleeping with the fishes."

Texas Rangers were said to "ride like a Mexican, shoot like a Kentuckian, and fight like the devil."

CANADIAN GANGLAND

*Canada: the land of big lakes, lots of snow, friendly people—
and a whole bunch of dangerous, violent gangs.*

BACKGROUND

Most people don't think of Canada as a place where violent gangs roam the streets, but in the past two decades, the number of gangs in the country has grown exponentially. Today there are today literally thousands of them, and their turf wars and drive-by shootings make the headlines more and more often. Here's a rundown of some of the most notorious—and dangerous—of them all.

Gang: Indian Posse (IP)

Base: Winnipeg, Manitoba

History: Indian Posse, believed to be the first "aboriginal gang" (or "First Nations" gang), was founded by a handful of disaffected teenagers in Winnipeg around 1990. IP quickly grew from a petty-theft operation into a criminal powerhouse specializing in drug trafficking, robbery, and prostitution on reservations, in cities, and inside prisons. Today it's the largest of the many existing aboriginal gangs, with hundreds of full-fledged members and many more "associates" who can be identified by their red bandannas and "IP" tattoos. IP members are believed to be responsible for hundreds of violent crimes, including many murders, mostly of rival gang members in drug wars. Co-founder Richard Wolfe was sentenced to 19 years in prison for armed robbery and attempted murder in 1996, and still maintains a leadership position from his cell.

Gang: The Galloway Boys, or G-Way

Base: Scarborough, a section of Toronto, Ontario

History: In 2000 this small but deadly gang was founded by a youth named Tyshan Riley, who, at the age of 18, became one of Scarborough's leading gangsters. In 2002 a high-ranking G-Way associate was shot to death by members of their main rivals, the Malvern Crew, from Toronto's nearby Malvern district. That led to a gang war that saw dozens of drive-by shootings and several murders. In 2004, after a two-year undercover police investigation, Riley and 16 other G-Way members were arrested.

Luminol, the chemical that makes blood glow, can destroy other crime scene evidence.

Riley alone was charged with 39 offenses, including three murders and five attempted murders. He and two other members were convicted of first-degree murder in July 2009, and each was sentenced to two consecutive life sentences.

Gang: Mad Cowz

Base: Winnipeg, Manitoba

History: This gang formed in the early 2000s around crack dealing in Winnipeg's crime-ridden west end. Members are African Canadians, most of them refugees from nations ruined by decades of civil war, such as Somalia and Sudan. New members are recruited from recently arrived immigrants, mostly teenagers already accustomed to violence. The gang quickly became a successful, wealthy, and dangerous force in the city. In late 2005, their success led to a split, and a new rival gang, the African Mafia, was born. That same year, the son of a prominent Manitoba surgeon was shot and killed in the streets by battling Mad Cowz and African Mafia members. His death dominated local news for weeks, and a resulting police crackdown put most of the Mad Cowz' leadership behind bars. Still, they continue to operate in the city and in prisons.

Gang: Ace Crew

Base: Ottawa, Ontario

History: Formed sometime in the early 1990s, the Ace Crew was involved in activities common to most gangs, including drug dealing and extortion, but they became infamous all over Canada in August 1995 when they abducted four teenagers in retaliation for a perceived slight to the gang by one of the teens. They tortured all four and murdered 17-year-old Sylvain Leduc. Ace Crew member John Wartley Richardson was sentenced to life in prison for the murder, with an additional 73 years added for other crimes. The gang faded, but some members are still active in Ottawa.

Gang: The Independent Soldiers, or IS

Base: Vancouver, British Columbia

History: IS became an organized gang in the early 2000s and is now one of Canada's most well-known gangs. The membership is multiracial, but the leaders are Indo-Canadians; the gang grew up out of Vancouver's large

Say hello to his little friend! Al Pacino was once arrested for carrying a concealed weapon.

Punjabi Sikh community. Dealing in drugs, prostitution, gun-running, and money laundering, the gang has spread across British Columbia and into several towns in neighboring Alberta. IS has been linked to hundreds of shootings and dozens of murders, mostly in Vancouver, since 2005. In January 2009, a crackdown on Mexican drug cartels led to a brutal war between the IS and other Vancouver gangs over dwindling drug supplies, with more than 100 shootings and stabbings and more than a dozen murders in just two months.

EXTRAS

• A 2008 report by the Royal Canadian Mounted Police (RCMP) said that gang members involved in international drug smuggling had infiltrated airports in major cities around the country. Most were working as baggage handlers.

• More than 130 gangs are based in Vancouver alone, vying for a drug business estimated to be worth more than $6 billion per year.

• In the late 1990s, Toronto police arrested four members of the Spadina Girls, a short-lived, all-female gang led by a 16-year-old girl. The gang consisted entirely of high schoolers, who, among other things, charged other students for protection. The arrests came after gang members brutally assaulted a fellow student at a billiard hall.

• A much more dangerous all-female gang has formed in recent years: the Indian Posse Girls, an offshoot of Indian Posse. They're believed to be in control of the sex trade in Winnipeg and Edmonton.

• Canada's Criminal Intelligence Service estimates that more than 11,000 Canadians are members of street gangs.

*   *   *

NOW YOU SEE HIM...

"In a Miami courtroom, while the lawyer for defendant Raymond Jessi Snyder was vociferously protesting a prosecutor's demand that Snyder be locked up pending trial because he was a 'flight risk,' the sly defendant slowly eased from his seat and bolted out the door. (He didn't get far.)"

—*Miami Herald*

NYPD lingo: A "cheese eater" is a cop who rats on other cops.

NAME THAT SLEUTH

*It took us a while, but using time-tested sleuthing
techniques, we finally solved…the mystery
of the fictional detective names.*

PERRY MASON (1933)
As a youngster, author Erle Stanley Gardner subscribed to a boy's fiction magazine, *The Youth's Companion*, and learned a lot about writing from the stories he read. *The Youth's Companion* was published by Perry Mason and Company.

SPENSER: FOR HIRE (1973)

Robert B. Parker first introduced his streetwise, Chaucer-quoting, beer-drinking, gourmet-cooking, Bostonian, ex-boxer private investigator in *The Godwulf Manuscript*. Parker saw Spenser as a tough guy but also as a knight in shining armor and named him after the English poet (and Shakespeare contemporary) Edmund Spenser.

MIKE HAMMER (1947)

Writer Mickey Spillane had been in and out of the comic book business for years when he tried to sell a new detective strip to some New York publishers in 1946. The character's name was Mike Danger. When no one would buy, he decided to turn it into a novel and changed the name to Mike Hammer, after one of his favorite haunts, Hammer's Bar and Grill.

SHERLOCK HOLMES AND DR. JOHN WATSON (1887)

Dr. Watson is believed to have been inspired by author Arthur Conan Doyle's friend Dr. James Watson. It's less clear how he named the famous sleuth whom he originally named *Sherringford* Holmes. Most experts say Doyle took "Holmes" from American Supreme Court justice, physician and poet Oliver Wendell Holmes, well-known for his probing intellect and attention to detail. Sherringford was changed to Sherlock, Doyle enthusiasts say, for a famous violinist of the time, Alfred Sherlock. Fittingly, Doyle made his detective an amateur violinist.

INSPECTOR MORSE (1975)

Morse's creator, Colin Dexter, was once a Morse Code operator in the English army—but that's not where he got the name for his character. Sir Jeremy Morse, the chairman of Lloyd's Bank, was a champion crossword-solver in England. Dexter, once a national crossword champion himself, named his melancholy inspector after Sir Jeremy.

HERCULE POIROT (1920)

Some say the meticulous Belgian detective was named after a vegetable—*poireau* means "leek" in French. But it's more likely that Poirot's creator, Agatha Christie, took the name from the stories of another female author of the time, Marie Belloc Lowndes. Her character: a French detective named Hercules Popeau.

TRAVIS MCGEE (1964)

John D. MacDonald began working on his Florida boat-bum character in 1962, calling him Dallas McGee. The next year, President John Kennedy was shot—in Dallas—and MacDonald changed the name to Travis.

KINSEY MILLHONE (1982)

Sue Grafton spent 15 years as a Hollywood scriptwriter before the birth of her first Kinsey Millhone novel, *A Is for Alibi*. Where'd she get the name? From the birth announcements page of her local newspaper.

JOHN SHAFT (1970)

Ernest Tidyman was trying to sell the idea of a bad-ass black detective to his publisher, but was stymied when the publisher asked the character's name—he didn't have one ready. Tidyman absent-mindedly looked out the window and saw a sign that said "Fire shaft." He looked back at the publisher and said, "Shaft. John Shaft."

*   *   *

"Police arrested two kids yesterday—one was drinking battery acid, the other was eating fireworks. They charged one and let the other off."

—**Tommy Cooper**

THE HATFIELDS VS. THE MCCOYS

The facts about one of the most famous feuds in U.S. history.

The Contestants: Neighboring clans living on opposite sides of a stream that marked the border between West Virginia and Kentucky. The Hatfields, headed by Anderson "Devil Anse" Hatfield, lived on the West Virginia side. The McCoys, whose patriarch was Randolph "Ole Ran'l" McCoy, lived on the Kentucky side.

How the Feud Started: There was already animosity between the two clans by 1878. For one thing, during the Civil War, the Hatfields sided with the Confederacy, and the McCoys sided with the Union. But in 1878 Ole Ran'l sued Floyd Hatfield for stealing a hog—a serious offense in a farm-based economy—and McCoy lost. In 1880 relations worsened when McCoy's daughter Rose Anne became pregnant by Devil Anse's son Johnse and went across the river to live—unmarried—with the Hatfields.

Then on August 7, 1882, Randolph's son Tolbert stabbed Devil Anse's brother Ellison multiple times in a brawl that started during an election day picnic; when Ellison died a few days later, the Hatfields retaliated by tying three of the McCoy brothers to some bushes and executing them.

The feud continued for six more years. It ended after a nighttime raid on the McCoys on January 1, 1888. That night, a group of Hatfields surrounded Ole Ran'l McCoy's house (he was away) and ordered the occupants to come out and surrender. When no one did they set the house on fire. Ole Ran'l's daughter Allifair finally ran out and was gunned down; so was her brother Calvin. The house burned to the ground.

And the Winner Is: No one. This last attack was so brutal that officials in both Kentucky and West Virginia finally felt compelled to intervene. One Hatfield who participated in the raid was convicted and hanged for the crime. Several others were sentenced to long prison terms. With most violent offenders behind bars and the rest of the clan members weary of years of killing, the feud petered out.

About 1 out of every 30 Americans is either in jail, on probation, or on parole.

JOHNNY CASH'S CAPTIVE AUDIENCE

Johnny Cash was one of country music's first "outlaws," but the music industry was still surprised in 1957 when he played a concert at Huntsville State Prison in Texas. Over the next decade, Cash performed 30 prison shows and recorded albums during at least three of them. (The shows at California's Folsom Prison and San Quentin became the most famous.) Here are 10 little-known facts about the Man in Black's prison concerts.

1. Columbia Records repeatedly rejected Cash's request to record a prison concert.

Cash started playing at prisons in response to fan mail from inmates who identified with his songs (especially "Folsom Prison Blues"). Soon he discovered that "prisoners are the greatest audience that an entertainer can perform for. We bring them a ray of sunshine into their dungeon, and they're not ashamed to respond and show their appreciation." He suspected that their excitement and gratitude combined with the thrill of performing in a dangerous venue would create the perfect setting for an album. His record company disagreed—they thought the concerts would kill Cash's career and hurt the label's image. But when Columbia brought on producer Bob Johnston—known for being a bit wild himself and for bucking authority (as well as for producing Bob Dylan)—that stance changed. Johnston readily approved the country star's idea. Columbia remained tight-lipped about the performance and the release of *Johnny Cash at Folsom Prison* in 1968, still believing the album would never sell. But it did...an incredible 500,000 copies in one year. Sales were boosted by Cash's tough-guy image (he wore solid black clothing, used profane language, had a gravelly voice, and fought an on-again, off-again addiction to drugs). To help the cause along, Columbia released exaggerated ads claiming Cash was no stranger to prison. Which brings us to...

2. Cash never served time at Folsom, or any other prison.

He did seven short stints in jail, though, for drug- and alcohol-related charges. His song "Folsom Prison Blues" was instead inspired by the 1951 movie *Inside the Walls of Folsom Prison*. According to biographer Michael Streissguth, another influence was Gordon Jenkins's song "Crescent City Blues," from which Cash "borrowed" so heavily that when his version was recorded on the *Folsom* album, the original artist demanded—and received—royalties.

3. Cash inspired future country star Merle Haggard.

Haggard was serving three years at San Quentin Prison for armed robbery and escaping from jail when Johnny Cash took the stage there in 1958. When Haggard later told Cash that he'd been at the concert, Cash said he didn't remember Haggard performing that day; Haggard replied, "I was in the audience, Johnny." In fact, he was sitting in the front row and was mesmerized by Cash. He and his fellow inmates identified with Cash's lyrics about loss and imprisonment. Haggard reminisced: "This was somebody singing a song about your personal life. Even the people who weren't fans of Johnny Cash—it was a mixture of people, all races were fans by the end of the show." Haggard also soon realized that he shared Cash's talent for making music and for speaking to the struggles of the working class. He joined the prison's country band shortly after Cash's concert and penned songs about being locked up. After his release in 1960, Haggard sang at clubs until he eventually became a country superstar himself.

4. The live "Folsom Prison Blues" was too grisly for radio play.

Cash's declaration "I shot a man in Reno/Just to watch him die," followed by an inmate's shriek of joy, was edited by radio stations. But the hollering wasn't real. It had been dubbed in by Columbia Records since the prisoners had been too enthralled by Cash's performance to whoop it up during songs.

5. Cash's band smuggled a gun into Folsom.

Johnny Cash and his bassist, Marshall Grant, often performed a comedy skit with an antique cap-and-ball gun that made smoke. It was a prop—but it was a real gun. Grant accidentally brought the weapon inside his bass guitar case to the 1968 show. A prison guard spotted it and politely

6. Folsom Prison inmate Glen Sherley wrote the song "Greystone Chapel" and credited Cash with changing his life.

Glen Sherley was in Folsom for armed robbery, but he also loved music.

True crime writer Ann Rule was Ted Bundy's co-worker while...

Before Cash arrived for the 1968 show, Sherley recorded the song "Grey-stone Chapel" at the prison chapel. Appropriately, it was about a man whose body is imprisoned but his soul is freed by religion. Cash's pastor, who also counseled inmates, smuggled the tape out to Cash, who learned to play the song the night before the show. After seeing Cash perform his song, Sherley vowed to make a mark with the musician. Once he was released from Folsom, he went to work for Johnny Cash's publishing company, House of Cash. Sherley later remarked, "I was a three-time loser when John reached out his hand to me in 1968, and since then I sincerely believe that I have become a worthwhile person and can contribute to society."

7. Cash's concert at Folsom landed him his own musical variety show: *The Johnny Cash Show.*

Cash noted, "I've always thought it ironic that it was a prison concert, with me and the convicts getting along just as fellow rebels, outsiders, and miscreants should, that pumped up my marketability to the point where ABC thought I was respectable enough to have a weekly network TV show."

8. When Johnny Cash recorded *At San Quentin* in 1969, he didn't know the lyrics to one of his most famous songs.

It was the first time Cash had performed "A Boy Named Sue," written by poet Shel Silverstein, so he had to read the lyrics from a sheet he'd stained with coffee. And before playing "Starkville City Jail," Cash explained that he was thrown in the slammer for picking daisies and dandelions at two in the morning. (By other accounts, he was breaking curfew, drunk in public, and trespassing.)

9. Cash brushed up on his Swedish for a show overseas.

In 1972 Cash went to Stockholm, Sweden, where he recorded the album *Pa Osteraker* at a Swedish prison. Between songs, he impressed and thrilled the inmates by introducing some of his songs in their language.

10. At the 1969 show, Cash's song "San Quentin" nearly incited a riot there.

He'd just written the song the night before, and its inflammatory lyrics like, "San Quentin, may you rot and burn in hell," clearly struck a chord

...she was researching the murders later found to be committed by him.

with the audience. The prisoners clamored and stomped until he repeated the song. Shrieking and jumping up on tabletops, they were so close to rioting that the guards drew and cocked their guns and the camera crew backed up toward the exit doors. According to producer Bob Johnston, Cash later said of that hair-raising moment, "I knew that if I wanted to let those people go all I had to do was say, 'The time is now.' And all of those prisoners would've broken...I was tempted." (But of course, he didn't.)

*   *   *

CON LETTER

An old man lived alone in the country. He wanted to plant a tomato garden, but it was difficult work, and his only son, Vincent, who used to help him, was in prison. The old man described the predicament in a letter to his son.

> Dear Vincent,
> I'm feeling bad. It looks like I won't be able to put in my tomatoes this year. I'm just too old to be digging up a garden. I wish you were here to dig it for me.
> Love, Dad

A few days later he received a letter from his son.

> Dear Dad,
> Sorry I'm not there to help, but whatever you do, don't dig up that garden. That's where I buried the BODIES.
> Love, Vincent

At 4:00 a.m. the next morning, FBI agents and local police arrived and dug up the entire area without finding any bodies. They apologized to the old man and left. That same day the old man received another letter from his son.

> Dear Dad,
> Go ahead and plant the tomatoes now. That's the best I could do under the circumstances.
> Love, Vinnie

Odds that a burglary in the United States will be solved: 1 in 7.

NICE CROOKS

If they were really nice, they probably wouldn't be crooks to begin with. But what else would you call a thief who apologizes?

GIMME TEN

At 5:00 a.m. on November 17, 2003, a man walked into a 7-Eleven in Santee, California, pulled out a gun, and told the clerk to give him $10. The clerk gave the man the money, and the man ran off. At 10:00 a.m. the same man returned to the store, put $10 on the counter, and apologized for the robbery. The clerk didn't wait for the apology—he immediately pressed the "panic" button under the counter. The police arrived and arrested the thief, who explained that he had stolen the money to buy gas for his car.

BEER NUT

Twenty-one-year-old Nicholas Larson stole a cash register from the Bonnema Brewing Co. in the town of Atascadero, California. Apparently he couldn't stand the guilt, because the next day he called the brewery to apologize. The kicker: He turned himself in for the theft—even though the register had been empty.

SHOOTING BLANKS

A man walked into a Kansas liquor store, pulled out a gun, and told the clerk, "Give me everything in the register." The clerk told him that it was empty—there was no money. "That's okay," the robber responded. "There aren't any bullets in the gun. I was just kidding."

CHANGE OF HEART

In January 2002, Ronald Van Allen went into the Savings Bank of Manchester in Manchester, Connecticut, and handed the teller a note. "This is a robbery!!" it read. "All I want is the money from the cash drawer. No one has to get hurt or shot but me. Sorry for your inconvenience." Van Allen left with $2,000, but four days later, he walked into the Manchester police department with a bag full of the money, apologized, and turned himself in. "I wish all of our cases were solved like this," said Detective Joseph Morrissey.

American crime rates have been falling steadily since 1980.

WAS IT...MURDER?

A mysterious death reveals a deep, dark secret. Lives are changed forever; the community is shocked. Mrs. Uncle John finds her husband in the arms of—no, wait! That's not part of the story.

LAST NIGHT

On the evening of March 18, 2003, a 75-year-old Tampa, Florida, socialite named Jean Ann Cone drove to the home of friends to help plan the annual benefit gala for the Tampa Museum of Art. She had a few drinks while she was there, and when it came time to leave, another woman, Bobbie Williams, followed behind Cone's Rolls Royce to make sure she got home safely. Cone's husband, Douglas, was away on business, so she appreciated the offer.

When the two women arrived at the Cone residence, Williams watched as Cone pulled into her garage and closed the automatic door behind her; then Williams drove home.

It was the last time anyone saw Mrs. Cone alive.

NOBODY HOME

At 5:00 p.m. the following day, the part-time housekeeper, Norma Gotay, arrived and noticed that Cone's bed was neatly made. That was unusual because it was Gotay's job to make it, but she assumed that Cone must have slept at a friend's house.

A little later, a friend of Cone's came by to take her to a baseball game they had planned to see together. All Gotay could tell the friend was that Cone was not home and that she had no idea where she was. At 7:00 p.m., Gotay finished her work and went home without ever seeing her employer. It wasn't until Cone missed a lunch appointment the next day that people began to worry.

Someone called Cone's daughter Julianne McKeel to ask if *she* knew her mother's whereabouts. McKeel promptly went over and searched the house but couldn't find any sign of her mother—until she checked the garage and saw the Rolls Royce parked in a puddle of green antifreeze. The windows were rolled up, all four doors were locked, and there, slumped in the driver's seat, was Jean Ann Cone. She was dead.

What domestic terrorist was a former UC Berkeley professor? Ted "Unabomber" Kaczynski.

WEIGHING THE EVIDENCE

Considering the unusual circumstances surrounding Mrs. Cone's death and her prominence in Tampa society, the investigation into her death was surprisingly short.

Facts of the case:

✓ There was no indication that Cone was despondent or suicidal in the days leading up to her death.

✓ The garage door was in the closed position when the body was discovered, and so was the door into the house.

✓ Cone was on medication, and the autopsy revealed that her blood-alcohol level at the time of her death was 0.18 percent—twice the legal limit. She had had a history of episodes of light-headedness caused by her medications, something that alcohol might have made even worse.

✓ Her car key was still in the ignition of the Rolls Royce, and it was turned to the on position, even though the engine was not running when she was found.

✓ Julianne McKeel confirmed that her mother was in the habit of pulling into the garage and closing the garage door behind her before shutting off the engine, unlocking the door, and getting out of the car.

The police considered all the evidence and concluded that Cone's death was accidental. They surmised that when she arrived home on the evening of the 18th, she pulled into her garage, closed the door behind her, and then passed out behind the wheel of her car before she could shut off the engine. The victim of too much alcohol and prescription drugs, she did not regain consciousness in time to turn off the ignition, and suffocated on the exhaust fumes that filled the closed garage. The car kept running until it overheated—which explained the puddle of antifreeze—and then stalled.

THE PLOT THICKENS

When Mr. Cone returned home, having heard of his wife's death, he was crying and inconsolable. He behaved just as you'd expect a man to behave after losing the woman he'd loved for 52 years. "He was really depressed," the housekeeper told reporters. "They cared about each other. They had been married for so many years." Nothing Mr. Cone said or did aroused even a hint of suspicion…at first.

Then, just 13 days later, friends of the family happened to read a baffling wedding announcement in the local newspaper. Less than two weeks after his wife's death, Douglas Cone had remarried—and he hadn't bothered to tell his three grown children. Now *that* could be considered suspicious behavior.

Had Mrs. Cone been murdered? Was Douglas Cone her killer? What was going on? Their son Doug Jr. asked the police to take another look into his mother's death.

MYSTERY MAN

The first thing they did was investigate the woman Cone had just married. Here's what they found:

✓ Her name was Hillary Carlson and she was already married.

✓ Few of her acquaintances had ever met her husband, Donald Carlson, who worked for the U.S. State Department and was always traveling.

✓ They had been married for more than 20 years, had two grown children, and lived on a 67-acre gated estate 20 miles north of Tampa.

Then the investigators discovered some bizarre coincidences: The Carlsons and the Cones traveled in the same exclusive social circles. The two families had both sent their children to the same prestigious Berkeley Preparatory School, and Hillary Carlson and Jean Ann Cone had served together on the school's board of trustees. Both families had given lots of money to the school—the library named in honor of Mrs. Cone was just yards away from the baseball field that was named for Mrs. Carlson.

Douglas Cone and Donald Carlson seemed to have less in common than their wives did. Cone didn't travel in diplomatic circles like Carlson—he was in road construction. But had Jean Ann Cone and Hillary Carlson compared notes about their husbands, they might have noticed something unusual: Jean Ann's husband was away on business during the week and home on weekends, while Hillary's husband was away on weekends but home during the week.

And just like Superman and Clark Kent, Douglas Cone and Donald Carlson were never in the same place at the same time.

THE JIG IS UP

With the cops (and the newspapers) hot on his trail, Douglas Cone had no choice but to reveal his incredible secret: for more than 20 years, he had been living a double life. On weekends he lived with his wife Jean Ann in town, but during the week he posed as Donald Carlson, living with his mistress, Hillary Carlson, and their two children on their large estate.

He and Hillary had made up the story about the State Department job so they would never have to appear together in public. Douglas Cone's "business trips" were simply a ruse so he could spend the week with Hillary. She knew everything, but Jean Ann Cone apparently died without realizing that her husband had been two-timing her for over two decades.

REST IN PEACE
The police still believe, and the Cone children now accept, that Jean Ann Cone's death was an accident. "The family was only suspicious because Douglas Cone remarried too quickly," says Tampa Police Sergeant Jim Simonson. "Turns out that can be easily explained; it's not like he met the woman two weeks before."

*   *   *

56 "BAT" THINGS FROM BATMAN COMICS, MOVIES, AND TV SERIES

Batalarm, Batanalyzer, Bat-a-rang, Bat-armor, Bat Awake, Batbeam, Batbeam Firing Button, Bat Blowtorch, Batboat, Batcamera's Polarized Batfilter, Batcave, Batcentrifuge, Batcharge Launcher, Batclaws, Batcommunicator, Batcopter, Batcostume, Batcuffs, Batcycle, Batcycle Go-cart, Batantidote, Batparachute, Emergency Tank of Batoxygen, Bat Earplugs, Bat Gas, Batguage, Bathook, Batkey, Batknife, Batladder, Batlaser Gun, Batmagnet, Batmissile, Batmobile, Batmobile Antitheft Device, Batmobile Mobile Crime Computer, Batmobile's Superpower Afterburner, Bat-o-meter, Bat-o-stat Antifire Activator, Batphone, Batpole, Batram, Bat Ray Projector, Batresearch Shelf, Batrope, Batscanner Receiver, Batscope, Batshield, Batsleep, Batsignal, Bat Terror Control, Batzooka, Compressed Steam Batlift, Homing Battransmitter, Memory Bat Bank, Superblinding Batpellets

30,000 people attended bank robber Pretty Boy Floyd's 1934 Oklahoma funeral.

THE BEIJING TEA SCAM (AND OTHER CONS)

We like to think that most people are decent. But not everybody is—some people make a living by scamming any victim they can find, and someday, it could be you. So here are a few of the oldest tricks in the con artist's book…just in case someone tries one on you.

THE CON: The Antique Toy

HOW IT WORKS: The first con man, or "grifter," buys a worthless old toy from a secondhand store. He goes into a bar, sets it down, and buys a drink. He then pretends to take an important call on his cell phone and steps outside, leaving the toy on the bar. After a few moments, the grifter's accomplice enters. He excitedly notices the antique toy, and asks where it came from, because "it's a rare antique worth a fortune." The accomplice tells the bartender that he's going to get some money—because he'll pay the owner of the toy $500 for it. The first con man then returns to the bar. If all goes according to plan, the bartender gets greedy and offers to buy the toy off the first con man for a modest fee, thinking he can turn around and sell it to the accomplice for $500. The grifter accepts; the accomplice never returns.

THE CON: The Human ATM

HOW IT WORKS: The grifter places an "out of order" sign on the screen of an ATM. Then, wearing a security-guard uniform, he stands next to it, straight as a rod and looking ahead. Whenever anyone comes by to make a cash deposit, he tells them that he works for the bank and is taking deposits by hand. He writes out a receipt and takes their cash, but also asks for their account number and PIN to secure the transaction. It's amazing that anyone would fall for this, but there are frequent reports of it happening.

THE CON: The Melon Drop

HOW IT WORKS: While carrying a sealed package full of broken glass,

---

FBI statistic: 74% of threats against federal workers are directed at IRS employees.

the con artist bumps into an innocent person and drops the package. When it hits the ground, it sounds like a precious glass object inside just broke into a thousand pieces (even though it was already broken). The con man angrily blames the clumsy bystander and demands money to replace the expensive item he's just broken. This ploy gets its name from a scam perpetrated on Japanese tourists. In Japan, watermelons are expensive, but in the United States they're cheap. So the scammer buys a watermelon at a grocery store, then deliberately bumps into a Japanese tourist, drops the watermelon, and demands a large amount of cash to replace it.

The Con: The Barred Winner

How It Works: A con man approaches the "mark" outside a casino, holding what he says is a bag of gambling chips worth several thousand dollars. The problem, he says, is that he was accused of cheating and thrown out of the casino without getting a chance to cash in his chips. He asks the victim to redeem them in the casino, promising a portion of the proceeds. When the mark agrees, the con man acts suspicious, afraid the mark will just walk away with all his money. (Oh, the irony!) The con man asks for collateral—his wallet or a piece of jewelry. The victim goes inside to cash in the chips, only to discover the the chips are fake and that the con artist has absconded with the collateral.

The Con: The Fake Mugger

How It Works: Two con artists spot an easy victim for a purse-snatching. The first one steals the purse and takes off running. The second one shouts, "Stop, thief!" and chases the mugger down the street as the mark looks on. The second con man wrestles the purse away, but in the melee, the "thief" escapes. The purse is returned to the mark, who gratefully gives the brave con man a cash reward. The two con men then split the haul.

The Con: The Beijing Tea Scam

How It Works: This tourist scam originated in China. Two young women approach, chat up, and befriend a traveler. After hitting it off with their new friend, the women will suggest that their new friend accompany them to a traditional Chinese tea ceremony. The tourist thinks this is a great idea (an authentic cultural experience) and agrees.

The three people then go to a small teahouse. They are never shown a menu—if asked, the two con women say that that is just how it's done. Then the tea is brewed, poured, and slowly consumed. At the conclusion, the tourist is given a bill for $100. The women hand over their money, and the tourist reluctantly does the same. The girls part ways with the tourist…then return to the teahouse, where they get their cut of the $100.

The Con: The Landlord Scam

How It Works: The con man takes a short-term sublet of an apartment, and then takes out a classified ad offering the apartment for rent at an amazing below-market rate. Potential tenants come to view the apartment, and since it's a great place for a great price, they are ready to sign a lease on the spot. The con man takes their deposit and first month's rent. And then he does this with another tenant, and another, and another. The con man tells each victim that they can move in on the first day of the following month. When all of the scammed tenants arrive at the same time with their furniture, ready to move in, the con man is long gone with their money.

The Con: The Street Mechanic

How It Works: At a stoplight or stop sign, the con artist flags down an expensive car. There's something wrong with the car, he tells the driver. There isn't, of course, but the con man says the problem is one that's difficult to see, like a "slightly crooked bumper," for example. He tells the victim that this kind of repair is usually very expensive, but he can fix it in just minutes—he's a mechanic—and the only payment he asks for is a ride to work. The con man "fixes" the bumper, and the victim drives him to work. While riding along, the con man "calls his boss" and a staged emotional conversation follows in which the con man is "fired" for being late again. The victim, feeling grateful (and guilty) that the man stopped to help him, offers up a hefty reward of thanks.

*　　　*　　　*

"There's only two people in your life you should lie to—the police and your girlfriend."

—**Jack Nicholson**

Bounty hunting is legal only in the US and the Philippines; elsewhere it's considered kidnapping.

SMUGGLERS' BLUES

*Lots of people try to bring home contraband. Some get away with it
(probably more than we'd like to think) and others get caught.
And sometimes the stories can be pretty entertaining.*

The Contraband: Chameleons

The Story: Dragos Radovic, 25, was arrested in April 2007 after
flying from Bangkok, Thailand, to Zagreb, Croatia, when customs
guards noticed his carry-on bag was "moving." A search turned up 175
chameleons stuffed into the parcel. Radovic told officials that the man
who sold him the lizards told him they would change color and camou-
flage themselves…and would be invisible to border guards.

The Contraband: $1 billion bills

The Story: Customs agents in Los Angeles got a tip in early 2006 that
Tekle Zigetta, a 45-year-old naturalized American citizen, was involved in
some kind of currency smuggling. They got a warrant to search his West
Hollywood apartment, where they were surprised to find $250,000,037,000
in cash. The $37,000 was real; the $250 billion was in the form of 250
billion-dollar notes. The bills were dated 1934, bore the likeness of President Grover Cleveland, and were stained yellowish to make them appear
old. Zigetta said he found them in a cave in the Philippines. (There is, of
course, no such thing as a billion-dollar bill.)

The Contraband: Human bones

The Story: In June 2007, Indian police announced that the discovery
of a "bone warehouse" near the Bhutanese border had led to the
uncovering of an extensive international bone-smuggling operation.
The smugglers claimed that the bones had come from bodies meant
for cremation in the Indian city of Varanasi. "During questioning they
confessed that there is great demand for femurs that are hollow, to be
used as musical instruments," officer Ravinder Nalwa told Reuters,
"and skulls as bowls for drinking during religious ceremonies." He
said the bones were headed to Buddhist monasteries in Bhutan and
Japan.

The Contraband: Critters

The Story: The smuggling of wildlife isn't uncommon, but in March 2007, a woman attempting to travel from Egypt to Gaza was caught taking it to bizarre heights. "The woman looked strangely fat," border spokeswoman Maria Telleria said, prompting guards to call for a strip search. According to Telleria, the female guard who performed the search "screamed and ran out of the room." The woman had three 20-inch-long crocodiles taped to her torso. She said she planned to sell the crocs to a zoo.

The Contraband: Cows

The Story: In India the majority Hindu population considers the cow a sacred animal. In bordering Bangladesh, the majority Muslim population considers the cow a food source. That may explain the huge cow-smuggling trade between the two nations: In 2006 more than 400,000 cows made their way from Indian villages to Bangladeshi dinner tables. In 2007 the Indian government came up with a plan to stop the trade: All cows living in villages near the border are now required to get photo IDs. "A bit strange it may sound," said Somesh Goyal, a top Indian Border Security Force officer, "but the photo identity cards of cows and their owners is helping."

The Contraband: Tobacco

The Story: In 2001 Indiana State Police arrested John Hester, 51, for smuggling tobacco into Pendleton Correctional Facility. The operation was troubling for two reasons: 1) Hester worked at the prison slaughterhouse, where he was in charge of acquiring cattle to be consumed by inmates; 2) he smuggled the tobacco into the facility in plastic bags…in the cows' rectums. "It was stuffed into the cow," said Indiana State Police Detective Gregory Belt, "and then the cow was brought onto the floor and it was removed."

*　　　*　　　*

LOUIS LOUIS

World's most counterfeited items: Louis Vuitton purses. The company estimates that only 1 percent of "Louis Vuitton" purses are authentic.

According to insiders, some Mafia bosses are appointed through yearly elections.

DID THE PUNISHMENT FIT THE CRIME?

They don't give judges awards for creativity—
but maybe they should. Do these guys
deserve a prize? You be the judge.

THE DEFENDANT: Edward Bello, 60, a vending machine repairman and small-time crook

THE CRIME: Conspiracy to use stolen credit cards, with which he racked up more than $26,000 in charges

THE PUNISHMENT: Federal District Court Judge Alvin K. Hellerstein sentenced Bello to 10 months of home detention…*with no TV*. The tube-free environment would "create a condition of silent introspection that I consider necessary to induce the defendant to change his behavior." Despite a 30-year history of committing petty crimes, Bello has never spent a day in prison and says he's grateful to the judge for sparing him from the slammer one more time. But he's appealing the no-TV sentence anyway, claiming that it's a form of censorship and violates his First Amendment rights. "Let's face it," he says, "a television is sort of like your umbilical cord to life."

THE DEFENDANT: Albert Brown, a repeat drug offender in San Francisco, California

THE CRIME: Selling drugs to an undercover cop

A NOVEL APPROACH: Rather than decide the sentence himself, Judge James Warren of San Francisco handed Brown one of his judicial robes and told him to put it on. "This is your life," he told Brown. "You are your own judge. Sentence yourself."

THE PUNISHMENT: Brown, in tears, gave himself six months in jail. Then, according to news reports, he tacked on a "string of self-imposed conditions such as cleaning himself up for his kids, and steering clear of the neighborhood where he got busted."

"The Probation Department recommended six months and a good lecturing," Judge Warren told reporters. "But I figured, I'm not that good

---

Butch Cassidy's first offense: Taking a pair of pants and some pie, for which he left an IOU.

at lecturing. He, on the other hand, was very good at lecturing himself. And maybe this time it will stick. I had the transcript typed up and sent over to him. Just in case he forgets."

THE DEFENDANT: Alan Law, 19, of Derwent, Ohio

THE CRIME: Disturbing the peace by driving through town with his truck windows rolled down and the stereo blasting

THE PUNISHMENT: Municipal Court Judge John Nicholson gave Law a choice: pay a $100 fine or sit and listen to polka music for four hours. Law chose facing the music. A few days later, he reported to the police station and was locked in an interview room, where he listened to the "Blue Skirt Waltz," "Who Stole the Kishka," "Too Fat Polka," and other hits by Cleveland polka artist Frankie Yankovic. Law managed to sit through it and has since abandoned his plans to buy an even louder stereo for his truck.

THE DEFENDANT: A youth in the Wake County, North Carolina, Juvenile Court (names of juvenile offenders are sealed)

THE CRIME: Burglary and theft

THE PUNISHMENT: Judge Don Overby sent the miscreant home to get his most-prized possession. The kid returned with a remote-controlled car, which he handed over to the court. The judge then took a hammer and smashed it to smithereens. Judge Overby has done this with other first time offenders as well. He says he got the idea after someone broke into his house and stole his CD player, his VCR, and $300 in cash. "I remember wishing these folks could feel the same sense of loss as I did," he says.

*   *   *

CAUGHT WITH THEIR PANTS DOWN

In January 2004, three men in Spokane, Washington, decided to have a little fun by running through the local Denny's at dawn, wearing just their shoes and hats. Their only mistake: leaving the car engine running. While they were streaking through the restaurant, someone stole their car and their clothes. The three naked pranksters had to hide behind parked cars until police arrived to take them to jail.

Most commonly requested item for death-row inmates' "last meals": French fries.

LAWYERS ON LAWYERS

Believe it or not, some lawyers are actually quite clever. Here are some quotes from the world's most famous lawyers.

"I bring out the worst in my enemies and that's how I get them to defeat themselves."
—**Roy Cohn**

"The court of last resort is no longer the Supreme Court. It's *Nightline*."
—**Alan Dershowitz**

"We lawyers shake papers at each other the way primitive tribes shake spears."
—**John Jay Osborn, Jr.**

"The ideal client is the very wealthy man in very great trouble."
—**John Sterling**

"An incompetent lawyer can delay a trial for months or years. A competent lawyer can delay one even longer."
—**Evelle Younger**

"I've never met a litigator who didn't think he was winning… right up until the moment the guillotine dropped."
—**William F. Baxter**

"I'm not an ambulance chaser. I'm usually there before the ambulance."
—**Melvin Belli**

"This is New York, and there's no law against being annoying."
—**William Kunstler**

"I get paid for seeing that my clients have every break the law allows. I have knowingly defended a number of guilty men. But the guilty never escape unscathed. My fees are sufficient punishment for anyone."
—**F. Lee Bailey**

"I don't want to know what the law is, I want to know who the judge is."
—**Roy Cohn**

"The 'adversary system' is based on the notion that if one side overstates his idea of the truth and the other side overstates his idea of the truth, then the truth will come out….Why can't we all just tell the truth?"
—**David Zapp**

The CIA developed a listening device for use in Vietnam, disguised to look like tiger droppings.

GO DIRECTLY TO JAIL

Four stories of dumb crooks who saved us all a lot of trouble.

SELF HELP

"A 22-year-old Green Bay man led police on a chase that moved as slowly as 20 mph and ended in the Brown County Jail's parking lot. The man parked his pickup in the jail's lot, smoked a cigarette, got out of the truck, and lay face-down on the ground to be arrested, police said. He told the officers he knew he was drunk and was going to be sent to jail, so he just drove himself there."

—Milwaukee Journal Sentinel

SUPPLY-SIDE ECONOMICS

"Sylvain Boucher of Quebec was spotted by prison guards standing between the prison wall and an outer fence. Assuming he was trying to escape, they grabbed him, but soon discovered he was not an inmate…and he was carrying a large amount of illegal drugs. Boucher was trying to break *in*, thinking the prison would be a good market for his drugs. He'll get to find out. Before he had the supply, but no market. Now he has the market, but no supply."

—Moreland's Bozo of the Day

IS THIS WHY THEY CALL IT "DOPE"?

"Philomena A. Palestini, 18, of Portland, Maine, walked into Salem District Court to face one criminal charge, but walked out in handcuffs with two. Court Security Officer Ronald Lesperance found a hypodermic needle and two small bags of what police believe is heroin in her purse as she walked through the security checkpoint. 'This doesn't happen very often,' said Lesperance."

—Eagle Tribune

THE "IN" CROWD

"A man who tried to break *into* a Rideau correctional center with drugs and tobacco was sentenced to two years in prison yesterday. Shane Walker, 23, was believed to be bringing drugs to a jailed friend last week when he was foiled by corrections workers who heard bolt-cutters snapping the wire fence and apprehended him."

—The National Post

Sherlock Holmes's nemesis, Professor Moriarty, was based on real-life criminal Adam Worth.

THE GREAT DIAMOND HOAX OF 1872, PART I

*Most stories have the moral at the end. But we'll put it right
up front: If it seems too good to be true, it probably is.*

NIGHT DEPOSIT

One evening in February 1871, George Roberts, a prominent San Francisco businessman, was working in his office when two men came to his door. One of them, Philip Arnold, had once worked for Roberts; the other was named John Slack. Arnold produced a small leather bag and explained that it contained something very valuable; as soon as the Bank of California opened in the morning, he was going to have them lock it in the vault for safekeeping.

Arnold and Slack made a show of not wanting to reveal what was in the bag, but eventually told Roberts that it contained "rough diamonds" they'd found while prospecting on a mesa somewhere in the West. They wouldn't say where the mesa was, but they did say it was the richest mineral deposit they'd ever seen in their lives: The site was rich not only in diamonds, but also in sapphires, emeralds, rubies, and other precious stones.

The story sounded too good to be true, but when Arnold dumped the contents of the bag onto Roberts's desk, out spilled dozens of uncut diamonds and other gems.

PAY DIRT

If somebody were to make such a claim today, they'd probably get laughed out of the room. But things were different in 1871. Only 20 years had passed since the discovery of gold at Sutter's Mill in California sparked the greatest gold rush in American history. Since then other huge gold deposits had been discovered in Colorado, as well as in Australia and New Zealand. A giant vein of silver had been found in the famous Comstock Lode in Nevada in 1859, and diamonds had been discovered in South Africa in 1867—just four years earlier. Gems and precious metals might be anywhere, lying just below the earth's surface, waiting to be dis-

---

About 1,500 New York residents are bitten every year...by other New Yorkers.

covered. People who'd missed out on the earlier bonanzas were hungry for word of new discoveries, and the completion of the transcontinental railroad in 1869 opened up the West and created the expectation that more valuable strikes were just around the corner. When Arnold and Slack rolled into town with their tale of gems on a mesa and a bag of precious stones to back it up, people were ready to believe them.

OPEN SECRET

The next morning the two men went to the Bank of California and deposited their bag in the bank's vault. They made another big show of not wanting anyone to know what was in the bag, and again they let some of the bank employees have a peek. Soon everyone in the bank knew what was in it, including the president and founder, William Ralston. He had made a fortune off the Comstock Lode, and had his eye out for the next big find. Ralston didn't keep the men's secret, and neither did George Roberts: Soon all of San Francisco, the city built by the Gold Rush of 1849, was buzzing with the tale of the two miners and their discovery.

Arnold and Slack left town for a few weeks, and when they returned, they claimed they'd made another trip to their diamond field. And they had another big bag of gems to prove it. Ralston knew a good thing when he saw it and immediately began lining up the cream of San Francisco's investment community to buy the mining claim outright. While Arnold played hard to get, Slack agreed to sell his share of the diamond field for $100,000, the equivalent of several million dollars today. Slack received $50,000 up front and was promised another $50,000 when he brought more gems back from the field.

Arnold and Slack left town again, and several weeks later returned with yet another bulging sack of precious stones. Ralston immediately paid Slack the remaining $50,000.

BIG TIME

Ralston didn't know it, but he was being had. The uncut gems were real enough, but the story of the diamond field was a lie. Arnold and Slack had created a fake mining claim in Colorado by sprinkling, or "salting," it with diamonds and other gems where miners would be able to find them. It was a common trick designed to make otherwise worthless land appear valuable. What made this deception different was its scale and the caliber of the people who were taken in by it. Ralston was a prominent and successful banker; he and his associates were supposed to be shrewd investors.

DUE DILIGENCE

To the investors' credit, they did take some precautions that they thought would protect them from fraud: Before any more money changed hands, they insisted on having a sample of the stones appraised by the most respected jeweler in the United States—none other than New York City's Charles Tiffany. If the appraisal went well, they planned to send a mining engineer out to the diamond field to verify first, that it existed, and second, that it was as rich as Arnold and Slack claimed. These precautions should have been enough, but through a combination of poor judgment and bad luck, both failed completely.

MAKE NO MISTAKE

In October 1871, Ralston brought a sample of the gems to New York so Tiffany could look them over. Ralston was already hard at work drumming up potential investors on the East Coast, and present at the appraisal were one U.S. Congressman and two former Civil War generals, including George McClellan, who'd run for president against Abraham Lincoln in 1864. Horace Greeley, editor of the *New York Tribune*, was there too.

Tiffany's expertise was actually in cut and polished diamonds— he knew almost nothing about uncut stones, and neither did his assistant. But he didn't let anyone else in the room know that. Instead, he made a solemn show of studying the gems carefully through an eyepiece, and then announced to the assembled dignitaries, "Gentlemen, these are beyond question precious stones of enormous value."

The investors accepted the claim at face value—the appraiser, after all, was *Charles Tiffany.* Two days later, Tiffany's assistant pegged the value of the sample at $150,000, which, if true (it wasn't), meant the total value of all of the stones found so far was $1.5 million (in today's money, $21 million)…or more.

IN THE FIELD

Now that the gems had been verified as authentic, it was time to send an independent expert out to the diamond field to confirm that it was everything Arnold and Slack said it was. As he'd done when he brought the stones to Tiffany, Ralston went with the most qualified expert he could find. He hired a respected mining engineer named Henry Janin to do the job. Janin had inspected more than 600 mines and had never made a mistake. His first goof would prove to be a doozy.

Janin, Arnold, Slack, and three of the investors traveled by train to Wyoming, just over the border from Colorado. Then they made a four-day trek by horseback into the wilderness, crossing back into Colorado. At Arnold and Slack's insistence, Janin and the investors rode blindfolded to keep them from learning the location of the diamond field.

The men arrived at the mesa on June 4, 1872, and began looking in a location suggested by Arnold. A few minutes was all it took: One of the investors screamed out and held up a raw diamond that he'd discovered digging in some loose dirt. "For more than a hour, diamonds were found in profusion," one of the investors later wrote, "together with occasional rubies, emeralds, and sapphires. Why a few pearls weren't thrown in for good luck I have never yet been able to tell. Probably it was an oversight."

SEEING IS BELIEVING

Janin was completely taken in by what he saw. In his report to Ralston, he estimated that a work crew of 20 men could mine $1 million worth of gems a month. He collected a $2,500 fee for his efforts, plus an option to buy 1,000 shares in the planned mining company for $10 a share. He used the $2,500 and somehow came up with another $7,500 to buy all 1,000 shares; then he staked a mining claim on 3,000 acres of surrounding land, just in case it had precious stones too.

One of the secrets of pulling off a scam is knowing when to get out. It was at this point that Arnold and Slack decided to make their exit. Slack had already cashed out for $100,000; Arnold now sold his stake for a reported $550,000, and both men skipped town.

For Part II of the story, turn to page 158.

All five of the biggest diamond heists in history have occurred since 2000.

A GREAT APE

The United States has McGruff the Crime Dog. But what about the rest of the world? Well, South Africa has Max the crime-fighting gorilla—and he's real, not a cartoon.

PIT STOP

In 1997 an armed criminal named Isaac Mofokeng tried to break into a house near the Johannesburg Zoo. The homeowner caught him in the act and called police. Mofokeng fled into the zoo, jumped down into the gorilla pit and he found himself face to face with two gorillas: a 400-pound male named Max, and a smaller female named Lisa.

Max had lived almost all of his 26 years in the zoo, so he was used to humans, but he'd never been confronted like this before. Sensing that he and his mate were threatened, he grabbed Mofokeng in a giant hug, then bit him on the butt and slammed him against the wall of the enclosure. Terrified for his life, Mofokeng fired three shots from his .38, hitting Max in the neck and chest.

By then Max was pretty agitated. He attacked police officers as they entered the enclosure to arrest Mofokeng, and zoo officials had to subdue him with a tranquilizer dart. Max was rushed to a nearby hospital and registered under the name "Mr. M. Gorilla." Surgeons successfully removed the bullet from his neck but decided it was safer to leave the one in his shoulder. Luckily Max made a full recovery. A month later he received an apology from Mofokeng. "I wanna say I'm sorry to the gorilla," the burglar told reporters as he was being led from court. "I was just protecting myself."

PRIME PRIMATE

Max became the star attraction of the Johannesburg Zoo, as well as a national hero and a symbol of defiance to South Africans frustrated by the country's high crime rate. For his courage under fire he was awarded a bulletproof vest and named an honorary officer by the Johannesburg police force. Max lived out the rest of his life in peace and quiet, enjoying his favorite snacks of garlic, onions, and the occasional beer before dying in his sleep of old age in May 2004. He was 33.

HAMBURGER 911

This may sound unbelievable, but it comes from the transcript of an actual 911 call made in Orange County, California.

Dispatcher: Sheriff's department, how can I help you?

Woman: Yeah, I'm over here at Burger King right here in San Clemente.

Dispatcher: Uh-huh.

Woman: Um, no, not San Clemente—sorry—I *live* in San Clemente. I'm in Laguna Niguel, I think. That's where I'm at.

Dispatcher: Uh-huh.

Woman: I'm at a drive-through right now.

Dispatcher: Uh-huh.

Woman: I ordered my food three times. They're mopping the floor inside, and I understand they're busy...they're not even busy, okay? I'm the only car here. I asked them four different times to make me a Western Barbeque Burger. They keep giving me a hamburger with lettuce, tomato, and cheese, onions, and I said, "I'm not leaving..."

Dispatcher: Uh-huh.

Woman: I want a Western Burger because I just got my kids from Tae Kwon Do. They're hungry, I'm on my way home, and I live in San Clemente.

Dispatcher: Uh-huh.

Woman: Okay, she gave me another hamburger. It's wrong. I said four times, I said, "I want my hamburger right." So then the lady called the manager. She...well, whoever she is, she came up and she said, "Do you want your money back?" And I said, "No, I want my hamburger. My kids are hungry, and I have to jump on that freeway." I said, "I am not leaving this spot," and I said, "I will call the police because I want my Western Burger done right!" Now is that so hard?

Dispatcher: Okay, what exactly is it you want us to do for you?

Woman: Send an officer down here. I want them to make me...

Bob Hope was jailed as a youth for stealing tennis balls.

Dispatcher: Ma'am, we're not going to go down there and enforce your Western Bacon Cheeseburger.

Woman: What am I supposed to do?

Dispatcher: This is between you and the manager. We're not going to enforce how to make a hamburger; that's not a criminal issue. There's nothing criminal there.

Woman: So I just stand here…so I just sit here and block…

Dispatcher: You need to calmly and rationally speak to the manager and figure out what to do between you.

Woman: She did come up, and I said, "Can I please have my Western Burger?" She said, "I'm not dealing with it," and she walked away. Because they're mopping the floor, and it's also the fact that they don't want to…they don't want to go and…

Dispatcher: Then I suggest you get your money back and go somewhere else. This is not a criminal issue. We can't go out there and make them make you a cheeseburger the way you want it.

Woman: Well, you're supposed to be here to protect me.

Dispatcher: Well, what are we protecting you from, a wrong cheeseburger?

Woman: No…

Dispatcher: Is this like…a harmful cheeseburger or something? I don't understand what you want us to do.

Woman: Just come down here. I'm not leaving.

Dispatcher: No ma'am, I'm not sending the deputies down there over a cheeseburger. You need to go in there and act like an adult and either get your money back or go home.

Woman: She is not acting like an adult herself! I'm sitting here in my car; I just want them to make my kids a Western Burger.

Dispatcher: Ma'am, this is what I suggest: I suggest you get your money back from the manager, and you go on your way home.

Woman: Okay.

Dispatcher: Okay? Bye-bye.

Read this and keep quiet: Demand notes are used in 57% of bank robberies.

NOT-SO-WISEGUYS

*When people enter the federal government's Witness
Protection Program, they're supposed to hide, right?*

WISEGUY: Henry Hill, a member of New York's Lucchese crime family and participant in the $5.8 million Lufthansa heist from New York's Kennedy Airport in 1978, the largest cash theft in U.S. history

IN THE PROGRAM: The Witness Protection Program relocated him to Redmond, Washington, in 1980, and Hill, who'd changed his name to Martin Lewis, was supposed to keep a low profile and stay out of trouble. He wasn't very good at either—in 1985 he and writer Nicholas Pileggi turned his mob exploits into the bestselling book *Wiseguy*, which became the hit movie *Goodfellas*.

WHAT HAPPENED: When the book became a bestseller, "Martin Lewis" couldn't resist telling friends and neighbors who he really was. Even worse, he reverted to his life of crime. Since 1980 Hill has racked up a string of arrests for crimes ranging from drunk driving to burglary and assault. In 1987 he tried to sell a pound of cocaine to two undercover Drug Enforcement officers, which got him thrown out of the Witness Protection Program for good. "Henry couldn't go straight," says Deputy Marshal Bud McPherson. "He loved being a wiseguy. He didn't want to be anything else."

WISEGUY: Aladena "Jimmy the Weasel" Fratianno, Mafia hit man and acting head of the Los Angeles mob. When he entered the Witness Protection Program in 1977, Fratianno was the highest-ranking mobster ever to turn informer.

IN THE PROGRAM: Fratianno has another claim to fame: he is also the highest-paid witness in the history of the program. Between 1977 and 1987, he managed to get the feds to pay for his auto insurance, gas, telephone bills, real-estate taxes, monthly checks to his mother-in-law, and his wife's facelift and breast implants.

WHAT HAPPENED: The Justice Department feared the payments made the program look "like a pension fund for aging mobsters," so he was thrown out of the program in 1987. But by that time, Fratianno had already soaked U.S. taxpayers for an estimated $951,326. "He was an expert at manipulating the system," McPherson said. Fratianno died in 1993.

WISEGUY: James Cardinali, a five-time murderer who testified against Gambino crime boss John Gotti at his 1987 murder trial. Gotti, nick-named the "Teflon Don," beat the rap, but Cardinali still got to enter the Witness Protection Program after serving a reduced sentence for his own crimes. After his release, federal marshals gave him a new identity and relocated him to Oklahoma.

IN THE PROGRAM: Witnesses who get new identities aren't supposed to tell anyone who they really are, and when Cardinali slipped up and told his girlfriend in 1989, the program put him on a bus to Albuquerque, New Mexico, and told him to get lost.

But Cardinali wouldn't leave quietly. When he got to Albuquerque, he made signs that read "Mob Star Witness" and "Marked to Die by the Justice Department." Then, wearing the signs as a sandwich board, he marched back and forth in front of the federal courthouse, telling reporters he would continue his protest until he was let back into the pro-gram or murdered by mobsters, whichever came first. "If I get killed," Cardinali told reporters. "I want everybody to see what they do to you."

WHAT HAPPENED: Cardinali flew to Washington D.C. to appear on CNN's *Larry King Live*. But leaving the state violated his parole, so when he got back to New Mexico he was arrested, taken to jail…and released into the custody of the U.S. Marshals Service. Then he vanished. Did he embarrass the Witness Protection Program into letting him back in? The Marshals Service "will neither confirm nor deny" that he did.

WISEGUY: John Patrick Tully, convicted murderer and member of the Campisi crime family of Newark, New Jersey

IN THE PROGRAM: Tully served a reduced sentence for murder and entered the Witness Protection Program in the mid-1970s. By the early 1980s, he was living in Austin, Texas, where, as "Jack Johnson," he worked as a hot dog and fajita vendor. (It was a "nostalgic" choice—years earlier, he'd robbed a bank and used the money to buy a hot dog cart.)

Tully's business thrived, but he had repeated run-ins with the police and was arrested numerous times for public intoxication and drunk driving. At some point the police figured out who "Mr. Johnson" really was and then, Tully alleges, they started harassing him.

WHAT HAPPENED: Tully fought back by publicly revealing his true identity. He wrapped himself—literally—in the American flag, and, standing on the steps of city hall with his seven-page rap sheet in one hand and a beer in the other, announced his entry in the 1991 race for mayor. His reasons for running: 1) As a reformed criminal he was a better candidate than typical politicians who "get into office and *then* start crooking," and 2) "If the police are going to hit me, they're going to have to hit me in the limelight."

Tully actually won 496 votes…but lost the race.

WISEGUY: Joseph "Joe Dogs" Iannuzzi, bookie, loan shark, and member of New York's Gambino crime family from 1974 to 1982

IN THE PROGRAM: Joe Dogs had a reputation for being an excellent cook—even in the mob. After turning State's evidence in 1982, he supported himself by opening a bagel shop in Florida.

Then in 1993 he wrote *The Mafia Cookbook*. How can someone in the Program promote a book? They can't—witnesses are forbidden from contact with the media, and Joe Dogs had to pass on several offers to appear on TV. But he was a huge fan of David Letterman, so when he was asked to appear on *The Late Show,* he agreed, even though he risked being thrown out of the program. Why would he take the chance? "Dave was my idol," Iannuzzi explained.

WHAT HAPPENED: It finally dawned on somebody at *The Late Show* that bringing a man marked for death by the mob into New York City and putting him on TV with Dave in front of a live studio audience might not be such a good idea. At the last minute, just as Joe Dogs was getting ready to cook Veal Marsala, show staffers told him his segment had been canceled.

Iannuzzi was furious—according to some accounts he even threatened to "whack" Letterman. And although he never actually went on the show, the U.S. Marshals Service kicked him out of the Witness Protection Program anyway.

"What am I going to do now? Well," he told reporters, "I can always cook."

THE MAN WHO WOULD NOT DIE

*Here's a real-life crime story that reads like something
out of a cartoon. Warning: It's pretty gruesome
…but it's also pretty fascinating.*

THE NEFARIOUS SCHEME

During the waning days of Prohibition, Tony Marino's speakeasy served illegal liquor in the Bronx, New York. Marino and his bartender, Joe "Red" Murphy, did some additional business on the side: They'd take out insurance policies in the names of vagrants and then feed them so much booze that they'd die. By December 1932, after having pulled off the scheme successfully a couple of times, Marino and Murphy set their sights on one of their regular customers, a 60-year-old Irish immigrant named Michael Malloy. A firefighter in his younger days, Malloy was now just another old drunk with no money, no home, and no family.

With three insurance policies secretly taken out in Malloy's name, the two conspirators offered him an open tab and a cot in the back in exchange for sweeping out the bar each morning. The men stood to collect $3,500 (nearly $60,000 in today's money), but only if Malloy's death was accidental. But no matter how much hooch he put down (reportedly more than enough to kill any other man), he'd just sleep it off and then ask for more. Not only that, but Malloy's health was actually *improving*—forcing Marino and Murphy to take their plan to the next level.

A TOUGH CONSTITUTION

• Murphy, a former chemist, mixed antifreeze with whiskey and told Malloy it was "new stuff." After drinking it down, Malloy said, "That was smooth!" Then he fell unconscious to the floor. The men dragged him into the back room and left him to die. But he didn't.

• The next morning, they found Malloy cheerfully sweeping the bar. So over the next few days, Malloy's drinks were spiked with more antifreeze—as well as turpentine, horse liniment, and rat poison. He didn't die.

The CIA once used pigeons to take aerial spy photos.

• Murphy gave Malloy a potentially lethal sandwich. The ingredients: sardines that had been left to spoil in an open tin for a week, along with some metal shavings and carpet tacks. Malloy happily ate the sandwich. He didn't die.

• Then they gave Malloy another rotten sandwich, this one containing oysters that had been soaked in a batch of whiskey and wood alcohol—a poison that, if it didn't kill you, would blind you. Malloy didn't go blind. And he didn't die.

• January brought a cold snap. One night, when the temperature was –14°F, the men fed Malloy so much hooch that he passed out. They then took him to a park, stripped off his shirt, and threw him onto a snowbank. Then they poured a few gallons of cold water over him for good measure. He didn't die.

• Then the men paid a cab driver named Hershey Green $50 to run over Malloy. Another accomplice, "Tough Tony" Bastone, held up Malloy's unconscious body in the road. Just before the cab hit Malloy at 45 mph, Bastone jumped out of the way. They left Malloy's mangled body in the road, believing he was finally dead.

HE LIVES!

Over the next few days, the gang scanned the obituaries and police reports for news of Malloy's death. It didn't come. And then, three weeks later, Malloy walked back into Marino's speakeasy, ordered a shot of rotgut, and explained to the astonished men, "I must have really tied one on, because I woke up in the hospital with a cracked skull and a busted shoulder!"

The men were at their wits' end. Bastone, a part-time hit man, offered to "fill the bum full of lead" for $500. Marino refused. He had another plan: He hired a fruit dealer named Daniel Kriesberg to rent a room, take Malloy there, and give him all the gin (mixed with wood alcohol) that he could drink. After Malloy passed out, Murphy brought in a length of rubber hose. He put one end in Malloy's mouth and the other into a gas jet, and then he turned it on. On February 22, 1933, Michael Malloy was finally dead.

That night, Marino paid a crooked doctor $50 to sign a death certificate listing Malloy's cause of death as "lobar pneumonia, with alcoholism as a contributing cause." Then another member of the gang, an undertaker named Frank Pasqua, buried Malloy in a $12 coffin without even embalming him. The next day, Murphy, posing as the deceased's brother, collected $800 from Metropolitan Life. One policy down, two to go.

CAUGHT!

But then the scheme began to unravel as the conspirators squabbled over who should get a bigger cut. Bastone even threatened to go public. The next day, two Prudential agents came to the speakeasy looking for Murphy but were told he was down at the police station being questioned about Bastone…who had mysteriously turned up dead the night before. The agents became suspicious and told the cops that it looked like a case of insurance fraud. Police exhumed Malloy's body and concluded that he was indeed gassed to death.

In a headline-grabbing trial, the Bronx's "Murder Trust" captured the attention of the public. In his opening statement, Bronx District Attorney Samuel J. Foley referred to the scheme as "the most grotesque chain of events in New York criminal history." While on the witness stand, each gang member tried to pin the whole thing on Bastone, testifying that he had forced them to kill Malloy. The jury didn't buy it. The verdict: Guilty. Green, the cab driver, turned state's evidence and was given a lesser sentence—life in prison. Marino, Murphy, Pasqua, and Kriesberg were each put to death in the electric chair at Sing Sing Prison in the summer of 1934.

And to this day, doctors still have no idea how Malloy could have possibly survived all of those murder attempts.

*　　　*　　　*

WEIRD CRIME NEWS

In April 2005, 18-year-old Nicholas Buckalew of Morrisville, Vermont, decided that he wanted to make a creative and unusual "bong" (large marijuana pipe). Late one night, Buckalew went to a cemetery, broke into an above-ground tomb, and took the skull from an interred body, along with the eyeglasses and bow tie that were with it. Police said he told friends he was going to bleach the skull and make a pipe out of it. In 2006 Buckalew pleaded guilty to "intentionally removing a tombstone and intentionally carrying away the remains of a human body." He was sentenced to one to seven years in prison.

There are about 45,000 private detectives in the US. Average inclome: $42,000.

THEY ALWAYS GET THEIR MAN

If the Americans hadn't disrespected Canadian borders, we might not have the Mounties.

LAWLESSNESS IN THE WEST

In 1869, with Canada about to take control of its interior from the Hudson's Bay Company, Prime Minister John A. Macdonald outlined his plan for a paramilitary police force to patrol the region. The idea didn't really get going, though, until 1873, after the Cypress Hills Massacre. That year, American wolf trappers in Montana lost a lot of horses to thieves who appeared to be headed for the Canadian border. The trappers followed and lost the trail, but stumbled on a camp of 300 Nakota natives. In a tense standoff full of accusations and alcohol on both sides, the wolf trappers opened fire on the Nakota camp, killing at least 20 people.

The massacre outraged Canadians for a number of reasons, including the fact that Americans were invading their territory with impunity. And it wasn't the first time either. Just a few weeks earlier, whiskey traders had started illegally selling alcohol at Fort Hamilton (nicknamed "Fort Whoop-Up" because of the whiskey trade) near what is now Lethbridge, Alberta, and rumors swirled that the traders had flown the American flag over the fort. They didn't really, but the incident was enough to speed up the formation of Macdonald's police force, which he named the North-West Mounted Police (NWMP), or Mounties. They got guns, horses, and red uniforms, in part to differentiate them from the blue of the American cavalry…just in case the recurring border incursions turned into a full-scale war.

ON THE MARCH…WITH A TRANSFER IN CHICAGO

The first squad of 309 Mounties was assembled in 1874. Scoring an early point for multiculturalism, if not for sensitive language, Macdonald had specified that the new force should be a "mixed one of pure white, and

British and French half-breeds." Pay was 75¢ a day, and recruits had to be between 18 and 40 years old, physically active and able, and literate in either English or French.

On June 6, the Mounties got their first orders to move out. They were headed for the wilds of Manitoba and were to be accompanied by Henri Julien, an illustrator/reporter from the *Canadian Illustrated News*. (Julien had been given an all-expenses-paid invitation to make sure the Mounties' heroic march west received adequate public attention.) The police, dressed in their scarlet best, mounted their horses and prepared for a journey…to the downtown train station. There, they loaded their horses onto train cars—an effort that Julien called "long, tedious, and amusing" in its disorder. At 3:30 p.m., the train whistle blew, and "amid the cheers of a vast crowd, we glided out of Toronto."

They headed across Ontario and straight into the United States. There was no cross-Canada train yet, so this police force, created in no small part to repel American incursions, headed for Chicago, where they transferred to a train that would drop them off in Fargo, North Dakota. After that, they boarded another train that took them to Fort Dufferin, Manitoba, the last outpost of civilization. From there, they marched 800 miles through plains, woods, rivers, and swamps on their way to Fort Whoop-Up in Alberta. Their mission: to clean out the whiskey sellers and horse thieves, keep peace between the Europeans and the people of the First Nations, combat general lawlessness, and enforce a firm border with the United States…by force if necessary.

TAMPING DOWN WHOOP-UP

It took three months for the Mounties to arrive at the fort. By then, the whiskey sellers, having heard the Mounties were coming, had cleared out. There was also no evidence of hostile natives or a gathering storm along the American border. It was an anticlimactic start for the NWMP, but for many, the best sort of anticlimax. Peace was established without a shot, and for their first few years, the Mounties had to deal with few crimes worse than horse theft. Since there was no judicial system set up, the commander at Fort Whoop-Up got himself sworn in as a justice of the peace so that he could judge civil and criminal cases there.

In 1876 the Mounties got their first real taste of combat when they defused a tense situation after 5,000 Sioux, led by Sitting Bull and pursued by the U.S. Army, fled over the Canadian border. The Americans were seeking revenge for the bloody defeat at the Battle of the Little Big Horn. Mountie commander James Morrow Walsh was assigned to deal with the situation. He organized an ad hoc NWMP headquarters at Wood Mountain, where the Sioux had set up camp, initiated a close friendship with Sitting Bull, and managed to keep the peace.

GOLDEN AGE

Keeping peace in Canada's Wild West continued to be the Mounties' primary mission. In 1895, they headed over the Rockies for the first time to regulate the influx of Americans crossing the Alaskan border during the Klondike gold rush. They collected customs duties, confiscated guns, and required that each miner be equipped with at least a ton of food and survivor gear to prevent mass numbers of needy people overrunning Canada. During this time, the Mounties managed to maintain a reasonable amount of order in a chaotic situation, expelling troublemakers while sensibly not making an issue of popular illegalities like prostitution and gambling. Prospectors, not necessarily a law-and-order bunch, were impressed by the Mounties' conduct, and their reputation spread across the world.

Around this same time, though, Canada's government started talking about dissolving the NWMP. Prime Minister Sir Wilfred Laurier thought the Mounties' golden age had passed; they'd done a good job of keeping order on the frontier, but Canada was moving into the 20th century and needed smaller, regional police forces. Despite discussions in Parliament and Laurier's push, the Mounties were popular, especially in the west, and the measure never caught on. Instead, the Mounties became the country's official police force in 1920 and got a name change to the Royal Canadian Mounted Police. They also were becoming the stuff of pop-culture legend.

THEY ALWAYS GET THEIR MAN

Today, the Mounties are one of Canada's best-known symbols, but it wasn't just their crime-fighting ways that made it so. The chief culprit behind the Mounties image in pop culture was a Winnipeg writer named Charles William Gordon, who wrote uplifting frontier adventures under the pen name Ralph Connor. In 1912, he wrote a novel called *Corporal Cameron of the North West Mounted Police: A Tale of the MacLeod Trail*. It sold like hotcakes…in Canada and abroad. The book starred an uncorruptible Mountie hero, some satisfying fisticuffs, and the rescue of a pretty girl. It also launched a whole line of Mountie adventures.

Where books went, Hollywood followed. By the 1950s, America's entertainment capital had made a total of 575 films set in Canada, and many of those—including the musical *Rose-Marie*, involved the Mounties. Hollywood's love did not go unrequited; from the early days, the Mounties cheerfully supplied technical advice to filmmakers, and even officers in active service. There were Mounties on the radio—including the popular 1930s show *Challenge of the Yukon*—and when television arrived, heroes like Sgt. Preston made a seamless transition to the new medium (though its snowy outdoor shots were filmed in Colorado and California, not Canada).

These days, the Mounties still appear in entertainment, but they're also a legitimate police force; they act as Canada's federal police as well as the provincial police for everyone except Ontario, Quebec, and Newfoundland and Labrador. (Those have their own provincial forces.) Not bad for a ragtag frontier police department whose first job was cleaning up a little fort called Whoop-Up.

MOUNTIE FACTS

• In popular culture, the Mounties' motto is "They always get their man," but that's actually a Hollywood creation. That phrase comes from an 1877 newspaper story in the *Fort Benton* (Montana) *Record* in which the reporter wrote, "They fetch their man every time." Hollywood producers read the story, jumped on the phrasing, and created the Mounties' "motto."

• The Mounties' distinctive outfit—wide-brimmed hat, red jacket, black riding pants, etc.—is called the Red Serge because the red jackets were originally made from a type of English twill called "serge." The Red Serge is only for special ceremonies and events, like the Musical Ride.

• Women became Mounties for the first time in 1974.

DUMB CROOKS: OHIO STYLE

We first collected these tales of not-so-wise guys for our book,
Uncle John's Bathroom Reader Plunges into Ohio.

MAN OF STEAL

The Crook: Matthew Binegar of Dayton
The Crime: The Ohio teenager decided to shoplift from a Kmart in Fairborn, so he shoved a DVD movie and a video game into his clothing and fled the scene. Binegar might have gotten away if not for his work "uniform." He was a street performer for a local apartment complex, and was wearing a Superman costume when he tried to fly, er…flee. After a brief chase, the police nabbed Binegar. Why so brief of a chase? Because several Kmart employees had watched Superman steal the merchandise and called the cops. Binegar was found guilty of one count of criminal theft, served 52 days in jail, and was fined $200. (According to reports, he also faced a lot of criticism from his older sister Michelle, who called him "America's Dumbest Criminal.")

IF YOU DON'T KNOW, JUST ASK

The Crook: Adam Brown of Columbus
The Crime: Brown, 17, broke into an elderly woman's home and ordered her to hand over the keys to her car. He would have succeeded in driving away…had he been able to open the garage door. He went back into the house and asked the lady how to get the garage door open. She told him; he went back and tried again, but couldn't get it open. So he went back inside and asked for a more detailed explanation. She slowly explained the procedure. Finally, on the third try, Brown got the garage door open. But then he realized he couldn't drive a car with a manual transmission. So he went inside the house *again* and asked the lady how to drive a stick shift. She slowly explained it to him—slowly, because 1) he wasn't that bright, and 2) the police were on their way. When they arrived, Brown was trying to back out of the driveway. He was arrested on the spot.

LEAVING THE SCENE

The Crook: Darren Wallace of Columbus

The Crime: Wallace thought he had what it takes to be a bank robber: a bank to rob, and a getaway driver. The only hang-up? His getaway driver was his mother…and she had no idea she was going to be used for that purpose. All Mrs. Wallace did was agree to drive him to the bank. After she dropped Darren off, she decided to run a few quick errands while he was inside. A short time later, Darren ran outside with his bag of money, but his mother was nowhere to be found. (She was actually two blocks away at the grocery store.) When she drove back up to the bank to retrieve her son, he was already in handcuffs.

GARBAGE COLLECTORS

The Crooks: An unidentified group of burglars from Fostoria

The Crime: The thieves broke into the Fostoria Bureau of Concern, an agency that serves the poor and needy and keeps little cash on hand. Apparently not knowing that, they stole a safe from the administrator's office. What happened to the thieves is unknown; they were never caught. But Susan Simpkins, the bureau's director, was thankful that the crooks took the old, empty safe that had no money in it, and left the new safe there that did contain cash. She'd hadn't got around to throwing out the old one. Simpkins told police, "They did us a favor by taking it."

THE SEQUINS OF EVENTS

The Crook: Larry Edmonds of Barberton

The Crime: Edmonds was under suspicion of burglarizing an Ohio home: The resident had caught him in her bedroom and gave his description to police. However, they found little tangible evidence that linked Edmonds to the crime. But he was acting suspicious, so the cops brought him in for questioning. During the interrogation, something sparkly caught an officer's eye. Edmonds's pants were hanging low, and sequins were showing around his waist. When the cop realized the sequins belonged to a pair of panties, he pressed Edmonds for an explanation. He admitted that the panties belonged to the victim…as well as the red string bikini he was wearing underneath the sequined panties. Officers then discovered he was wearing *seven more* pairs of underwear. Edmonds went to jail; the woman's panties were returned. (No word on whether or not she kept them.)

On average, 80 people shoot at the Goodyear blimp each year.

DRAKEN TO THE CLEANERS

Here's a classic scam from our archives.

THE SIR FRANCIS DRAKE ASSOCIATION

Background: In 1913 thousands of people with the last name Drake received a letter from the "Sir Francis Drake Association," an organization founded for the purpose of settling the estate of the legendary British buccaneer who had died 300 years earlier. The letter claimed that the estate was still tied up in probate court, and that since Drake's death in 1596 the value had grown to an estimated $22 billion. Any Drake descendant who wanted a share of the estate was welcome—all they had to do was contribute toward the $2,500-a-week "legal expenses" needed to pursue the case. When the estate was settled, each contributor would be entitled to a proportional share. There was no time to waste—the fight was underway and any Drake descendant who hesitated risked being cut out entirely.

Exposed: The Sir Francis Drake Association was the work of Iowa farmer-turned-conman Oscar Merrill Hartzell. But he didn't invent the hoax—the first of hundreds of similar swindles took place within months of Drake's death in 1596. Hartzell got the idea for his version after his mother was conned out of several thousand dollars in another Drake estate scam. When he tracked down the crooks who had swindled her and realized how much money they were making, Hartzell decided that rather than call the police, he would keep quiet…and launch his own scam. Using the money he'd recovered for his mother, Hartzell promptly sent out letters to more than 20,000 Drakes. Thousands took the bait. Hartzell eventually expanded the scam to target people who weren't even named Drake.

Final Note: By the time the feds caught up with him 20 years later, Hartzell had swindled an estimated 70,000 people out of more than $2 million. Rather than admit they'd been duped, many of the victims donated an additional $350,000 toward his legal defense. Hartzell was convicted of mail fraud and sentenced to 10 years in federal prison; a few years later he was transferred to a mental institution, where he died in 1943.

Do you? 1 in 4 Facebook users leave themselves open to crime by revealing personal details.

UNCLE JOHN'S STALL OF SHAME

*Don't abuse your bathroom privileges…or you may
wind up in Uncle John's "Stall of Shame."*

Honoree: Joseph Carl Jones, Jr., an alleged burglar

Dubious Achievement: Landing in the can after a trip to the can

True Story: On the morning of February 7, 2003, Janie Sidener of Mineral Wells, Texas, arrived to open the store where she worked. She should have been the first one in the building that morning, but shortly after she entered she noticed something unusual, so she looked around. That's when she saw Joseph Carl Jones, fast asleep on a bed that the store had for sale. "Apparently he needed to take a break," said police spokesperson Mike McAllister.

Sidener quietly called her employer, who called the police. They woke the burglar, arrested him, and hauled him off to the slammer. So what was it that alerted Sidener to the fact that something was amiss? Before his nap, Jones had used the bathroom…and hadn't flushed.

Adding Insult to Injury! The store Jones had picked to rob was owned by the wife of the district attorney.

Honoree: Jon Carl Petersen, 41, head of the Iowa office of the U.S. Bureau of Alcohol, Tobacco and Firearms (ATF)

Dubious Achievement: Wrecking his own career with alcohol, toilet paper, and firearms (ATPF)

True Story: During Homecoming Week 2002, a pickup truck full of Indianola high school sophomores decided to TP some houses in town, an unofficial Homecoming tradition for many years. Too bad they chose the street where Petersen lived. And too bad Petersen had been drinking.

When he saw the kids throwing toilet paper in his yard, he jumped in his patrol vehicle and chased them with lights flashing and sirens blaring. When they finally stopped, he ordered the sophomores out of their truck and held them at gunpoint until police arrived…and arrested *him*. A sobriety test showed that Petersen had a blood alcohol level of 0.22%, twice the legal limit. He was charged with drunk driving, 10 counts of assault with a weapon, and two counts of simple assault. If convicted on all counts, he faces up to 20 years in prison and a $50,000 fine.

"He deserves what he gets," said one of the kids involved. "It's kind of stupid that he's an Alcohol, Tobacco and Firearms agent, and he was doing two of the things he's trying to prevent."

Honoree: Catherine Tarver, the mother of an accused murderer

Dubious Achievement: Using a public restroom to influence the outcome of a trial

True Story: In May 2003, Judge Walter McMillan ordered that Tarver be barred from Georgia's Washington County Courthouse. Reason: A courthouse employee saw Tarver cracking open eggs and sprinkling chicken feathers, chicken blood, and what has been described as "voodoo powder" in the restroom. So Judge McMillan imposed a ban, telling her, "If I find any more eggs in this courthouse, you will face criminal charges."

Sheriff Thomas Smith speculates that Tarver was trying to influence the outcome of the trial. "I think it's a curse against the prosecution," he told reporters. "There's been four incidents of it in the courthouse bathroom where brown eggs have been busted. It always happened on the day of Brandon Tarver's hearings."

Tarver denies using voodoo. "I don't even know what that is," she claims.

Honoree: Dr. Michael Warren, a South Carolina dermatologist

Dubious Achievement: Turning his bathroom into an ICU—a peekaboo ICU

True Story: When the staff restroom went out of order in 2002, Dr. Warren cheerfully allowed female employees to use his private restroom. But when months went by without Dr. Warren making an attempt to get the restroom fixed, his staff became suspicious. That's when they found a hidden camera in the doctor's bathroom. Dr. Warren admits that he installed the camera but claims that he did so "as a security measure, after cash and checks were stolen from his office." (No word on what a thief would steal from the doctor's bathroom.)

THE REAL ZORRO?

*Every cultural legend has to start someplace, even if it's from just a kernel
of truth, expanded and embellished until it bears no resemblance
to the original. Here's the possible origin of Zorro, the
"bold renegade" who "carved a Z with his blade."*

BACKGROUND

Pulp fiction writer Johnston McCulley created the swashbuckling character Zorro for a tale called "The Curse of Capistrano" that appeared in *All-Story Weekly* magazine in 1919. Literary historians believe McCulley based him on a number of characters, most of them fictional…and at least one real human being. It turns out that the story of the real man's life was just as unusual—and probably every bit as embellished—as Zorro's.

THE MAN

Not long after gold was discovered at Sutter's Mill in California in 1848, a young Mexican man named Joaquin Murrieta came to California with his wife, Rosa Feliz, and her brothers Claudio, Reyes, and Jesus. They hoped to strike it rich in the gold fields, but none of them did; the closest any of them got was when Claudio was arrested for stealing another miner's gold.

In 1850 Claudio escaped from jail and led his brothers and Murrieta in what became one of the most violent bandit gangs ever to terrorize the California gold country. The group was known to raid isolated ranches, but they preferred to rob lone travelers and Chinese miners (they thought the Chinese were less likely to be armed than whites or Mexicans). The gang murdered most of its victims after robbing them, to ensure that there were no witnesses.

The law began to catch up with the gang in September 1851, when Claudio was killed in a shootout following a robbery in Monterey County. Murrieta happened to be in Los Angeles at the time, and when Claudio died he assumed control of the gang. Not long afterward the bandits made the mistake of killing Joshua Bean, a major general in the militia. Murrieta then compounded the error by abandoning Reyes to his fate—Reyes was arrested for Bean's murder and hanged.

Outlaw "Ma" Barker's real name was Arizona Clark.

THE END

Jesus, the youngest of the Feliz brothers, apparently never forgave Murrieta for Reyes's death, because when the posse of state rangers caught up with him he willingly gave them the location of Murrieta's hideout. On July 25, 1853, Murrieta died in a gun battle not far from where Interstate 5 now intersects Highway 33 outside of Coalinga, California. After Murrieta died, Jesus gave up his life of crime, moved to Bakersfield, and started a family. He lived to a ripe old age and died in 1910.

Murrieta was not as lucky. After he died in the shootout, the posse cut off his head and preserved it in a giant glass jar filled with brandy—there was a bounty on his head (so to speak), and in the days before fingerprinting and DNA evidence, posses had to be a little more creative in documenting that they'd gotten their man.

Murrieta's brandied head made the rounds of the "$1-a-peek, crime-doesn't-pay" lecture circuit for a few years; then it ended up as a feature attraction behind the bar of San Francisco's Golden Nugget Saloon, where for the price of a drink you could sit at the bar and stare at the head for as long as you could stand the sight of it staring back at you. The head was still floating there in its jar on the morning of April 18, 1906, when it, the jar, and the saloon were all destroyed in the San Francisco earthquake and fire.

THE LEGEND BEGINS

By then Murrieta's image had already been completely remade into a Robin Hood-like figure who robbed from the rich, killed them, and gave to the poor. (His infamy as a killer was so well-established that a complete whitewash would not have been believable.) The makeover had begun less than a year after his death, when a newspaperman named John Rollin Ridge wrote *The Life and Adventures of Joaquin Murrieta, the Celebrated California Bandit.* Ridge himself was on the lam for a murder he'd committed in Arkansas, which must have given him sympathy for his subject. He painted a picture of Murrieta as a good man at heart who embarked on his life of crime only after seeing his brother lynched and his wife gang-raped by a band of vicious gringos. Murrieta then got his revenge by killing every white man he met until he was finally hunted down and killed by a drunken, sadistic ranger who was only in it for a $5,000 bounty.

Ridge's book sold so well that five years later the *California Police Gazette* published an even more exaggerated version of the tale. That in turn led to new versions being published in France, Spain, and Chile, where a statue was erected in honor of Murrieta, who—in that version of the story, at least—was a native of Chile. These fictionalized accounts of Murrieta's life gained even more credibility when a historian named Herbert Howe Bancroft fell for them and passed them along uncritically in one of his volumes on the American West. Now that a prominent historian had signed off on them as true, the tales were accepted as unvarnished fact by just about everyone. Joaquin Murrieta became a folk hero, one whose fame continues to this day. He has been the subject of a play by the Nobel Prize-winning author Pablo Neruda, and in 1976 he even became the inspiration for the Soviet Union's first-ever rock opera, *The Star and Death of Joaquin Murietta, a Chilean Bandit Foully Murdered in California on 25 July 1853.*

HEAD COUNT

So was Joaquin Murrieta ever really captured and killed? Was that really his head floating in the jar behind the bar in the Golden Nugget Saloon? Even that detail has been called into question. According to one version of the story, the posse on Murrieta's trail had only 90 days to catch the bandit and collect the reward. When the time was nearly up and they still hadn't captured their man, the party murdered the first Mexican they came upon and put *his* head in the jar so that they could claim the reward. "It is well known that Joaquin Murrieta was not the person killed," the editor of the San Francisco newspaper *Alta* wrote in August 1853. "The head recently exhibited in Stockton bears no resemblance to that individual, and this is positively asserted by those who have seen the real Murrieta and the spurious head."

EPILOGUE: Z MARKS THE SPOT

Seventy-five years after Murietta's death, writer Johnston McCulley was working as a crime reporter for the *Police Gazette*. After World War I, he switched to pulp-fiction writing. An amateur history buff, he based many of his stories in old California, and was undoubtedly familiar with the legend of Murrieta. But in addition to Joaquin Murrieta, McCulley is believed to have drawn inspiration from *The Count of Monte Cristo*, by Alexandre Dumas (1844–45), and *The Scarlet Pimpernel*, by Baroness

---

...for her book *Portrait of a Killer: Jack the Ripper, Case Closed*: $6 million.

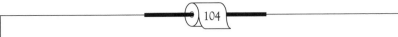

Orczy (1905), both of which feature wealthy gentlemen who don disguises to fight evil.

McCulley created dozens of characters over the course of his career, and as was the case with so many of the others it is doubtful that he intended for Zorro to be more than a just one-story character. That all changed when United Artists, the film studio founded by Charlie Chaplin, Douglas Fairbanks, Mary Pickford, and D. W. Griffith, decided to base their first film, *The Mark of Zorro* (1920), on "The Curse of Capistrano." Why mess with success? McCulley happily went on to write more than 60 stories featuring Zorro, the most popular character he'd ever create.

Zorro, in turn, was one of the major inspirations for another character: Batman, who appeared in comics beginning in 1939. In the original version of the Batman story, Bruce Wayne's parents are murdered after leaving a movie theater. The movie they'd just seen: *The Mark of Zorro*.

*   *   *

MORE REAL POLICE BLOTTERS

"A caller reported that someone was on a porch yelling 'Help!' from a residence on Bank Street. Officers responded and learned the person was calling a cat named 'Help.'"

"Dispatch received a report of a chicken pot pie running east on Main Street."

"Suspicious people were reportedly doing something with flashlights by the side of North 5th Street. A deputy checked and found the people were not suspicious, but merely Canadian."

"The Learning Center on Hanson Street reported a man across the way standing at his window for hours watching the center, making parents nervous. Police identified the subject as a cardboard cutout of Arnold Schwarzenegger."

"Two students of unspecified gender told police they were assaulted in some way on their way home from an unspecified number of assailants, perhaps sustaining unspecified injuries or none at all, police didn't say."

The Kalashnikov AK-47 (and variants of it) has been used in more than 75 wars.

QUEEN OF THE JAIL

*From our Dustbin of History files: Here's a true story of
danger, seduction, betrayal, and a deadly escape.*

THE SETTING

Allegheny County Jail, Pittsburgh, Pennsylvania, 1901

THE CAST

Katherine Soffel	**Ed Biddle**	**Jack Biddle**	**Peter Soffel**
The warden's beautiful wife	Famous outlaw	Ed's accomplice and younger brother	The prison warden

PROLOGUE

Jack and Ed were "the Biddle Boys," leaders of a gang of small-time outlaws who relied more on brains than brawn to carry out their nefarious crimes. Sometimes they used chloroform to render their potential victims unconscious; sometimes they used beautiful women as distractions. They carried guns, too…just in case.

On April 12, 1901, the gang was robbing a house next to a small grocery store in Mt. Washington, Pennsylvania. A female accomplice kept the grocer occupied while the boys searched the adjoining house, looking for a pile of cash. The distraction didn't work, though—the grocer heard a noise and went to investigate. A struggle ensued, shots were fired, and the grocer ended up dead on his living-room floor. The Biddle brothers fled the scene and holed up in a safehouse, but the police soon caught up with them. After a violent shootout, the outlaws were arrested, but not before a policeman was killed. The trial was quick and the sentence severe: the Biddle Boys were to be hanged for their crimes on February 25, 1902.

SECRET LOVE AFFAIR

Peter and Katherine Soffel were in the midst of a divorce when the Biddles arrived at the Allegheny County Jail. Katherine, who had previously spent time in an asylum, showed no interest in her husband. Instead, she spent most of her time visiting the prisoners, offering them spiritual advice and bringing them Bibles. For the inmates, Katherine Soffel was a welcome sight. They called her "Queen of the Jail."

She first went to see the Biddles out of curiosity; their exploits throughout the Midwest had made them somewhat notorious. Ed's charm and good looks soon won her over, though. She became infatuated and visited him more and more often, at least 25 times over the next few months, sneaking him food and books. The warden knew his wife had taken an interest in the outlaw but must not have realized just how keen an interest. He allowed her to keep visiting.

After a few months, Ed and Jack convinced Katherine that they were innocent and asked her to help them escape so they could live honest lives as coal miners in Canada. She agreed.

DARING ESCAPE

As luck would have it, Ed's cell could be seen from Katherine's bedroom window. The two designed a secret alphabet code with which Katherine could point to various body parts, representing different letters, and spell out messages about the warden's movements. This allowed the Biddles to devise a plan. Then they had Katherine—at great risk to herself—smuggle in two saws and a revolver.

On Wednesday night, January 29, 1902, the boys cut through their cell bars. They apprehended three guards and locked them in a cell. As they were leaving the prison, they were met by a waiting Katherine, which was *not* a part of the plan. She was supposed to lay low and meet them in Canada a month later. But Katherine, mad with love, took a page out of the Biddles' book and chloroformed her husband, then snuck away in the night. She didn't want to be away from Ed Biddle.

The warden awoke to a nasty headache and an empty house. When he was told the Biddle Boys had escaped, he knew Katherine was involved and immediately put out an all-points-bulletin on the three of them.

ON THE RUN

Meanwhile, Ed agreed to let Katherine come along, much to the dismay of Jack, who thought she'd slow them down. But Ed was the boss. They stole a horse and a sleigh from a nearby farm and made it to Coopers-

---

Killed by cops in 1934: Bonnie & Clyde, John Dillinger, Pretty Boy Floyd, Baby Face Nelson.

town, 38 miles north of Pittsburgh. They planned to have a quiet breakfast there and slip away unnoticed, but news of the breakout had beat them to the town. The Pennsylvania winter was harsh, and the three fugitives didn't have any warm clothes. They were easily identified and the police were now hot on their trail. They stopped for lunch in Mount Chestnut, 54 miles from Pittsburgh, and Ed and Katherine consummated their relationship. Time, however, was running out.

FINAL SHOWDOWN

With their horse and sleigh, the Biddle Boys and Katherine Soffel left Mount Chestnut on the snowy afternoon of January 31, 1902. They had only traveled a few miles when a posse met them head-on at the crest of a hill. Ed stopped the sleigh, handed the reins to Katherine, and he and Jack jumped off, each with gun in hand. The sherriff ordered the two men to surrender. Ed told them to go to hell and opened fire. The lawmen responded with a hail of bullets.

When the shootout was over, Ed was shot twice, Jack 15 times, and Katherine—who had grabbed a gun and joined in the fray—was shot once by Ed after pleading for him to take her life. She didn't want to live without him.

The three were taken to nearby Butler Hospital. Katherine's wound was treatable; Ed and Jack were not so lucky. As they lay on their deathbeds, they told police varying accounts of what had happened. Ed claimed he'd never loved Katherine, that he just used her to help him escape. Katherine claimed that Ed was just saying that to protect her. Love letters he wrote her while still in prison backed her up, but only Ed knew for sure. He and Jack both died on the night of February 1, 1902.

POSTMORTEM

The Biddle Boys' bodies were put on display at the Allegheny County Jail for two hours. More than 4,000 people came to see the famous bandits. Katherine served 20 months in prison and lived out the rest of her life in shame. She died a brokenhearted woman on August 30, 1909.

*   *   *

"We wouldn't have been captured if we hadn't stuck to the woman."

—Jack Biddle

1st known official autopsy: Julius Caesar's. The coroner ruled that the second stab was the fatal one.

WHERE'S JIMMY?

One of the 20th century's most notorious men disappeared nearly four decades ago...and hasn't been heard from since.

THE MAN

Born in 1913, James Riddle "Jimmy" Hoffa was president of the Teamsters Union from 1957 to '67. In that time, he turned it into America's largest, richest, and most corrupt union—with overt connections to the Mafia. In a highly publicized 1967 trial, Hoffa was convicted of jury tampering and sent to federal prison. Four years later, he was released—on condition that he not hold union office until 1980.

But Hoffa didn't stay inactive for long: In 1972 he filed a lawsuit to overturn the arrangement and began a campaign to return to power. By 1975, he'd gained enough support in the union to pose a threat to the leaders who'd replaced him...if his lawsuit succeeded.

THE MYSTERY

On July 30, 1975, Hoffa told his wife he was going to a Detroit restaurant for a meeting with two men—an eastern Teamster official and a Detroit mobster. Hoffa never returned. Police dug up fields, ripped up cement floors, and dredged rivers, but besides Hoffa's car—which was discovered at the restaurant—no trace of him was ever found. The two men he was supposed to have met with both had alibis, and neither admitted to knowing anything about the meeting.

THE THEORY

Most experts, including the FBI, believe the Mafia had Hoffa killed. Why? The mob had switched allegiance to Hoffa's successors while he was in prison and didn't want him messing things up. Hoffa's bodyguard, however, insists it was the government that killed the union boss. The reason? They were still trying to cover up the fact that they used the Mafia to try to kill Fidel Castro, and Hoffa knew too much.

He was officially declared dead seven years to the day after he disappeared. A tip in 2006 led police to dig up a Michigan field, but they found nothing. Hoffa's fate remains unknown, but his legacy lives on: His son, James P. Hoffa, is currently in charge of the Teamster's Union.

Most successful police dog: Trepp, a Florida golden retriever, has over 100 arrests to his credit.

CAUGHT IN THE ACT

A few tales of dishonest people getting their comeuppance.

CULPRIT: Nigel Hardman, a.k.a. "Prince Razaq," of Warton, England

GRAND SCHEME: After a number of civil servant jobs—mail sorter, meter reader, and accident insurance advisor—Hardman was ready for something different. His chance came after a 2002 car accident, when he applied for disability payments and housing assistance, claiming he was "too ill to work." Now, with a supplemental income, Hardman started training to be a magician. After he recovered, he stuck with his act...but kept on receiving government payments. Donning a turban, long robes, curly-toed sandals, and the name "Prince Razaq," he appeared on the British TV show *The Big Breakfast* (he escaped from a straight jacket while standing on a bed of nails), and his career took off. With newfound fame, Hardman started living in lavish style, even purchasing a 31-foot-long stretch limousine so he could, according to the *Guardian*, "drive stag and hen party guests around Blackpool."

EXPOSED! British fraud investigators, it turned out, had also seen the talent show and soon learned that the man who was "too ill to work" was moonlighting as a death-defying daredevil who swallowed swords and tamed lions. In 2008 Hardman, 40, pleaded guilty to 11 counts of fraud—in all, he bilked £18,000 ($35,000) from the British benefits system. (He was also nearly bankrupt.)

OUTCOME: Hardman was tagged for six months, which means he can't leave his home from 7 p.m. to 7 a.m. If he does, the magistrate warned him, the court will come down on him "like a ton of bricks."

CULPRIT: Martino Garibaldi, a 45-year-old shop owner from Montecalvo, Italy

GRAND SCHEME: Garibaldi's wife (first name not released) thought her marriage was fine...until one day in 2007, when she discovered that all of her money—37,000 euros ($73,000)—was missing from her bank account. And Martino was missing, too. Did he run off? Was he kidnapped? Mrs. Garibaldi hired a private investigator to track down her

---

First Sherlock Holmes movie: *Sherlock Holmes Baffled* (1900).

husband, but the search yielded nothing. Her husband and her money were both gone.

EXPOSED! A few months later, in early 2008, Mrs. Garibaldi received a call from one of her friends: watch the new movie, *Natale in Crociera* (*Christmas on a Cruise*), said the friend, and pay close attention to the background people. Mrs. Garibaldi watched it, and sure enough, there was Martino—along with his mistress—sitting at a table enjoying themselves in the background of a scene that was filmed in the Dominican Republic.

OUTCOME: Thanks to the new evidence, Mrs. Garibaldi was able to track Martino down and has since served him with divorce papers…and is suing him to get all of her money back.

CULPRIT: Michael Cosmi, a 29-year-old man from Wayne, New Jersey

GRAND SCHEME: From December 2005 to February '06, Cosmi would routinely wander around New York City's JFK Airport while speaking loudly into his cell phone: "Yes, yes, I've been robbed! And my patient doesn't have much time!" When a concerned citizen showed interest, Cosmi introduced himself as "Dr. Michael Harris" or "Dr. Michael Stanley" and explained that he desperately needed cab fare to get to Brigantine Hospital in New Jersey to perform emergency surgery. "I promise I'll pay you back," he'd say. "It's a matter of life and death!" In all, Cosmi conned ten people out of more than $800, including a flight attendant; a rabbi; a cop's widow; and an off-duty NYPD captain named Bill Tobin, who gave the scam artist $100.

EXPOSED! A week after he'd been unknowingly conned at the airport, Tobin was riding on the LIRR (Long Island Railroad) and heard Cosmi giving the same spiel to an elderly woman. "I wasn't carrying my gun, which was probably good, because I wanted to stick it in his ear," said Tobin, who arrested Cosmi for fraud.

OUTCOME: Authorities were able to track down Cosmi's other victims (he still had all of their names and addresses in his notebook because he'd promised to pay them back). It was later revealed that Cosmi is the son of a New Jersey prosecutor…and that there is no "Brigantine Hospital" in New Jersey or anywhere else. Cosmi was ordered to pay $2,165 in restitution and undergo drug counseling to avoid a jail term.

First FBI agent killed in the line of duty: Edwin Shanahan (1925).

THE GANG'S LAST STAND

When the James-Younger gang rode into Northfield, Minnesota, on September 7, 1876, their plan was to rob a bank. The townspeople, however, had other ideas, and the band of burgling brothers was never the same.

BROTHERS IN ARMS

After the Civil War ended in 1865, Confederate guerrilla fighters Jesse and Frank James were in a bind: They couldn't surrender for fear of being shot by the conquering Union army, and they certainly didn't want to ally themselves with their former enemies. Figuring there was safety in numbers, the James brothers teamed up with another group of brothers that had sided with the South during the war: the Youngers, specifically Cole, Bob, and Jim. The James and Younger brothers (and a few other outlaws) formed the James-Younger gang. They made it their mission to strike back at the Northern victors.

For the next 10 years, the James-Younger gang went on a violent crime spree throughout the reunified United States. They robbed banks, stores, stagecoaches, and individuals and even committed murder. In 1873 they pulled off their first train robbery, killing the engineer and stealing $3,000 from the passengers. These dastardly deeds quickly earned the James-Younger gang a reputation as the most notorious—and wanted—criminals of their time.

GO NORTH, YOUNG MEN

In 1876 Bill Stiles, a gang member from Minnesota, suggested that his home state would be an easy target for a bank robbery. Stiles boasted that the banks there were full of money and that the locals (mostly farmers) would be poor shots and unable to defend themselves.

The gang posed as railroad surveyors and cased varous Minnesota cities, including Red Wing, St. Paul, and Mankato, before deciding on the First National Bank of Northfield. It seemed like a good choice; the bank was rumored to hold a lot of Union money, and the former Confederates were always looking for ways to get back at their old enemies. Given the relatively small size of the town and the experience of the gang, the men looked forward to a quick and profitable job.

THE JOB

On the afternoon of September 7, 1876, eight gang members rode into Northfield wearing long coats that concealed their weapons. Frank James, Bob Younger, and Charlie Pitts entered the bank around two o'clock in the afternoon. Cole Younger and Clell Miller stood guard at the front door, while Jesse James, Jim Younger, and Bill Stiles protected the planned escape route.

Inside the bank, one of the robbers (possibly Frank James, though no one is certain) ordered cashier Joseph Lee Heywood to open the safe. Heywood refused. Things heated up when merchant J. S. Allen walked by the bank and noticed the commotion. He tried to get past Miller at the front door but couldn't; Miller shoved him away. Allen then ran off yelling, "The bank is being robbed! The bank is being robbed!" That's when Miller and Cole Younger started shooting at him.

NOT IN OUR TOWN!

The unexpected gunfire outside startled the robbers and the hostages inside the bank. Mayhem broke out. During the battle, bank clerk A. E. Bunker made a mad dash out the back door, but not before taking a bullet in his shoulder. Then Frank James shot and killed Heywood, who went down *still* refusing to open the safe.

Meanwhile, several Northfield citizens had armed themselves and taken up strategic positions around the town. As the outlaws tried to get away, they were met by a barrage of bullets from the townsfolk. Clell Miller and Bill Stiles fell dead in the street. Frank James was shot in the leg; Jesse James rode by on a horse, grabbed his brother's arm, and pulled him along. The Younger brothers and Pitts also took some bullets. A local named Nicolas Gustafson was caught in the crossfire and fatally shot. When the smoke cleared, two gang members and two townies were dead.

LIVING ON THE LAM

The wounded outlaws headed for the woods to regroup. For the next week, the gang members sneaked through several tiny Minnesota towns. But they were lost; they couldn't find their way around without their guide, Bill Stiles. As the days went by, the gang—slowed by their injuries—grew increasingly tired and hungry. It got so bad that their exhausted horses had to be abandoned. All the while, posses of angry

Minnesotans—regular folk and lawmen alike—were hunting them down. As a last resort, the members of the James-Younger gang decided to split up. The James bothers stole two horses from a farm and headed for Dakota Territory, while Charlie Pitts and the wounded Younger brothers went west, eventually hiding near Madelia, Minnesota.

Time was running out for the Youngers and Pitts. The posses were hot on their trail, and just outside Madelia, bareley 50 miles from Northfield, the search party closed in on them. Shots rang out. Pitts was killed. The Youngers thought better of trying to run again, and surrendered. The Youngers were each arrested and tried on four counts, including murder, attempted murder, and robbery. To avoid execution, the brothers pleaded guilty to the crimes. (At the time, Minnesota law would not allow a death sentence for people who pleaded guilty.) All three Youngers were sentenced to life in prison.

THE ASSASSINATION OF JESSE JAMES

But the James brothers escaped from Minnesota. They kidnapped a doctor to treat their wounds, released him, and then Jesse and Frank traveled to their home state of Missouri. There, they formed a new gang and continued on with their lives of crime. But there was a huge price on their heads, and they knew it. Lawmen all over the Midwest were looking for them. The governor of Missouri even offered a $10,000 reward for their capture. (Back then, that amount would set someone up for life.) In 1881 James was shot and killed by the youngest member of the gang, Bob Ford. Frank later turned himself in. He was tried but acquitted for his crimes.

NORTHFIELD'S LEGACY

Today, the memory of the raid lives on in Minnesota. The First National Bank of Northfield has been restored as a museum, and each September the town's citizens celebrate the "Defeat of Jesse James Day." Festivities include a reenactment of the raid, a parade, and a graveside memorial service at the burial sites of J. L. Heywood and Nicolas Gustafson.

Final Irony: The bank job that marked the end of the James-Younger game only netted the boys $26.70.

*   *   *

"A thief believes everybody steals." —**Edgar Watson Howe**

The insanity defense was used in court as early as the 13th century.

HELLO, 911?

*Here's are some of our favorite emergency-call
stories. Believe it or not, they're all real.*

NINE-ONE-YAWN

In August 2004, an unidentified person called 911 in Millersville,
Maryland, and was asked the nature of their emergency. The
caller explained the situation, and the dispatcher responded…by snoring.
It was the middle of the night and the dispatcher had fallen asleep. For
the next two minutes the caller tried to wake up the dispatcher but could-
n't. Police captain Kim Bowman told reporters that, luckily, the call
wasn't a *dire* emergency and nothing bad had come of it (but added that
the department was implementing a program to teach employees how to
stay awake during the night shift).

IT'S A LOVE EMERGENCY

In July 2006, a sheriff's deputy in Aloha, Oregon, responded to a noise
complaint at the home of Lorna Jeanne Dudash. He spoke with the
woman for just a moment and then left. A short time later Ms. Dudash
called 911—and asked if that "cutie-pie" officer could return. "He's the
cutest cop I've seen in a long time. I just want to know his name," she
said. The confused dispatcher asked again what her emergency was and
Dudash responded, "Honey, I'm just going to be honest with you, I'm 45
years old and I'd just like to meet him again." So the dispatcher sent the
officer to Dudash's home—and he promptly arrested her for abuse of the
emergency-dispatch system. She faces several thousand dollars in fines
and up to a year in prison.

GIMME A NINE…GIMME A ONE…

In 1999 a 911 dispatcher in Fayetteville, Arkansas, received a call, but
there was nobody on the line—all she could hear was a football game in
the background. She hung up and called the number back, but nobody
answered. A short time later it happened again, and again there was
nobody on the line. A few minutes later it happened again…and
again…and again. Dispatchers were called 35 times before police finally
traced the call…to a football fan who had his cell phone set to speed-dial

---

911. It was in his pocket and had been going off every time he stood up to cheer.

PIZZA 'N' NUTS

In May 2005, 86-year-old Dorothy Densmore of Charlotte, North Carolina, called 911 and complained to the dispatcher that she had called a nearby pizza shop, and they had refused to deliver a pizza to her. The dispatcher advised Densmore that calling 911 for non-emergencies was a crime and hung up on her. Densmore called back, and kept calling back. She called more than 20 times. An officer was finally sent out to her home to arrest her…but not before being kicked, punched, and bitten on the hand by Densmore. (She had also complained to the dispatcher that someone in the pizza parlor had called her a "crazy old coot.")

GAS LEAK

Officers in Janesville, Wisconsin, responded to a 911 call about a domestic disturbance after a husband and wife got into an argument. When they arrived at the couple's home, the wife explained to the officers that the argument had started after the husband had "inappropriately passed gas" while they were tucking their son into bed. (The man was not charged with a crime.)

*   *   *

DIAL "M" FOR MURDERER

"Murderers and Mafia mobsters have been employed by Italy's state telephone company to run a call center from prison. Telecom Italia has opened a new directory assistance service inside the notorious Rebibbia prison, which is Rome's largest jail, with 1,600 inmates. Twenty-six prisoners in the program work from 8 a.m. to 8 p.m. and are paid the equivalent of 20 cents for every call they answer. 'It is good because people do not know who we are, so we do not feel like we are in a ghetto anymore,' said a man serving 13 years for murder. There are plans to open another call center at Poggioreale prison in Naples. Although inmates have access to a nationwide database of phone numbers, they are unable to dial out."

—*Sydney Morning Herald*

Every year, more than 20,000 art thefts are reported in Italy.

YAKUZA!

It's difficult for Westerners to understand the Yakuza, often referred
to as the Japanese Mafia. We were confused ourselves, so we sent
Uncle John on a covert mission to Tokyo to infiltrate the Yakuza.
He returned with some great info…but he also had a lot of
tattoos and only nine fingers. Now he's kind of menacing.

YA-WHAT-A?

Did you see the movie *Kill Bill*? The "Crazy 88s" depicted in the film were a fearsome Japanese Yakuza gang…which were summarily dismembered by Uma Thurman's character. In real life, Thurman wouldn't have stood a chance against the Yakuza. With their full-body tattoos, expensive sunglasses, flashy black suits, and slicked-back hair, Yakuza gang members are highly trained outlaws—as organized as they are criminal. Taking a page from the Yakuza's book, we've carefully organized this two-part article into tidy little sections.

ORIGIN

• Dating back to the 1600s, the "official" Yakuza history describes the crime syndicate's ancestors as if they were "Robin Hoods," descended from the *machi-yokko* (servants of the town) who protected villagers from out-of-control rogue samurai.

• Another theory: The original Yakuza were rogue samurai. Whether they began as heroes or villains, the Yakuza are proud to be outcasts—a fact reflected in their name: *ya* means 8, *ku* means 9, and *sa* means 3, which add up to 20—a losing hand in the card game *hana-fuda* (flower cards). The Yakuza are the "bad hands" or "losers" of society, an image they embrace.

STRUCTURE

• The Yakuza is not a single entity, but rather a collection of separate gangs, much like the Mafia, but with a much more intricate hierarchy. Within the crime syndicate are several powerful "families"; the most powerful is the Yamaguchi-Gumi family, with about 45,000 members. In all, there are 2,500 families and more than 110,000 Yakuza, making it the largest criminal organization in the world.

2008 newspaper study: 36% of recent Atlanta Police Academy graduates have a criminal record

• Yakuza activity is not limited to Japan; they have a presence in other Asian countries, as well as in Europe, Mexico, and the United States. Hawaii has an especially large Yakuza presence (members cover their tattoos and pose as tourists). The Yakuza own casinos in Las Vegas, operate construction companies in Chicago and London, and produce movies in Hollywood and Hong Kong.

HIERARCHY

• Each family is made up of many smaller sub-gangs, or clans. At the head of each family is a *kumicho*, what Westerners might refer to as the "godfather." There are several other subgroups of leadership, all the way to the *oyabun*, who are clan bosses. They each have a group of trusted men, who act as local bosses, and so on, down to the bottom rungs, the *kobun* (children).

• Once accepted, each kobun is assigned to an oyabun. The elder member instructs and watches over his apprentice, and is also responsible for his apprentice's actions. This relationship is considered more sacred than that of father and son.

THE UPSIDE

• Acceptance by a community and free health care (not many criminal organizations have a dental plan). Those are great perks, but what *really* draws young men into the life are Japanese Yakuza movies—which thrived in the 1960s and '70s. They glorified the outlaws and their fancy cars and black suits. The message is clear: To be Yakuza is to be a badass.

• The money can be quite good, too. Yakuza families earn around $60 billion annually, nearly 2 percent of Japan's gross domestic product. But it can take a while for new recruits to start seeing big dividends. (In fact, they have to hand over all profits to their oyabuns.) However, recruits who show an aptitude for learning may receive a free education.

THE DOWNSIDE

• Beyond the obvious risks brought on by a life of crime, there are some other dangers involved, such as hepatitis. Japanese tattoo artists use a technique called *tebori*—attaching a small bundle of needles to a bamboo handle, which is dipped in ink and tapped into the skin by hand or with a small hammer. This method is notorious for spreading infections. In addi-

Ancient Aztecs guilty of public drunkenness had their heads shaved and their homes destroyed.

tion, the ink inhibits the sweating out of toxins. These issues, combined with heavy drinking, lead to a high incidence of liver disease among Yakuza members. (Tattoos are also very expensive, costing upward of $10,000, not to mention the years of painful pinpricks.)

• If an obun angers or embarrasses his oyabun, he is obligated to cut off the tip of his pinkie finger and present it to him gift-wrapped. A second offense requires the severing of the second joint of that finger, and so on. This punishment, called *yubizume*, comes from the traditional way of holding a Japanese sword—removing the pinkie and ring fingers progressively weakens a warrior's grip. A family member knows that he must commit yubizume when his superior gives him a knife and a piece of string—the knife to cut off the finger, and the string to stop the bleeding. Of course, if a Yakuza *really* screws up, he is expected to commit suicide by way of *seppuku*—ritual disembowelment with a sword.

• Japan is a society of rigid social rules, and the Yakuza break many of them. Although at times the families have been beneficial to their communities, they remain outcasts. Because of this, tattoos and missing fingers are strictly taboo among Japanese citizens, and those who flaunt them are often shunned.

CODE OF CONDUCT

• In the ongoing attempt to keep public relations smooth, Yakuza codes of behavior are very important: Theft is frowned upon, as it harms the community. Although they smuggle and sell firearms, members seldom use them. And if a gang member kills someone, by Yakuza standards he should take the murder weapon to the police and confess to the crime.

• Harmony within the groups is also paramount to keeping order, requiring a few basic tenets: Never reveal any secrets of the organization, never harm wives or children, don't use drugs, don't withhold money from the gang, always obey your superior, and don't ask the police for help. Above all else, loyalty to the family is the glue that holds the Yakuza together.

But that glue isn't as strong as it once was, and the Yakuza are in a state of flux.

For that story, and for instructions on how to join the Yakuza (they accept applications), grip your sword and turn to page 211.

Good night: In the 1840s, French criminals couldn't be arrested from sundown to sunup.

MURDER, HE WROTE

*How did New York City, a famous cigar girl, and Edgar
Allan Poe combine to create one of the world's first
murder mystery stories? Read on.*

PROLOGUE

Anyone who enjoys murder mysteries owes a debt of gratitude to
Edgar Allan Poe. Before there was a Sherlock Holmes or a Nancy
Drew, before the word "detective" was even in common usage, Poe created
the character of C. Auguste Dupin, an eccentric Parisian genius who
solved murder cases that baffled the city's police force. Dupin first
appeared in April of 1841 in a short story called "The Murders in the
Rue Morgue" and reappeared in two more stories after that. To create his
detective stories, Poe did plenty of research on real crimes, including one
of his century's most notorious murder mysteries.

CHAPTER ONE: THE BODY

On July 28, 1841, the body of 21-year-old Mary Cecilia Rogers was found
floating in the Hudson River near Hoboken, New Jersey. The discovery
was shocking, not just because the body was battered beyond recognition
(she could be identified only by her clothing and a birthmark on her
arm), but because Rogers was famous in New York City. One of America's
first celebrities, she was nicknamed the "beautiful cigar girl."

Until shortly before her death, Rogers had worked at a huge
tobacco and cigar shop on Broadway. She had an unusual job: enticing
men into the shop. According to legend, she was so beautiful that men
would come inside just to see her, and wouldn't leave without buying
tobacco. Some of those admirers even published poems in local papers,
singing of her charms. One besotted "poet" wrote, "She's picked for her
beauty from many a belle / And placed near the window Havanas to sell."
Other patrons were more talented, including New York City newspaper
reporters and a writer named Edgar Allan Poe.

CHAPTER TWO: THE DISAPPEARANCE

By July 1841, Rogers had quit her job at the tobacco shop to help her

---

Until David Berkowitz called himself "Son of Sam," the press called him the ".44 Caliber Killer."

mother run a boarding house on Nassau Street. She had plenty of admirers there, too, including a sailor named William Kiekuck, clerk Alfred Crommelin, and the dashingly handsome (but hard-drinking) Daniel Payne. To her mother's dismay, Rogers chose Payne and accepted his marriage proposal, though there were rumors later that the young woman was planning to leave him.

On Sunday, July 25, Rogers told her fiancé that she was going to visit her aunt, who lived uptown. She never made it. When she hadn't returned home the next morning, Payne took out a missing-persons ad in the *New York Sun*. Reporters jumped on the story—search teams formed and started combing the city. But Rogers was nowhere to be found...until Wednesday, when her body was pulled from the river.

The coroner found strangulation marks on Rogers's neck, and part of her dress had been torn off and tied around her mouth and neck with a sailor's slipknot. Another piece of her dress was missing, and the coroner speculated that it had been used to drag the body to the river. He also noted that Rogers was not pregnant, she had been severely beaten and sexually assaulted, and her body still showed signs of rigor mortis (when a corpse's limbs go stiff). He concluded that she'd been murdered on Sunday night, just after she left home, and that she may have been killed by more than one assailant, perhaps one of the gangs that plagued New York City's streets at the time.

CHAPTER THREE: THE INVESTIGATION

The discovery of the beautiful cigar girl's body launched an intensive inquiry to find out who had killed her. Some people thought she'd drowned accidentally, but that didn't explain her injuries. One witness claimed to have spotted her on Sunday on the Hoboken Ferry with a "dark-complected man." Daniel Payne and the other men she knew from the boarding house came under suspicion immediately; newspapers even published libelous stories accusing them of her murder. Payne had to bring witness affidavits to several city newspaper offices to get them to stop calling for his arrest.

About three weeks after Rogers disappeared, a woman named Frederica Loss, who ran a tavern in Hoboken near the spot where Rogers's body was found, came forward and produced some stained, mildewed pieces of clothing that she said her sons had found nearby. The items looked like things Rogers had owned—one handkerchief was even monogrammed with the initials "MR." But no one could say for sure that the items had belonged to Mary Rogers, and there were rumors that the belongings had been planted to lure gawkers. Loss's tavern had been doing a brisk business serving tourists who came to visit the site of Rogers's demise.

CHAPTER FOUR: THE REVELATION

Despite having several leads, police couldn't find Rogers's killer. Every suspect they questioned (including her fiancé, Daniel Payne) had an alibi. But events began to take a strange turn. In October 1841, a few months after Rogers's death, Payne walked to the thicket near Hoboken where Rogers's clothes had been found. There, he penned a vague note about his "misspent life" and drank a fatal overdose of laudanum, a liquid form of opium.

Then, in the fall of 1842, one of Frederica Loss' sons accidentally shot her. On her deathbed, a delirious Loss confessed that on that fateful Sunday, Mary Rogers and a doctor had rented a room in the tavern. Rogers was pregnant, Loss said, and she died in the rented room from complications after the doctor performed an abortion.

That story appeared in all of New York City's major newspapers and churned up reader interest again. Police found nothing to corroborate the confession, but the case was back in the spotlight. Questions abounded: A botched abortion contradicted the coroner's report that Rogers had died of strangulation. Had the coroner been lying? Or had the mysterious doctor tried to cover the whole thing up by beating Rogers's body, simulating a strangulation, and dumping her in the river? Could the wounds from the abortion have looked to the coroner like sexual assault? Maybe Mary Rogers was planning to leave Daniel Payne after all, and when he found out about that and the abortion, he killed her in a fit of rage. Or was Frederica Loss simply a delusional dying woman still trying to drum up business for her tavern? No one knew, and no one ever figured it out. To this day, Mary Rogers's murder remains unsolved.

CHAPTER FIVE: THE DETECTIVE STORY

In 1841 Edgar Allan Poe wasn't yet the legend he is today, but he was an up-and-coming writer. He'd held jobs at various literary magazines and had published several short stories, including "The Murders in the Rue

Morgue," starring that early fictional detective C. Auguste Dupin. Poe had always been attracted to stories of supernatural melancholy and horror, and Mary Rogers's murder caught his attention. He decided to try to solve the case in fictional form, and to write a compelling story in the process. The result was "The Mystery of Marie Rogêt," a three-part serial that appeared in a magazine called *Snowden's Ladies' Companion* in late 1842 and early '43. Poe wrote later, "Under the pretense of showing how Dupin...unraveled the mystery of Marie's assassination, I, in fact, enter into a very rigorous analysis of the real tragedy in New York."

Poe's story went like this: The body of a young woman named Marie Rogêt was pulled out of the Seine River in Paris. The young perfume-shop worker had been brutally beaten and died as the result of some kind of "accident." Part of her dress had been removed and tied in a sailor's knot, which was used to drag the body to the river. In the story, Dupin essentially "solved" the crime by implying that Rogêt had been killed by a "naval officer with [a] dark complexion." But Poe never named names.

"The Mystery of Marie Rogêt" was a hit for Poe, and so was the final Dupin story, "The Purloined Letter," published in 1845. It also spawned an entirely new fictional genre: the detective novel, which turned crime-solving into literature.

*　　　*　　　*

SPEEDY JUSTICE

Defendant: John Cracken, a Texas personal injury lawyer

The Crime: Flaunting his wealth in public

Background: In 1991 Cracken represented a disabled widow in a lawsuit against her husband's employer, the Rock-Tenn Company. Rock-Tenn was a recycling company, and the man was killed in a baling machine. Cracken sued for $25 million, but Rock-Tenn's case was so weak that there was talk that the jury might award as much as $60 million. Shortly before deliberations were to begin, however, some of the jurors happened to spot Cracken in the courthouse parking garage, driving a brand-new red Porsche 911.

The Sentence: The jury awarded Cracken's client only $5 million. Why so little? One juror explained, "There was no way I'm going to buy that lawyer another fancy car."

Odds that someone caught shoplifting is a teenager: 50%.

KALASHNIKOV PAT & THE HELICOPTER JAILBREAKS

Since 1986 there have been 11 helicopter-assisted jailbreaks from French prisons. Three of them involved the same man.

BACKGROUND: Pascal Payet, a.k.a. "Kalashnikov Pat," is one of France's most notorious criminals. In 1997 he was arrested for armed robbery and murder after an attack on an armored truck, during which he shot a guard 14 times. Payet was sent to Luynes Prison in southeast France to await trial.

ESCAPE! On October 12, 2001, a helicopter appeared above the prison exercise yard. A rope ladder was lowered, Pascal and one on other inmate climbed it, and the chopper flew off. The daring escape shocked French authorities and made headlines worldwide.

ESCAPE II! In May 2003, Payet was still on the loose when he and some associates decided to go *back* to Luynes Prison (in a hijacked helicopter) to pick up a few friends. Two of the men belayed commando-style down to the steel net that had been put over the exercise yard after Payet's previous escape, sawed a hole in it and dropped a ladder through, and three inmates, all cohorts of Payet, climbed up. The helicopter landed in a nearby sports stadium, and the men left in a waiting car. The three friends were recaptured a week later; Payet, some months later. In 2005 he was sentenced to 30 years in Grasse Prison in southeast France.

ESCAPE III! On July 14, 2007, Payet escaped again—and again it was with a helicopter. This one was hijacked in the nearby seaside resort town of Cannes; it landed on the roof of a building at Grasse Prison half an hour later. Three armed men jumped out and overtook the guards, went straight to Payet's cell, took him back to the chopper, and flew away. The chopper eventually landed at a local hospital's heliport, and the men all disappeared. Payet was arrested in Spain two months later and is currently serving a lengthy sentence in a French prison. Where is the prison? Cautious French authorities refuse to disclose its location.

The FBI was created by Napoleon Bonaparte's great-nephew.

CELEBRITY MUMMIES

A few famous folks that got a bad wrap.

JOHN WILKES BOOTH (aka John St. Helen)

After he shot Lincoln, Booth was a fugitive for 12 days. The U.S. government announced that federal troops had tracked him down and shot him in a Virginia tobacco barn. Then, to prevent his gravesite from becoming a Confederate shrine, they quickly buried him in an unmarked grave at the Washington Arsenal. But this made people suspicious. Why so fast—were they hiding something? Was the man they buried really Booth…or had the assassin escaped?

Over the years, more than 40 people made deathbed "confessions" claiming they were Booth. One of these was John St. Helen. In 1877, thinking he was about to die, St. Helen confessed to a man named Finis L. Bates that he was Lincoln's assassin.

St. Helen actually survived and lived until 1903. When he finally died, Bates had St. Helen's body mummified and moved to his basement, where it was stored for the next 20 years. Then, when Bates died in 1923, his wife sold the mummy. It ended up in the hands of carnival operators who exhibited it as Booth until the mid-1970s. It then disappeared, and hasn't been seen since.

ELMER J. MCCURDY

In 1976 an episode of TV's *The Six Million Dollar Man* was filmed at the Nu-Pike amusement park in Long Beach, California. There was a dummy hanging from a fake gallows in the fun house; when a technician tried to move it out of the way, its arm came off at the elbow…exposing human bones. It was a mummy, not a dummy!

The film crew was horrified. The mummy's face had been painted and shellacked so many times that the amusement park owners thought it was made of *wax*. But who was the mummy? And how did it wind up in the park?

The L.A. County coroner had one clue: The mummy's mouth was stuffed with carnival ticket stubs. They were traced to Oklahoma, and, working with Oklahoma historians, the coroner finally identified the

---

There is a robbery in London every 4.5 minutes.

body as Elmer J. McCurdy, a long-forgotten bandit. According to a 1993 *Wall Street Journal* article:

> Eighty years ago, [McCurdy] robbed the wrong train and rode off with $45 and a load of whiskey. When the posse caught him two days later, the whiskey was gone and he was having a nice nap. According to local legend, he decided to shoot it out anyway. That was another mistake. An…undertaker in Pawhuska, OK, mummified his body and put it on display for 5¢ a view until 1916, when two men posing as Mr. McCurdy's brothers claimed the corpse. They were actually carnival promoters. For decades, the unfortunate Mr. McCurdy crisscrossed the country as a sideshow attraction.

The town of Guthrie, Oklahoma, paid for McCurdy's trip back to the state and gave him a Christian burial. His grave (which has been sealed in concrete to ensure that it is his final resting place) is now the town's biggest tourist attraction.

EVA "EVITA" PERÓN

Juan Perón was the president of Argentina from 1948 to '54. His wife, Eva, a former actress and a crusader for the poor, was extremely popular. When she died of cancer in 1952 at age 33, Perón had her mummified and put on public display. The procedure took about a year and cost $100,000. Peron fell from power while his wife was still lying in state, and went into exile in Spain before he could arrange for her burial. Evita was put in storage in Buenos Aires. Then her body disappeared.

It turned out that anti-Perónists—making sure the body was never again used as a pro-Perón political symbol—had stolen the coffin, sealed it in a packing crate, and eventually buried it in a Milan cemetary. In 1971—19 years later—a sympathetic Spanish intelligence officer told Perón where his wife was buried. Perón had her exhumed and brought to Spain. When the ex-dictator pried open the coffin, his wife was so well preserved that he cried out, "She is not dead, she is only sleeping!"

Rather than bury his Evita again, Perón kept her around the house; he and his third wife, Isabel, propped her up in the dining room and ate in her presence every evening, even when they entertained guests. The arrangement lasted until 1973, when Perón returned to power in Argentina and left his beloved mummy in Spain. Later, Evita was brought across the Atlantic and buried in Argentina.

What's a *melcryptovestimentaphiliac*? Someone who compulsively steals ladies' underwear.

LEMME EXPLAIN...

*Free advice from Uncle John: When you're caught red-handed,
it's often better just to fess up and take your lumps. Here are
a few people who would have done well to follow his advice.*

SCOOBY-DOOFUS

In August 1996, in Tampa, Florida, police arrested Robert Meier
and charged him with credit fraud after he married his comatose
girlfriend only hours before she died. Why? So he could rack up more
than $20,000 in charges on her credit cards. Meier's excuse: It was his
girlfriend's dog's fault. According to a police spokesperson, "He said the
dog told him she would want him to have a better life, so it would be OK
to use her credit cards."

WHO'S KIDDING WHO?

In February 1997, Cathleen Byers, former manager of the Oregon Urban
Rural Credit Union, was arrested for embezzlement. Was she guilty? Byers
admitted stealing $630,000 over six years but claimed that she wasn't *really*
guilty because she suffers from multiple personality disorder. One of her
other personalities—Ava, Joy, Elizabeth, Tillie, Claudia, C. J., Katy,
Roman, Cookie, Mariah, Frogger, Chrissy, or Colleen—must have done it
without her knowledge. An expert testified that whichever alter-personal-
ity took the money didn't know right from wrong and that Byers
wasn't even aware of what her alter-self was up to. The judge didn't buy
it, arguing that Byers "should have been clued in by the new house and
the luxury cars."

DRIVEN TO DRINK

After only one month on the job, Calgary, Alberta, school bus driver
Marvin Franks was arrested for driving his bus while under the influence
of alcohol. Police pulled Franks's bus over and administered a breath test
after a terrified student called 911 using her cell phone. The bus driver
was found to have a blood-alcohol level three times the legal limit. In an
interview with the *Calgary Sun*, Franks admitted to having two beers
before starting his route, on top of being hungover from drinking the

night before. But he blamed his drinking on job stress, which he blamed on the kids he drives to school. "If you had these kids on your bus, you'd drink too," he explained.

LOUNGE LIZARD

In March 2002, 47-year-old Susan Wallace, a former British Airways flight attendant, was convicted of animal cruelty after she threw Igwig, her three-foot-long iguana, at a doorman and then later at a policeman following an altercation in a pub. Wallace maintains that she is innocent because Igwig acted of his own volition. "He probably jumped in defense of me. He's done that before," she said. (Igwig is now banned from the pub.)

STRAIGHT SHOOTER

David Duyst of Grand Rapids, Michigan, was convicted of murdering his wife and was then sentenced to life without parole. Yet to this day, Duyst insists that he's not guilty, despite a mountain of forensic evidence against him. So how'd she die? According to Duyst, she committed suicide by shooting herself…*twice,* in the *back* of her head.

SIDE ORDER OF COMPASSION, PLEASE

Professional boxer Waxxem Fikes, 35, served five days in an Akron, Ohio, jail after assaulting a waiter at Swenson's restaurant in 2001. According to testimony, Fikes was "aggressively complaining" that the onions on his double cheeseburger were unsatisfactory. "I told him that I expect the onions to be crisp, tender and succulent, and bursting with flavor," Fikes testified. "They were not. My hands are lethal weapons or whatever, I know that. But he had no compassion for what I was talking about."

BODY OF EVIDENCE

In March 2001, a woman in Munich, Germany, saw a neighbor carrying a dead body into his apartment. She called the police. When the suspect answered the door in a "surprised and disturbed state," officers thought for sure that they had a murderer on their hands. Not quite. As the embarrassed man explained, the "dead body" was actually a life-sized silicon doll that he'd just purchased from an adult bookstore.

Pittsburgh cops once investigated a crime scene for 8 hours before realizing it was a movie set.

D. B. COOPER

*Modern-day Robin Hood? Or high-flying robber? He hijacked
an airplane, stole a small fortune, then parachuted
out of sight…and straight into legend.*

DAREDEVIL
The day before Thanksgiving in November 1971, a nondescript man wearing a plain dark suit, white shirt, narrow black tie, and sunglasses stepped up to the Northwest Orient Airlines ticket counter in Portland, Oregon. He paid $20 in cash for a one-way ticket to Seattle on Flight 305.

Once the 727 was airborne, the man summoned the flight attendant, Tina Mucklow, introduced himself as "Dan Cooper," and handed her a note. It said he had a bomb in his briefcase and would blow up the plane if they didn't grant his demands. He wanted two parachutes and $200,000 in $20 bills. When the plane landed in Seattle, Cooper kept the pilot and crew hostage but let the passengers off in exchange for the chutes and the loot. Then he ordered the pilot to take off and set a course for Mexico with these instructions: Keep the landing gear down, and the flight speed under 170 mph. Somewhere over the Lewis River, 25 miles northeast of Portland, Cooper strapped on a parachute, tied the money to his waist, and jumped out the rear stairway of the plane. He was never seen again.

THE BIGFOOT OF CRIME

In the ensuing investigation, the FBI questioned a man named Daniel B. Cooper. Although that person was never a serious suspect, the FBI reported to the press that they'd interrogated a "D. B. Cooper." And those initials became forever linked with the skyjacker.

The FBI manhunt that followed was unprecedented in scope and intensity. It was a showcase investigation, meant to display the competency of the world's greatest law enforcement agency. Every inch of ground in the vicinity of the purported landing site was searched from the air and land, with teams of trackers and dogs, for 18 days. So it was a humbling moment when, after weeks of tracking down leads, the FBI admitted that they had come up with…nothing. No credible suspect. No trace of the loot or the parachute. No further leads to follow. A complete dead end.

First high-profile kidnapping in Canada: beer baron John Sackville Labatt in 1934.

One frustrated FBI agent referred to Cooper as the "Bigfoot of crime" because there was no proof of his existence anywhere.

If Cooper survived, he'd pulled off the crime of the century.

A STAR IS BORN

Something about the hijacking caught the public's imagination, as the media reports raved about the audacity of the crime and the calm, competent way in which Cooper carried it out. According to the flight attendants, Cooper behaved like a gentleman throughout the ordeal, even requesting that meals be delivered to the crew while they were stuck on the ground in Seattle, waiting for the ransom money to be delivered.

He became a folk hero, a latter-day Jesse James. Songs were written about him, and a movie was made, starring Treat Williams as Cooper and Robert Duvall as the FBI agent on his trail. Half a dozen books, mostly by former FBI agents, provided theories about what happened to him. He was living the high life on a beach in Mexico. Or he'd slipped back into his former life somewhere in the States, undetected and unnoticed.

On February 13, 1980, a family picnicking on the Columbia River, 30 miles west of Cooper's landing area, found three bundles of disintegrating $20 bills ($5,800 total). The serial numbers were traced to the ransom. The rest of the cash has never been found.

...SO WHO DUNNIT?

• *Possible Suspect #1.* On April 7, 1972, four months after Cooper's successful hijacking, another hijacker stole a plane in Denver, using the same M.O. as D. B. Cooper. The Denver flight was also a 727 with a rear stairway, from which the hijacker made his getaway by parachute. A tip led police to Richard McCoy Jr., a man with an unusual profile: married with two children, a former Sunday school teacher, a law enforcement major at Brigham Young University, a former Green Beret helicopter pilot with service in Vietnam, and an avid skydiver. When FBI agents arrested McCoy two days after the Denver hijacking, they found a jumpsuit and a duffel bag containing half a million dollars. McCoy was convicted and sentenced to 45 years.

In August 1974, McCoy escaped from prison (he tricked the guards into letting him out of his cell with a handgun made from toothpaste and then crashed a garbage truck through the prison gate). The FBI tracked him down and three months later killed him in a shootout in Virginia.

Officially, the murders of Lizzie Borden's parents remain unsolved. (Lizzie was acquitted.)

In 1991 former FBI agent Russell Calame claimed in his book *D. B. Cooper: The Real McCoy* that McCoy and Cooper were the same person. He quoted Nicholas O'Hara, the FBI agent who tracked down McCoy, as saying, "When I shot Richard McCoy, I shot D. B. Cooper." But there's no conclusive evidence. In fact, McCoy's widow sued for libel and won.

Possible Suspect #2. In August 2000, Jo Weber, a Florida widow, told *U.S. News and World Report* that shortly before her husband Duane died in 1995, he told her, "I'm Dan Cooper." Remembering that he'd talked in his sleep about jumping out of a plane, she checked into his background and discovered he'd spent time in an Oregon prison. Then she found a Northwest Airlines ticket stub from the Seattle-Tacoma airport among his papers. She found a book about D. B. Cooper in the local library—it had notations in the margins matching her husband's handwriting.

She relayed her suspicions to FBI agent Ralph Himmelsbach, chief investigator on the D. B. Cooper case. To this day he insists Weber is one of the likeliest suspects he's come across. More recently, facial recognition software was used to find the closest match to the composite picture of Cooper. Of the 3,000 photographs used (including Richard McCoy's), Duane Weber's was identified as the "best match."

Possible Suspect #3. Elsie Rodgers of Cozad, Nebraska, often told her family about the time she was hiking near the Columbia River in Washington in the 1970s and found a human head. They never really believed her until, while going through her things after her death in 2000, they found a hatbox in her attic...with a human skull in it. Was it Cooper?

Possible Suspect #4. In 2011 an Oklahoma woman named Marla Cooper told the FBI that when she was eight years old in November 1971, her uncle, L. D. Cooper, said he was planning "something big." He returned two days later with severe wounds. As Marla's father was tending to him, L.D. said, "We did it. We hijacked an airplane." They told little Marla her uncle was in a car accident. She never saw L.D. again after that, and put it out of her mind for nearly 40 years. Then in 2009, Marla's elderly mother talked about her "long-lost brother who'd hijacked that plane." Marla gave the FBI a guitar strap belonging to her uncle, as well as a Polaroid of him. Like Weber's, it looks eerily like the suspect in the composite drawing. The Feds couldn't get any prints off the strap, however, and L. D. Cooper has been dead since 1999. The case remains open.

In 2006 a Florida school's mock CSI field trip accidentally discovered a real dead body.

HOW TO RIG A COIN TOSS

A long-held secret of carnies and hucksters.
With a little practice, it really works.

WHAT YOU NEED

A large coin. The bigger and heavier, the better. When you get really good at it, you can use a quarter, but until then, a fifty-cent piece or silver dollar is best. The trick is nearly impossible with a nickel, dime, or penny.

HOW TO DO IT:

1. Place the coin in the middle of your palm with the side you want to win face down. For example, if you want "heads" to win the toss, put the heads side of the coin face down in your palm.

2. Hold your arm straight out and clench all the muscles in your arm so it's as stiff as possible.

3. While holding that arm out tight, toss the coin into the air.

4. Here's the tricky part: As you keep your arm clenched and toss the coin up, jerk your hand slightly back. In other words, very subtly pull your hand ever so closer to your body. The move may be somewhat noticeable, but don't worry. Nobody will be watching your hand—all eyes will be on the coin in the air.

5. Catch the coin in your palm. Result: The coin will turn over in the air exactly one whole time. It will land exactly the same as it was before the toss—with the predetermined winning side face down in your hand.

6. Slap the coin onto your forearm to reverse the coin and reveal the winning side—which is what was face down in your palm when you started and what you rigged it to be.

It takes some practice to learn when and how hard to jerk back your hand to spin the coin only once. The heavier the coin, the easier it is—a small coin weighs so little that it tends to spin too many times. With a heavier coin, you've got more control. Now get out there and cheat…er, uh…amaze your friends.

What do Fiji, Chile, and Egypt have in common? You can be jailed there for not voting.

INFAMOUS WEAPONS

*We couldn't find Uncle John's old Fart Bazooka, but
we managed to find some other famous weapons.*

THE SARAJEVO PISTOL

On June 28, 1914, Gavrilo Princip shot and killed the heir to the Austro-Hungarian throne, Archduke Franz Ferdinand, and his wife, Sophie, in Sarajevo, Bosnia. The assassinations caused a chain reaction of events which, within less than five weeks, led to the start of World War I. The gun was a Browning semiautomatic pistol, model M1910, serial #19074.

Princip, just 19, was a member of the Serbian nationalist group called the Black Hand. He fired seven shots into the royal couple's car from five feet away, then attempted to shoot himself, but was stopped by passersby and quickly arrested. Princip died in prison of tuberculosis in 1918 (the disease was one reason he took the mission). After his trial, the pistol was presented to Father Anton Puntigam, the Jesuit priest who had given the archduke and duchess their last rites. He hoped to place it in a museum, but when he died in 1926 the gun was lost…for almost 80 years.

In 2004 a Jesuit community house in Austria made a startling announcement: they had found the gun (verified by its serial number). They donated it to the Vienna Museum of Military History in time for the 90th anniversary of the assassination that started a war that would eventually kill 8.5 million people. Also in the museum are the car in which the couple were riding, the bloodied pillow cover on which the archduke rested his head while dying, and petals from a rose that was attached to Sophie's belt.

JOHN WILKES BOOTH'S GUN

The gun that Booth used to assassinate President Abraham Lincoln now resides in the basement museum of Ford's Theatre, in Washington, D.C. The gun is a single-shot flintlock, made by Philadelphia gunsmith Henry Derringer. It's tiny—just six inches total in length with a 2½" barrel—but it's powerful, firing a .44- caliber bullet. The gun was found on the floor of the theater box where Lincoln sat. Also in the museum is the knife with which Booth stabbed one of Lincoln's companions, Major Henry Rathbone, in the arm before Booth jumped from the box to escape.

What about the bullet that killed one of the most revered figures in American history? You can see that, too. It was removed during a post-mortem autopsy and was kept by the U.S. War Department until 1940, when it went to the Department of the Interior. It can be viewed today at the National Museum of Health and Medicine in Washington, D.C.

THE MUSSOLINI MACHINE GUN

On April 28, 1945, Italian dictator Benito Mussolini and his mistress, Claretta Petacci, were captured while trying to flee into Switzerland. They were executed by an Italian communist named Valter Audisio, who shot the pair with a French-made MAS (Manufacture d'Armes de St. Etienne) 7.65mm submachine gun.

The gun disappeared until 1973, when Audisio died. He'd kept it in Italy until 1957, when, during a resurgence of Mussolini's popularity, he secretly gave it to the communist Albanian government for safekeeping. With Audisio's death, the Albanians proudly displayed the gun "on behalf of the Italian people." Its home is now Albania's National Historical Museum. Audisio once wrote that the only reason he used the machine gun was that the two pistols he tried to use had jammed. He also said that he had no orders to shoot Petacci—but she wouldn't let go of Il Duce.

LEE HARVEY OSWALD'S GUNS

The gun that Lee Harvey Oswald allegedly used to assassinate President John F. Kennedy is a Mannlicher-Carcano .38 bolt-action rifle, 40 inches long, and weighs eight pounds. He bought it through a mail-order company for $12.78. Something with as much historical significance as Oswald's rifle would become the property of the people of the United States, right? Wrong. Murder weapons are normally returned to the families of their owners, and Oswald's gun was no exception—it was returned to Oswald's widow. The National Archives purchased the rifle from Marina Oswald. The Archives also has the .38 Special Smith & Wesson Victory revolver that Oswald had with him that day and used (allegedly) to kill Officer J. D. Tippett before being arrested. Two days later, Oswald was shot and killed by Jack Ruby.

JACK RUBY'S GUN

Ruby was a Dallas strip-club owner and small-time mobster who killed the alleged killer of the president. Just why he did it remains a mystery. But on November 24, 1963, in the basement of the Dallas jail—which at the time was crowded with police officers, reporters, and cameramen—Ruby walked right up to Oswald and shot him once in the side. The gun he used was a .38-caliber Colt Cobra revolver that he bought at Ray's Hardware and Sporting Goods (on the advice of Dallas police detective Joe Cody).

The gun was returned to Ruby's family, where it promptly became tangled in a legal battle over Ruby's estate between the lawyer who was appointed executor and Ruby's brother, Earl. It wouldn't be resolved until 1991, when a judge found for Earl Ruby, who immediately put the gun up for auction and it sold to a collector named A. V. Pugliese. Price: $220,000. In 1992 a friend of Pugliese's brought it to Washington, D.C., and offered to show it to Speaker of the House Thomas Foley. The gun was seized by police and almost destroyed, per D.C.'s strict gun-control laws, but lawyers were able to get it back. On November 24, 1993, the 30th anniversary of the shooting, Pugliese had Earl Ruby fire 100 shots with the gun and offered the spent shells for sale. Price: $2,500 each. (They only sold a few.)

SADAAM HUSSEIN'S PISTOL

When former Iraqi president Sadaam Hussein was captured in a "spider hole" in Iraq in December 2003, he had several weapons with him. One was a pistol. Major General Raymond Odierno reported that Hussein was holding the loaded pistol in his lap when he was captured, but didn't make a move to use it. The Army had the pistol mounted and, in a private meeting, the Special Forces soldiers who took part in the capture presented it to President George W. Bush.

When news of the war souvenir broke in May 2004, reporters asked President Bush if he planned to give the pistol to the next Iraqi president. No, he said, it "is now the property of the American government." The gun is kept in a small study off the Oval Office, and, according to one White House visitor who later spoke to *Time* magazine, the president "really liked showing it off. He was really proud of it."

Is this some kind of joke? In Quitman, Georgia, it is illegal for a chicken to cross the road.

COPS STORY

COPS *has been a Saturday night TV staple for so long—24 seasons as of September 2011—that it's easy to forget what a groundbreaking show it was when it debuted in 1989.*

FIRST-PERSON PERSPECTIVE

In the early 1980s, an aspiring filmmaker named John Langley began work on *Cocaine Blues*, a documentary about the crack cocaine epidemic sweeping the country. As part of the project, he filmed law-enforcement operations, including drug busts and police raids.

At first Langley obtained the footage as an objective bystander, but that ended when an officer invited him to suit up in tactical gear and follow the police as they moved in. For the first time, Langley understood the stress and danger (and the adrenaline rush) that police experience daily. And the footage he shot during the raid was some of the most compelling he'd ever seen. He thought it might be possible to build an entire show around it.

KEEPING IT REAL

As Langley developed the idea for a show he called *Street Beat*, he decided it should be presented in a minimalist, *cinema verité* style—the edited footage would be presented as-is, without a narrator, script, music, staged reenactments, much editing, or any other standard TV storytelling conventions to distract the viewing audience. He didn't want a host or anyone else telling people what to think about what they were seeing.

Langley believed that such a show would be successful, but ABC, CBS, and NBC weren't convinced and passed on the idea. Even Langley's business partner, Malcolm Barbour, was skeptical. The concept was *so* unusual, and even if it was a good idea, it wasn't clear that a beginner like Langley would be able to pull it off.

With no takers for *Street Beat*, Langley and Barbour's production company spent the next few years producing a series of crime-themed syndicated TV specials (which included footage of police ride-alongs) hosted by Geraldo Rivera. The specials were very successful and helped to raise Langley's profile in the TV business. But if he thought that would make it

Duane Chapman (*Dog the Bounty Hunter*) cannot own a gun. Reason: felony conviction.

easier for him to find a buyer for the show he now called COPS, he was wrong: ABC, CBS, and NBC still said no.

THE ROOKIE

By 1987, however, there was a new player in network television: Fox. The upstart network had been on the air since October 1986, but few of its shows were successful. Fox was struggling not just to stay afloat but also to forge an identity distinct from the Big 3 networks—its survival strategy was to put unusual new shows on the air. And thanks to a looming TV writers' strike that looked like it might drag on for months, Fox was particularly interested in shows that didn't require writers or scripts.

Langley and Barbour put together a reel of the best police-raid footage from the Geraldo crime specials and made a sales pitch to three Fox executives: CEO Barry Diller; programming head Steve Chao; and a third, unidentified man who sat in the corner taking notes—Langley assumed he was an accountant. After they made their presentation, the man taking notes, who turned out to be Fox chairman Rupert Murdoch, told Diller, "Order four of 'em." Langley and Barbour had a deal.

COP-SPAN

To film the pilot, Langley went to the same person he'd gone to when he needed police footage for his Geraldo specials: Sheriff Nick Navarro of Broward County, Florida. Navarro was bothered by the fact that the public's understanding of law enforcement was informed by fictional and wildly inaccurate movies and TV shows such as *Dirty Harry* and *Miami Vice*. He saw COPS as an almost C-SPAN-like chance to depict law enforcement as accurately and honestly as possible, and he believed that such transparency was essential in a free society. He happily allowed Langley to film his officers at work.

If you watch the hour-long COPS pilot, you may be surprised at how different it is from the modern version of the show. The most glaring difference is the inclusion of scenes of the officers in their own homes—cooking dinner with their families, watching TV, and playing with their children. One officer and his wife even argue about their relationship in front of the COPS camera crew. Langley says Fox forced him to insert the cops-at-home footage into the pilot against his better judgement, theorizing that if the *cinema verité* footage didn't hook the audience, the real-life soap opera storylines would. The COPS pilot aired on Saturday, March 11, 1989. Ever since then, the show has aired on Saturday night.

ONE, TWO, THREE

Fox didn't promote COPS very heavily, but the show still managed to find an audience, which grew quickly thanks to positive word of mouth. As it did, Langley set to work stripping out all the features the network had forced on him—background music, the "soap opera" subplots, and the scenes shot at police headquarters, which he believed were unnecessary and much less interesting than scenes of police in the field. In the process, he also developed the three-stories-per-episode format that continues to this day:

• The first segment is a dramatic "action" sequence of some kind, often involving a police chase of a vehicle, or of a suspect on foot.

• The second segment is slower and often contains emotional or humorous content (such as the scene where a suspect repeatedly denies that he uses drugs, not realizing that he has a marijuana cigarette tucked behind his ear until the officer plucks it out).

• The third segment aims to give the audience something to think about, such as the methods used to take an uncooperative suspect into custody, or the social costs associated with treating drug addiction as a criminal problem instead of a public health issue.

BAD BOYS, BAD BOYS

Twenty-three years and more than 800 episodes later, COPS remains the most successful reality series on network television. Its role in shaping the public's perception of law enforcement has been profound, and it has produced an entire generation of officers who first developed an interest in police work while watching COPS when they were kids.

Perhaps the show's most unusual claim to fame is how it turned its "Bad Boys" theme song into the most quotable, if not the most famous, reggae song in history. From the beginning, Langley wanted COPS to be the first-ever network show with a reggae theme song, and while filming the pilot in Florida he had his field producers scour local record stores in search of just the right song. Someone found "Bad Boys," sung by the Jamaican band Inner Circle. "I said, 'That's it, that's the song,'" Langley

---

J. Edgar Hoover once gave his mother a canary bred by the "Birdman of Alcatraz."

remembers. "I mean, it was just too good. You know, '…bad boys, bad boys, what you gonna do, what you gonna do when they come for you?' It was just too perfect." The song was released as a single in 1993 and hit the Top 10.

MAKING THE SHOW

• In a typical week of production, as many as a dozen two-person COPS film crews are riding along with police officers all over the U.S. Most production takes place during warmer months, when crooks are more likely to be out and about. That explains why you hardly ever see a police chase in the snow…but you see plenty of suspects who are sweaty and shirtless.

• On average, it takes about 18 hours of unedited police footage to produce the 22 minutes of material that make up an episode.

• COPS has been filmed in Hong Kong, Great Britain, Russia… but never in Canada. Why not? "Canada has far less crime than we do in the States," Langley told the Ottawa Citizen in 2008.

"I'M ON TV!"

• If you (like Uncle John) live in terror of COPS filming in your town on that one worst day of your life, when you're drunk, half naked, and screaming in the middle of the street, fear not: COPS can't show your face on TV without your consent. Every face shown on the program is the face of a person who has signed a release form.

• In the early years, getting suspects to sign the release forms wasn't easy; many faces had to be digitally blurred as a result. But now that the show is famous, more than 90% of suspects sign them. "When they hear that we're not a news camera, that we're COPS, they generally exclaim, 'Oh, that's great! When will I be on?'" Langley says.

*   *   *

THE WORLD'S MOST STOLEN PAINTING

The Ghent Altarpiece is a Dutch panel painting known as Het Lam Gods ("The Lamb of God") that was completed in 1432. It weighs two tons, measures 14 feet by 11 feet, and has been stolen 13 times, the most of any famous piece of artwork.

ETHICALLY DISABLED

*There are few things more pathetic than people pretending to be
disabled—and few things more satisfying than catching them.*

FUTBOL FAKERS

Their dream was to watch their country's soccer team play in a
World Cup game in Germany in 2006, but the admission price was
more than the three Argentinians wanted to pay. Determined to see the
match, they found a loophole: Discounted seats were being offered to disabled people. So they somehow got themselves three wheelchairs and
rolled into the match against Holland, claiming a handicapped viewing
spot near the field.

The ruse probably would have worked, too, if one of them
hadn't gotten so excited after a play that he jumped out of his chair with
his arms raised in the air. "A person near us thought there was a miracle
happening," one of the fakers told reporters outside the stadium—which
is where the three fans spent the second half of the game after security
escorted them out (on foot).

PARALYMPIC FAKERS

The 2000 International Paralympics were a resounding success for Spain:
The country won 107 medals overall, highlighted by the gold medal
awarded to its developmentally disabled basketball team. A few months
later, one of the players, Carlos Ribagorda, made the shocking admission
that "of the 200 Spanish Paralympic athletes, at least 15 had no physical
or mental handicap." Ribagorda, a journalist for the Spanish magazine
Capital, had joined the intellectually disabled basketball team to expose
the corruption. In the two years Ribagorda played for the team, no one
ever tested his I.Q. Not only that, says Ribagorda, the team was told to
slow down their game so they wouldn't attract suspicion.

A subsequent international investigation concluded that only two
members of the basketball team were intellectually disabled. In addition, as Ribagorda had discovered, some members of Spain's Paralympic
track, tennis, and swimming teams were found to be only...*morally*
handicapped.

Until 1819 in the United Kingdom, felling a tree illegally was punishable by hanging.

LAWSUIT FAKER

In 2006 Las Vegas authorities suspected that wheelchair-bound Laura Lee Medley was taking them for a ride. After four separate lawsuits against four California cities over faulty handicapped access to public buildings, investigators smelled fraud. They tracked Medley to Las Vegas, where they arrested the 35-year-old woman, who was sitting in her wheelchair. Medley immediately began complaining of pain and begged for medical attention. Skeptical—but not wanting to doubt her if she really was in pain—police officers drove her to a nearby hospital. But moments after she was wheeled through the entrance, the "paralyzed" woman got up and started sprinting through the hospital corridors. She was quickly apprehended and cuffed. Medley was charged with four counts of fraud and resisting arrest.

BEAUTY PAGEANT FAKER

Dee Henderson was crowned Mrs. Minnesota International in a 1999 beauty pageant, thanks in part to the aerobic exercises she performed for the talent competition. Henderson owned and operated two businesses selling beauty pageant supplies, *and* was the director of three Midwest beauty pageants. Those are amazing accomplishments, especially considering the fact that at the same time, she was getting disability payments from the government. Henderson claimed she couldn't work, couldn't sit for more than 20 minutes at a time or lift anything heavier than her mail. She also had difficulty with "walking, kneeling, squatting, climbing, bending, reaching, and personal grooming." The injuries, she said, stemmed from a 1995 car accident. From 1996 to 2003, Henderson received Social Security benefits totaling $190,000.

But her case unraveled when a video taken by a private investigator showed her doing activities such as snorkeling and carrying heavy luggage (not to mention the aerobics). More damning evidence: an email in which Henderson claimed she would "keep going and going and going and going" like the Energizer Bunny. She did keep going...to prison for 46 months.

*   *   *

If I die, I forgive you. If I recover, we shall see.
—**Spanish proverb**

McGruff the Crime Dog was named in a 1980 contest. Runner-up name: "Shurlocked Homes."

HOLLYWOOD SCANDAL, PART I

A woman is found dead…a well-known celebrity is charged with murder…the whole world follows the trial. O. J. Simpson? Nope—Fatty Arbuckle. In the early 1920s, the Arbuckle trial was as big as the Simpson trial. Here's the story.

A KNOCK AT THE DOOR

On the morning of Saturday, September 10, 1921, two men from the San Francisco sheriff's office paid a visit to Roscoe "Fatty" Arbuckle, then Hollywood's most famous comedian, at his home in Los Angeles. One of the men read from an official court summons:

"You are hereby summoned to return immediately to San Francisco for questioning…you are charged with murder in the first degree."

Arbuckle, thinking the men were pulling a practical joke, let out a laugh. "And who do you suppose I killed?"

"Virginia Rappé."

Arbuckle instantly knew that this was no joke. He'd just returned from a trip to San Francisco, where he'd thrown a party over the Labor Day weekend to celebrate his new $3 million movie contract—then the largest in Hollywood history—with Paramount Pictures. A 26-year-old bit actress named Virginia Rappé had fallen ill at the party, presumably from drinking too much bootleg booze. Arbuckle had seen to it that the woman received medical attention before he returned to L.A., but now Rappé was dead—and Arbuckle had somehow been implicated in her death. Whatever doubts he may still have had about the summons vanished the following morning as he read the three-inch headlines in the *Los Angeles Examiner*:

ARBUCKLE HELD FOR MURDER!

The autopsy report showed that Rappé died from acute peritonitis, an inflammation of the abdominal lining brought on by a ruptured bladder. Why was Arbuckle a suspect in the death? Because Maude "Bambina" Delmont, another woman at the party, had filed a statement with San Francisco police claiming that she had seen Arbuckle drag Rappé into his bedroom against her will and assault her. As she later explained to newspaper reporters,

> I could hear Virginia kicking and screaming violently and I had to kick and batter the door before Mr. Arbuckle would let me in. I looked at the bed. There was Virginia, helpless and ravaged. When Virginia kept screaming in agony at what Mr. Arbuckle had done, he turned to me and said, 'Shut her up or I'll throw her out a window.' He then went back to his drunken party and danced while poor Virginia lay dying.

The 265-pound comedian had supposedly burst Rappés' bladder with his weight during the assault. And because the injury had gone untreated, it developed into a massive abdominal infection, killing Rappé.

Pressing Charges

After Delmont's statement was filed, San Francisco District Attorney Matthew Brady had ordered Arbuckle's arrest and had issued a public statement to the press:

> The evidence in my possession shows conclusively that either a rape or an attempt to rape was perpetrated on Miss Rappé by Roscoe Arbuckle. The evidence discloses beyond question that her bladder was ruptured by the weight of the body of Arbuckle either in a rape assault or an attempt to commit rape.

FALSE WITNESS

Brady's case was based almost entirely on Delmont's police statement. And the case certainly *appeared* substantial—at least until Brady looked into Maude Delmont's background after she gave her statement. Then he discovered a police record containing more than 50 counts of bigamy, fraud, racketeering, extortion, and other crimes (including one outstanding bigamy warrant, which Brady would later use to his advantage).

WHAT REALLY HAPPENED

Brady later learned from other guests at the party that a very drunk Maude Delmont had actually been locked in a bathroom with Lowell Sherman, another party guest, during the entire time that she claimed to have witnessed Arbuckle with Rappé. She could not have seen any of the things she claimed to have seen—and if that were not bad enough, Brady later discovered that on Wednesday, September 7, Delmont had dashed

off the following telegram to two different friends as Virginia Rappé lay
dying at the St. Francis Hotel:

> WE HAVE ROSCOE ARBUCKLE IN A HOLE HERE
> CHANCE TO MAKE MONEY OUT OF HIM

BLIND AMBITION

District Attorney Brady had no case—there wasn't a shred of physical
evidence to indicate that Arbuckle had committed any crime against
Rappé; his only "witness" was a woman with a long criminal record; and
the telegrams demonstrated clearly that Delmont's police statement was
part of an attempt to blackmail Arbuckle. Despite all this, Brady decided
to bring the case to trial. Why? One theory: Brady, whom acquaintances
described as a "self-serving, arrogant, ruthless man with blind ambition
and a quick temper," was gearing up to run for governor of California. He
probably figured that winning a murder conviction against Hollywood's
biggest comedian would score points with the public.

JUDGE NOT

Still, the case could not have gone to trial if the police judge, Sylvain
Lazarus, had dismissed the case due to lack of evidence. But Judge Lazarus
refused to throw it out, citing the "larger issues" surrounding the case:

> I do not find any evidence that Mr. Arbuckle either committed or
> attempted to commit rape. The court has been presented with the mer-
> est outline....The district attorney has presented barely enough facts to
> justify my holding the defendant on the charge which is here filed
> against him.
>
> But we are not trying Roscoe Arbuckle alone; we are not trying the
> screen celebrity who has given joy and pleasure to the entire world; we
> are actually, gentlemen, trying ourselves.
>
> We are trying our present-day morals, our present-day social condi-
> tions, our present-day looseness of thought and lack of social balance...
>
> I have decided to make a holding on the ground of manslaughter.

The judge suspected Arbuckle was innocent, the district attorney knew
Arbuckle was innocent, and yet the case still went to trial.

> *Would Arbuckle be sent up the river?*
> *Turn to page 228 to find out.*

...billiards room. (Billiards were illegal in Virginia.)

I CAN'T TAKE IT ANYMORE!!!

Uncle John presents these true stories of extreme overreactions to serve as a reminder: Always keep your cool.

THE ANNOYED: George Furedi

SITUATION: A local church's public address system was keeping Furedi awake at night.

FREAK-OUT: Furedi drove his SUV to the church and slammed into the front of it. He was arrested a short time later for malicious mischief, driving while intoxicated, and numerous hit-and-run charges (he rammed into several cars on the way). How did the cops find Furedi? They ran a check on his license plate. (He left his truck wedged in the church doors.)

THE ANNOYED: Chris Baugh

SITUATION: Someone vandalized the building Baugh was renovating. He was convinced that local skateboarders were responsible.

FREAK-OUT: There was a community skate park not far from Baugh's building site. Seeking retribution, Baugh drove a bulldozer to the park and demolished ramps, rails, and fences. Police charged Baugh with second-degree criminal mischief. (No charges were ever filed against the skateboarders—Baugh didn't have any proof that they were responsible for vandalizing his building.)

THE ANNOYED: Charles Booher

SITUATION: An Internet company swamped Booher's computer with e-mails and Internet pop-up ads for male enhancement.

FREAK-OUT: Booher, who'd battled testicular cancer, contacted Doug Mackay, one of the people whose name appeared on one of the ads, and asked him to stop sending them. When they continued to arrive, Booher barraged Mackay's company with e-mails and phone calls for the next three months, threatening to torture and kill him and his employees. Mackay called the FBI; they placed Booher under arrest. He faces five years in prison and a $250,000 fine. "I blew my cool," he says.

In Jack the Ripper's day, many blamed the growing crime rate on violence in the theaters.

THE ANNOYED: A 45-year-old German man

SITUATION: In the apartment next door, the man heard the tell-tale signs of redecorating: furniture being moved across the floor and pictures being nailed to the walls.

FREAK-OUT: After an hour or so, the man went to the apartment and found two teenage boys fixing up the place. He threatened them at gunpoint: "Stop this racket or you'll be sorry." It worked…kind of. He didn't hear any more noise because the police came and took him to jail.

THE ANNOYED: Ashley Carpenter, a bicyclist from Dorset, England

SITUATION: Carpenter always tried to share the road with cars, but often felt that motorists ignored him.

FREAK-OUT: When a car splashed him with water in December 2003, the 37-year-old Carpenter snapped and started a vigilante campaign to rid the road of rude drivers. His method: slashing tires. In all, Carpenter slashed more than 2,000 tires on 548 cars, causing more than £250,000 ($447,000) worth of damage. He was nabbed by police after being caught in the act by surveillance cameras.

THE ANNOYED: A 30-year-old Norwegian man

SITUATION: His girlfriend liked to drink alcohol. He didn't. So he spent night after night after night as her designated driver.

FREAK-OUT: Apparently not knowing how to say no, he decided his only way out was to lose his driver's license. So on the way home one night, he passed a police car at 85 mph in a 50 mph zone. It worked: He was banned from driving for a year. (He also got a two-week vacation from his girlfriend—in jail.)

*　　　*　　　*

OTHER FREAK-OUTS

• After a neighbor's dog pooped on his lawn, Walter Travis, 68, shot the neighbor several times (but not the dog).

• Danny Ginn stole a garbage truck at gunpoint because the truck's driver kept using his driveway to turn around.

• Kevin French, 45, shot his neighbor in the head with an air rifle because he "mowed his lawn too often." (The neighbor recovered.)

California's license plates have been manufactured at Folsom prison since the 1930s.

HOW TO STAY ALIVE

In our Uncle John's Fast-Acting Long-Lasting Bathroom Reader, we presented the "BRI Survival Guide"—tips for how to make it through a natural disaster. Here are a few people-related disasters that you'll hopefully never experience, but if you do, you can protect yourself.

STREET ATTACK
• When walking at night, stay in well-lit areas and travel with friends whenever possible.

• If you feel that someone is following you with ill intentions, speed up and listen carefully for the footsteps of your pursuer. If he speeds up too, start running and shouting as loudly as you can, drawing as much attention to yourself as possible.

• If you're accosted, try to determine the attacker's intent. If it's a simple robbery, calmly give them what they want—especially if they have a weapon. None of your possessions are worth your life. Without making too much eye contact, try to note as many details as you can about their appearance, voice, and mannerisms.

• If the attacker intends to cause you bodily harm and doesn't have a gun, then try one of these weapons:

• **Pepper spray.** A good idea if you live in a potentially dangerous area.

• **Your keys.** Bunch them in your hand with the ends sticking out between your fingers. A successful strike to the neck, eye, or groin could end the attack right away.

• **Your foot.** Go for the groin—it will give you a longer reach than your assailant, especially because you'll be leaning back when kicking.

• **Other weapons:** comb (drag it underneath the nose); umbrella (for puncturing); makeup (blow powder in the assailant's face to blind him); also nail files, pens, or anything with a point.

Using any of these makeshift weapons will, if successful, give you only one chance to escape. So once you've made your move, get yourself away as fast as possible—and as *loudly* as possible. The best thing to yell is, "Call the police! I'm being attacked!" And yell it over and over.

UNRULY CROWDS

At any sporting events, concerts, or other public gathering there's always the possibility that a mob mentality will break out and people will get trampled. Keeping calm can save your life in this situation.

• Know where the nearest exit is. Try to make a habit of looking for possible escape routes whenever you enter a new place. (This isn't paranoia, it's common sense.) At the first sign of trouble, start heading for the exit.

• If you find yourself trapped in a mob, the most important thing is to stay on your feet and move with the crowd. Stopping for even a second may cause you to lose your footing and get trampled.

• Staying on your feet is of utmost importance. So if you are stopped, take a deep breath and tense up your shoulders, biceps, and chest. Bunch your arms up against your stomach to make yourself as solid as possible.

• If you have a small child, carry him or her in front of you. If at all possible, don't let the child walk.

• Keep quiet for two reasons: 1) You'll call less attention to yourself, which could save you from pepper spray, flying fists, or bullets; and 2) It can be hard to see through a mob, so keeping quiet may allow you to hear escape instructions from police or venue officials.

BEING TIED UP

Although this rarely occurs outside the movies, it does happen. If it happens to you, here's a neat magician's trick (Houdini used it) that may help you escape:

• While your captor is tying you up, make yourself as large as possible by inhaling and pushing your chest out. Flex any muscles that are being tied up, but do it as subtly as possible so as not to raise suspicion. When your captor leaves, relax. You'll get at least a half an inch of slack in the ropes, which should be more than enough for you to wiggle your way to freedom.

"STRONG ENOUGH TO FLOAT A PISTOL"

Howdy, pardner. Time to lock the outhouse door and settle in to these rootin-tootin' lines from classic Hollywood Westerns...unless yer yella.

Young Eddie: "He don't look so tough to me."

Cowboy: "If he ain't so tough, there's been an awful lot of sudden natural deaths in his vicinity."

—*The Gunfighter* (1950)

"I always say the law was meant to be interpreted in a lenient manner. And that's what I try to do. Sometimes I lean to one side of it, sometimes I lean to the other."

—**Paul Newman**, *Hud* (1963)

"Sonny, I can see we ain't going to have you 'round long enough to get tired of your company."

—**Richard Widmark**, *The Law and Jake Wade* (1958)

Cowboy: "For a long time I was ashamed of the way I lived."

Dance hall girl: "You mean to say you reformed?"

Cowboy: "No, I got over being ashamed."

—*Goin' to Town* (1935)

J. W. Grant: "You bastard!"

Hired gun Henry "Rico" Fardan: "Yes, sir. In my case an accident of birth. But you, you're a self-made man."

—*The Professionals* (1966)

Fletch McCloud: "Ever hear what William Shakespeare said? 'All's well that ends well.'"

Cowboy Bob Seton: "Shakespeare, huh? He must have come from Texas. We've been saying that for years."

—*The Dark Command* (1940)

Trampas: "When I want to know anything from you, I'll tell you, you long-legged son of a—"

"The Virginian": "If you want to call me that, smile."

—*The Virginian* (1929)

Sheriff Bullock: "How is he, Doc?"

Doc: "Well, he suffered lacerations, contusions, and a concussion. His jugular vein was severed in three places. I counted four broken ribs and a compound fracture of the skull. To put it briefly, he's real dead."

—*Rancho Notorious* (1952)

"I like my coffee strong enough to float a pistol."

—**Ernest Borgnine**, *Jubal* (1955)

"I don't want trouble with anybody— unless I start it."

—**"Wild Bill" Elliott**, *The Showdown* (1950)

The bandit Black Bart wrote poems and left them in empty strongboxes to confuse lawmen.

LADY OF THE LOCKUP

This story from Uncle John's Tales to Inspire *is neither about cop nor crook—but a wannabe nun who wanted to make a difference.*

SOUTH OF THE BORDER

In 1965 a Southern California housewife named Mary Brenner got a phone call from her local priest, Father Henry Vetter. Father Henry knew that Brenner did a lot of charity work in the Los Angeles area, so he invited her to join him on a trip to Tijuana, a Mexican city just south of San Diego. A few days later, they filled a station wagon with donated medicine and other supplies, and headed south. After dropping off the medical supplies at various city hospitals, they made a stop at Tijuana's notorious La Mesa prison.

AN EYEFUL

There's a lot of poverty in Tijuana, and Brenner, who grew up in Beverly Hills, was shocked at every stop they made. But it was the prisoners at La Mesa who moved her the most. Built in the 1950s to house 600, the prison now held more than 7,000 men and women in appalling conditions. It had a reputation as one of the most dangerous jails in Mexico.

Even though Brenner was holding down two jobs and raising seven children, she resolved to return to La Mesa as often as she could. And over the next several years she managed to make the three-hour drive fairly regularly, bringing with her carloads—and sometimes even truck-loads—of donated medical supplies, toiletries, used clothing, furniture, and fast food that restaurants saved for her instead of tossing out at the end of the day. Yet after having accomplished so much, each time she left the prison she felt there was still more to do.

A CHANGE OF HABIT

When her second marriage ended in divorce in 1972, Brenner started thinking about what she wanted to do with the rest of her life. A devout Catholic, she thought about becoming a nun. But when she approached an order called the Maryknolls, they told her she was too old—only women aged 35 or younger were allowed to join. (Her two divorces didn't help her case, either.)

In 2000 the CIA built a robotic catfish called Charlie. His mission remains classified.

After talking it over with priests and nuns who knew of her work, she decided to take private vows and become a sort of "freelance" nun—one who didn't belong to any established religious order. She sewed her own habit and took the name Mother Antonia, in honor of Father Anthony Brouwers, a priest she admired. From then on the prisoners, the prison guards, and all their families would be her life's work.

GETTING STARTED

When the warden of La Mesa told Mary Brenner years earlier to come back anytime and stay as long as she liked, he probably never imagined that one day she'd show up at the front gate dressed as a nun, asking for permission to live in the prison. But he lived up to his offer and granted "Mother Antonia's" request; in March 1977 she took up residence in the women's block and began living at La Mesa full time.

Believing that every person has an innate capacity for good, Mother Antonia refused to judge the prisoners—she only wanted to help them. And her approach to serving the prison community was simple: If an inmate or guard needed anything, she'd do her best to get it for them. She focused on the most basic needs at first—collecting and distributing food, blankets, toiletries, and medicine to the inmates, as well as caring for the sick and tending to the spiritual needs of both the inmates and the guards. But over time "Madre Antonia," as the prisoners called her, became more ambitious:

• She recognized that bad or missing teeth were more than just a cosmetic problem, they were also a major barrier to parolees finding decent jobs and putting their criminal pasts behind them. So Mother Antonia recruited dentists to come to the prison and cap teeth and fit bridges and dentures for inmates and guards. The dentists donated their time; Mother Antonia paid for materials and other expenses out of charitable contributions she raised. It typically cost more than $200 to treat each case, yet so far Mother Antonia has managed to obtain treatment for 4,000 people.

• She also arranged for plastic surgeons to visit La Mesa to remove prison tattoos, repair cleft palates (the cause of some speech impediments), and perform other surgeries that improved the appearance of inmates and made it easier for them to reenter life outside the prison walls.

• Inmates were routinely being beaten during Mother Antonia's early trips to La Mesa, something she attributed to the guards' limited education, poor job training, and low pay. By befriending the guards and their families, she has been able to improve the treatment of inmates not just at La Mesa, but also at local police stations and jails. Mother Antonia is credited with ending three prison riots over the years.

• Many petty criminals were serving months or even years of hard time simply because they couldn't afford to pay fines—some as low as $25. Mother Antonia has used donated money to get thousands of nonviolent offenders out on bail or released from prison altogether.

LIFE SENTENCE

Now in her 80s, Mother Antonia has spent more than three decades living in a cell at La Mesa prison. Advancing age has taken its toll: She suffers from heart trouble and sleeps with an oxygen tank next to her bed, but she insists on living at the prison. As word about her triumphs has spread over the years, she has attracted other women to the cause. The Catholic Church officially recognized her work about a year after she started, and in 2003 she formed a new religious order called the Eudist Servants of the Eleventh Hour, which accepts women aged 45 to 65. In 2005 she was the subject of a best-selling book titled *The Prison Angel*. In 2010 filmmaker Jody Hammond released a documentary about her narrated by Susan Sarandon called *La Mama: An American Nun's Life in a Mexican Prison*.

Though not a household name in the U.S., Mother Antonia's work has made her one of the most famous and revered women in Mexico, but she says she has trouble seeing what all the fuss is about. "I don't understand why people are so amazed. To give help is easy," she says. "To ask for it is hard."

*　　　*　　　*

HAPPINESS IS A WARM GUN

"Madison, Wisconsin, police chief Richard Williams turned on his oven to roast some turkey but forgot that was one of his favorite hiding places for his gun. 'Shortly thereafter: boom!' police spokesperson Jeanna Kerr said, adding that Williams was given a one-day, unpaid suspension for violating his department's firearms policy."

—*News of the Weird*

Los Angeles County has 10,000 cops who patrol 500 sq. miles and serve a pop. of 4.1 million.

ISN'T IT IRONIC?

*Just like guns and ammo, or death and taxes,
the law and irony go hand in hand.*

IRONY HITS THE STREETS

• "If you didn't see me put this flyer on your windshield, I could have stolen your car," read the ads for Ray Wright's Philadelphia burglar alarm business. While he was placing them on other people's windshields, his own car was stolen.

• In 1999 Roger Russell began a 2,600-mile walk across South Africa to promote crime prevention. Two days into his walk, Russell was robbed at gunpoint.

• Two plainclothes German police officers were making their way through a crowd of protesters to meet up with some uniformed cops. But the uniforms met them halfway and beat the two with nightsticks. The bruised officers sued the police department.

IRONY BEHIND BARS

• In 1853 a contractor named John Coffee built a new jail in the town of Dundalk, Ireland. During the project, Coffee went bankrupt. He became his jail's very first inmate.

• In 2002 Albion State Prison in New York offered a class that became so popular among the most violent criminals that there was a waiting list to sign up. The subject of the class: quilting.

LEGISLATING IRONY

• A new anti-pornography law could not go into effect in Winchester, Indiana, because the editors of the town's only newspaper refused to print the wording of the law on the basis that it was pornographic. For a new law to be official, it has to be printed in the newspaper.

• New York state assemblywoman Nancy Calhoun pled guilty to charges that she harassed her ex-boyfriend in 1999. According to testimony, she "burst into his home in the middle of the night, tailgated him in a car, and posed as a cosmetics seller to get his new girlfriend's phone number." Calhoun was co-sponsor of the state's new anti-stalking legislation.

Good news for Wiccans: Witchcraft hasn't been a crime in the New World since 1750.

• On October 30, 2003, Congress released findings of a study that said toy guns don't have any relationship to crime. That same day, the Capitol was locked down for an hour because two workers had brought toy guns to work as part of their Halloween costumes.

IRONY IN THE COURT

• A 1986 court case did not go well for the Otis Elevator Company. It might have had something to do with the fact that the jury—on their way to hear the case—got stuck for 20 minutes in an Otis elevator.

• A similar thing happened to the Pacific Gas & Electric Company in 2000. While on trial for "failure to trim vegetation around power lines," a branch fell off a tree and knocked out power to the courthouse.

• In 1992 the U.S. Postal Service was defending itself against an unemployment discrimination lawsuit. In order to proceed, the defense had to mail a list of expert witnesses from Washington, D.C., to Dayton, Ohio. The list was sent via the USPS's Overnight Express Mail delivery service, but did not arrive in Dayton for ten days.

• A production company won a $1.8 million judgment against a former employee accused of stealing the concept for a television game show. Name of the stolen show: *Anything for Money*.

DEATHLY IRONY

• Myra Davis was Janet Leigh's body double in the 1960 Hitchcock classic *Psycho*. It was her hand that was seen in the famous shower scene in which Leigh's character is stabbed to death. On July 3, 1988, Davis was found strangled in her Los Angeles home, murdered by a 31-year-old "caretaker and handyman"…just like Norman Bates.

• A 22-year-old California skier stole a piece of padded yellow foam from a ski lift pole, dragged it up the hill, and used it as a makeshift sled. He crashed into the newly unpadded pole, hit his head, and died.

CAN'T WE ALL JUST GET IRONIC?

• "Human Kindness Day" took place in May 1975, in Washington, D.C. Afterward, the cops announced that during the festivities, there were "600 arrests, 150 smashed windows, and 42 looted refreshment stands."

• Love Your Neighbor Corp. of Michigan sued Love Thy Neighbor Fund of Florida for trademark infringement.

DRIVE LIKE YOU STOLE IT

*Here are some real-life bumper stickers (with attitude)
that our perps…er, readers have sent us over the years.*

MY CHILD WAS INMATE OF THE
MONTH AT THE COUNTY JAIL.

Dangerously under-medicated!

Honk at me if you've never seen
an UZI from a car window

99% of Lawyers Give the
Rest a Bad Name

**Bad Cop,
No Donut!**

*If it weren't for physics and law
enforcement, I'd be unstoppable.*

Drive it like you stole it

Forget Gun Control, Ban Crime

THE ONLY DIFFERENCE BETWEEN
A RUT & A GRAVE IS THE DEPTH

**Hello, Ossiffer.
Just put it on my tab.**

I NEED SOMEBODY BAD.
ARE YOU BAD?

**man cannot live on bread
alone…unless he's in a cage
and that's all you feed him**

It is as bad as you think
and they are out to get you

***EVERYTHING I NEED TO KNOW
I LEARNED IN PRISON***

REMEMBER: IT'S PILLAGE FIRST,
THEN BURN.

Skateboarding is NOT a crime!
(but most skateboarders are criminals)

*Don't like the way I drive?
Stay off the sidewalk!*

```
Four out of five
voices in my head say,
     "Kill!"
```

Come to the dark side:
We have cookies

**Don't you make me release
the flying monkeys!**

TO ERR IS HUMAN.
TO ARR IS PIRATE.

Support Your Local Police
(Leave fingerprints)

JAIL SUCKS

If a cop refers to you as "EDP," it means you're an "Emotionally Disturbed Person."

THE WORLD'S MOST DANGEROUS BAND

Marilyn Manson, Alice Cooper, Ozzy Osbourne—those "wild children"
of rock 'n' roll are downright tame compared to the craziest musical act we've
ever heard of. Murder, suicide, and sheep heads are all part of the package
with the Norwegian "black metal" band known as…Mayhem.

DISILLUSION
In the early 1980s, a radical underground music scene was form-
ing in Europe. As far as these young musicians were concerned,
rock was too tame, punk had gone mainstream, and the supposed
"Satan-worshipping" heavy-metal acts like Black Sabbath, Dio, and
KISS were all faking it. So, with no bands that were "heavy" enough for
their taste, these young people made their own music that reflected
their bitter attitude toward…well, everything. The two most prominent
styles to emerge from the scene came to be known as "death metal" and
"black metal." To the untrained ear, both sound pretty much the same—
blisteringly fast tempos; distorted guitars; screeching, unintelligible
vocals; morbid lyrics (when you could hear them); and elaborate, gruesome stage acts. But of the two, black metal was the most melodic…
and the most blasphemous.

THE GATHERING
One of the pioneering bands of black metal was an Oslo band called Mayhem. Formed in 1984, the original lineup consisted of guitarist/vocalist
Øystein Aarseth (also known as "Euronymous"), bassist Jorn Stubberud
("Necrobutcher"), and drummer Kjetil Manheim. After going through a
few singers ("Messiah" and "Maniac"), Mayhem was joined by Swedish
vocalist Per Yngve Ohlin, who adopted the nickname "Dead."

Dead was *the* quintessential black-metal singer: He buried his clothes
for weeks underground to give them a "grave" scent; he slashed his own
skin during performances; and, for inspiration, he inhaled rancid air from
a plastic bag containing the decomposed remains of a crow. In 1990 Dead
and the rest of Mayhem moved into a house together to work on their

---

High caliber? More Americans in their thirties own firearms than any other age group.

first full-length album, *De Mysteriis Dom Sathanas*—a Latin phrase that loosely translates to "Lord Satan's Secret Rites." During those album sessions, a style emerged that would come to define black-metal music. According to *Dark Legions* magazine:

> [The music] was metamorphosing into a sleeker, melodic variant with more dynamic change in the songs, producing different "settings" to tell a tale, somewhat like a micro-opera in harsh guitars and howling vocals. Similarly, the band's appearance went from t-shirts and jeans to black clothing, black boots, and black-and-white facepaint, or "corpsepaint," to make them all appear dead.

THE SPLINTERING

Life in the Mayhem house was as intense as the music: Dead, who continually battled depression, didn't get along with Euronymous. And on April 8, 1991, Euronymous came home to find Dead dead—with slit wrists and a self-inflicted gunshot to the head. (Next to him was a suicide note that read, "Please excuse all the blood.") Before calling the police, however, Euronymous ran to the store and bought an instant camera...and then photographed Dead's body in a variety of positions. (One of the photos later found its way onto the cover of Mayhem's bootleg live album, *Dawn of the Black Hearts*.) According to legend, Euronymous also kept chunks of Dead's scattered brain and mixed them into a stew, and used bone fragments from his skull to make necklaces that he gave to musicians whom he "deemed worthy."

The well-publicized tragedy gave a huge boost not only to Mayhem's popularity but to all of black metal. "People became more aware of us after that," said Necrobutcher, the bassist. "It really changed the scene." But the "scene" became too much for Necrobutcher to handle, and he soon quit the band.

THE REFORMATION

But Mayhem lived on...for a while. Singer Attila Csihar took over for Dead, while Varg Vikernes ("Count Grishnackh," named after a *Lord of the Rings* villain) stepped in on bass. But once again, there was trouble in the band—Count Grishnackh, who suffered from paranoid delusions, became convinced that Euronymous was secretly conspiring to torture and kill him. On August 10, 1993, less than a year after joining the band,

Grishnackh went to Euronymous's apartment and stabbed him 23 times, killing him.

The ensuing murder trial put Mayhem in the news again. And the trial revealed that not only did the bassist kill the guitarist, but Grishnackh was also responsible for a spate of infamous church-burnings that had plagued Norway for the past few years. He was sentenced to 21 years in prison. (He was released on parole 15 years later, in 2009.)

THE SHEEP OFFENSIVE

It seemed that with two members dead and one in jail, Mayhem would never rock again. Not so—in 1995 Hellhammer got a lineup together to start anew, this time with guitarist Rune "Blasphemer" Eriksen and original member Sven Erik "Maniac" Kristiansen on vocals. He even lured Necrobutcher out of retirement to play bass. Soon after, Mayhem *finally* released *De Mysteriis Dom Sathanas*—an album that had been stalled amidst all of Mayhem's mayhem. That was followed by *Wolf's Lair Abyss* in 1997 and *Grand Declaration of War* in 2000. Mayhem were back in business—and were now a bona fide legend in the black-metal world. They managed to stay below the radar of the mainstream press… for a time.

But in 2003 the band made headlines again. During a show in Bergen, Norway, Maniac was cutting up a dead sheep on stage—a ritual that had become a regular part of their act—when its head somehow catapulted into the crowd, hitting 25-year-old Per Kristian Hagen. The sheep's head knocked the young man to the floor, and he ended up with a fractured skull. Hagen filed assault charges against Mayhem. "The whole thing was an accident," claimed Blasphemer (although he added, "but maybe it *would* be an idea for another show"). In the end, Hagen dropped the charges and the band had weathered yet another storm.

LONG DIE ROCK

With the band members now in their 40s, Mayhem is still at it. They made the news again in 2009 when they were arrested for trashing a hotel room in the Netherlands. And though they don't expect everyone to like their music, they don't want to be thought of as just a gimmick. According to vocalist Attila Csihar, "It took us 20 years of doing this before people realized we weren't joking."

Serial killer Rodney Alcala once appeared on *The Dating Game*.

THE GREAT DIAMOND HOAX OF 1872, PART II

*Here's the second installment of our tale of what may
have been the biggest con job of the 19th century.
(Part I is on page 79.)*

EMPIRE BUILDER

As Arnold and Slack made their getaway, William Ralston was hard at work putting together a $10 million corporation called the San Francisco and New York Mining and Commercial Company. He'd already lined up 25 initial investors who contributed $80,000 apiece, and now he was preparing to raise another $8 million. New York newspaper publisher Horace Greeley had already bought into the company; so had British financier Baron Ferdinand Rothschild.

A *Rothschild* investing in the diamond field? The house of Rothschild was a world-renowned banking firm and experienced at spotting good investments. With Tiffany and Rothschild involved, the excitement surrounding the diamond field grew to a fever pitch. No one but Arnold and Slack knew where the mine was, but so what? When rumors began spreading that it was somewhere in the Arizona Territory, fortune seekers by the hundreds began making their way there in the hope of finding strikes of their own.

LOCATION, LOCATION, LOCATION

The stage was now set for the swindle to grow much bigger, which meant that a lot more people would have lost a lot more money. That it didn't happen was due purely to chance: When Arnold and Slack picked the location of their "diamond field," they unknowingly chose an area where a team of government geologists had been conducting surveys for five years.

The leader of the geological team was a man named Clarence King. When he learned of the diamond strike, he couldn't believe what he was hearing. He'd been all over the territory and had already filed a report stating that there were no deposits of precious gems of any kind anywhere in the area. If the story were true, he and his team of experts had missed a significant diamond field that two untrained miners had been able to find on their own. His professional reputation was on the line: If there really was a diamond field and word of it got back to Washington, D.C., he would be exposed as incompetent and funds for the survey would be cut off.

TOO GOOD TO BE TRUE?

King arranged to meet the engineer Henry Janin over dinner to get a firsthand account of the diamond field story. As he listened to Janin describe his trip to the site, he started to smell a rat. Janin reported finding diamonds, rubies, and sapphires next to each other, and as a geologist, King knew that was impossible. The natural processes by which diamonds are created are so different from those that create rubies and sapphires that they are never found in the same deposits.

Because Janin had been blindfolded on the trip to the site, he couldn't tell King where it was. But King was so familiar with the area that after quizzing Janin, he was able to figure out exactly which mesa he was talking about. The next day he and some other members of his team set out to visit the site themselves.

ON THE SPOT

They arrived at the site a few days later. It was fairly late in the day, so they set up camp and then started exploring the area. As had been Janin's experience, it didn't take long for them to find raw diamonds, rubies, and other gems. By the time King was ready to turn in for the night, he'd found so many precious stones that even *he* had a touch of diamond fever. He went to bed wondering if the field really was genuine, and maybe even hoping a little that it was. That hope vanished early the next morning.

• Shortly after sunrise, another member of the party found a diamond that was partially cut and polished. Nature is capable of many things, but it takes a jeweller to cut and polish a diamond—the stone had been planted there by human hands.

• King noticed that wherever he found diamonds, he found other precious stones in the same place, and always in roughly the same quantities, something that does not happen in nature.

• Upon close examination, the team also noticed that the crevices in which the gems were found had fresh scratch marks, as if the gems had been shoved into place with tools.

• When precious stones were found in the earth, it was always in places that had been disturbed by foot traffic. When they went to areas that were undisturbed, they never found anything.

DIGGING DEEP

King knew that if the field was real, diamonds would also be found deep in the ground as well as on the surface. As a final test, he and his men went to an undisturbed area where they thought diamonds might occur naturally and dug a trench 10 feet deep. Then they carefully sifted through all of the dirt that had been removed from the trench, and found not a single precious stone in any of it. There was no question about it: the find was a hoax. Arnold and Slack had planted the gems.

As soon as King got to a telegraph station, he sent word to Ralston in San Francisco that he'd been conned. Ralston was shocked and angry. He closed the company and returned the unspent capital to the original 25 investors. Then, because his reputation was on the line, he refunded the rest of their investment out of his own pocket, which cost him about $250,000. It turns out that Ralston's bad judgment wasn't limited to diamonds: He poured millions into the building of San Francisco's Palace Hotel and other money-losing schemes, which contributed to the Bank of California's collapse in 1875. His body was found floating in the San Francisco Bay the following day, though the cause of death remains a mystery.

THE HOAX EXPOSED

The Great Diamond Hoax of 1872, as it came to be known, received widespread newspaper coverage not just in America but also in Europe. As reporters in the United States and abroad researched the story, details of how the hoax had been perpetrated began to emerge:

• Arnold had once been a bookkeeper for the Diamond Drill Company of San Francisco, which used industrial-grade diamonds in the manufacture of drill bits. He apparently stole his first batch of not-so-precious gems from work, then bought cheap, uncut rubies and sapphires from other sources and added them to the mix. None of the people he duped had been able to tell industrial-grade diamonds and second-rate gems from the real thing.

• When Ralston and the other early investors paid Slack the first install-ment of $50,000 for his share of the mine, he and Arnold made the first of two trips to London, where they bought $28,000 worth of additional uncut stones from diamond dealers there. Most of the gems were used to salt the claim in Colorado; the few that were left over were the ones that Tiffany and his assistant had foolishly valued at $150,000.

AFTERMATH

Philip Arnold and John Slack made off with $650,000, which in 1872 should have set them up for life. Neither of them fared very well, though: Arnold moved to Kentucky and bought a 500-acre farm. When the law eventually tracked him down, he paid a reported $150,000 to settle the claims against him, then used the remaining money to start his own bank. Six years after the diamond hoax, he was injured in a shootout with another banker; he died from pneumonia six months later at the age of 49.

Less is known about Slack. He apparently blew through his share of the loot and had to go back to work, first as a coffin maker in Missouri and then as a funeral director in New Mexico. When he died there in 1896 at the age of 76, he left an estate valued at only $1,600.

Uncovering and exposing the fraud gave Clarence King's career a huge boost; in 1879 he became the first director of the U.S. Geological Survey. But he was a better geologist than he was a businessman, as he learned to his dismay in 1881 when he quit working for the government and took up ranching. He failed at that, then went on to fail at mining and banking. He died penniless in 1901 at the age of 59.

FOOL'S GOLD

So did anyone come out ahead from the experience? Apparently only Henry Janin, the mining engineer who had vouched for the authenticity of the diamond field. He suffered a blow to his reputation when the hoax was exposed, but by then he'd already sold his $10,000 worth of shares to another investor for $40,000. Janin was never implicated in the scam; as far as anyone knows, his good fortune was just a case of dumb luck.

...has committed a violent crime—also known as "Bonnie and Clyde Syndrome."

JAIL FOOD FOLLIES

Are you sick of the cafeteria? Tired of the same old fast food? Then maybe you'd like to sample the cuisine at your local prison. Bon apétit!

PRISON: Rockwood Institution, Winnipeg, Canada
FOOD: Lobster and liquor
STORY: In August 2002, prison officials reported that a "well-connected" inmate had managed to make prison a four-star dining experience for his fellow inmates. They said that Ronald Hickey, 48, who was serving a nine-year sentence for drug convictions, had somehow smuggled over a ton of gourmet seafood and liquor into the prison. The officials couldn't prove it, though: the accusations were based solely on tips from inmate informants—any actual evidence is believed to have been eaten.

PRISON: Pozo Almonte jail in Santiago, Chile
FOOD: French bread sticks
STORY: Prison officials couldn't figure out why prisoners were suddenly so fond of French baguettes, prompting a huge rise in deliveries from certain local bakeries. But a November 2002 search of one of the bakeries discovered the secret ingredient: the bread sticks were being hollowed out and filled with marijuana.

PRISON: Caledonia County Work Camp, Vermont
FOOD: Beer and cigarettes
STORY: In December 2001, Mark Delude, a prisoner at this work camp for nonviolent offenders, crawled under the fence surrounding the site, and took off. How far did he get? About a mile and a half, to the nearest convenience store. Delude wasn't trying to escape, he just wanted some beer and smokes. He bought a case of beer and a carton of cigarettes, and had a few of both before trying to sneak back into prison with the rest of his booty. Guards caught the slightly inebriated Delude standing outside his tent…and shipped him off to a more secure facility. "I don't remember ever trying to catch people trying to break back in before," said State Police Officer George Hacking. "But nothing surprises me."

In 2001 William Petersen (CSI's Gil Grissom) lobbied Congress for more crime-lab funding.

HEY! I'M BEING ATTACKED WITH...

Okay, drop the pork chop and come out with your hands up.

...A FISH. In 2005 a woman in Saginaw, Michigan, was charged with assault after she attacked her boyfriend with a mounted swordfish. She had pulled it off the wall during an argument and stabbed him with the fish's long, sharp bill. He was treated at the scene; she was arrested.

...A CHIHUAHUA. In June 2006, a woman in St. Peters, Missouri, bought a Chihuahua puppy from a dog breeder. When the animal died a short time later, the woman went to the breeder's house, walked in, and, according to news reports, "hit the breeder over the head numerous times with the dead puppy." Then, as she fled in her car, she waved the dead Chihuahua out of the sunroof while yelling threats and obscenities at the breeder.

...A POOPER-SCOOPER. In 2006 Leisa Reed, 47, walked into a Waukesha, Wisconsin, home in the middle of the night, wildly swinging a pooper-scooper. The home owners, John and Linda Dormer, tried to tell Reed she was in the wrong house, but Reed wasn't listening. John Dormer was hit in the face with the pooper-scooper and then fought for his life as the crazed woman came at him with two pairs of scissors. Police finally arrived and, although Reed was only 5'2" and weighed a mere 105 pounds, it took five officers, three stun gun shots, leg straps, and a large bag to finally subdue her. The fact that she was high on crack cocaine made her seemingly superhuman, police said. (She got two years in prison.)

...A PORK CHOP. A 45-year-old Australian man in Roma, Queensland, was helping his son move out of an apartment he had been evicted from when an argument broke out over a refrigerator. The fridge apparently belonged to one family, and the meat inside it to another. During the melee that followed, a woman grabbed a frozen pork chop and hit the father in the head. He was taken to the hospital to get stitches. The Australian Broadcast Company reported that the woman was charged with "assault with a pork chop," adding that the "the weapon has been removed from the scene…and probably eaten."

…A PROSTHETIC LEG. A teenager with a prosthetic leg in Cape Girardeau, Missouri, was attacked by two other teens in September 2006. The two boys pulled 17-year-old Michael Williams out of his car, pulled off his prosthetic leg, and beat him with it. Alexander Harris, 17, and an unnamed 16-year-old were charged with felony assault. Williams thinks the two probably attacked him simply because he was disabled. "What motivates someone to do that, I have no idea," he said.

…A FISH (AGAIN). Alan Bennie was walking through a park in Grangemouth, Scotland, when 22-year-old David Evans approached him, holding a fish. According to prosecutor Neil MacGregor, Evans then asked Bennie, "Do you want to kiss my fish?" MacGregor continued, "Mr. Bennie made no reply, at which point the accused said: 'You answer me next time I ask you to kiss a fish,' and slapped him round the face with it." Evans pleaded guilty to "assault with a fish" and was sentenced to six months in prison.

…A TOILET. In February 2006, a father and son were in their home in Chamberlain, Texas, watching the Super Bowl when they heard a noise outside. Looking down the street, they saw a man and woman in a heated argument that looked like it might turn violent, so they rushed over to intervene. The man pulled out a knife and was able to wound both the father and son. Luckily, a discarded toilet was lying nearby, so the father grabbed a piece of the bowl and clobbered the man, who was taken to the hospital… for *head* injuries. Then he was *throne* in jail, the *loo*-ser. (He's in the *can* now.)

*   *   *

A POLICE WORD ORIGIN

The term "M.O." from the Latin *modus operandi* ("mode of operating") was first applied to catching crooks based on their habits in the 1880s. The theory was developed by English constable Major L. W. Atcherley.

Police dogs are sometimes trained in a foreign language so that criminals can't command them.

ARGH, MATEYS!

Here's a swashbuckling article from Uncle John's Bathroom Reader Plunges Into
Canada *about pirates and privateers. Both occupations require the same skills:
looting, murdering, plundering, and kidnapping. The only real difference
is sponsorship—a pirate works for himself and his crew, but a privateer
is sanctioned by his own government as long as he pays a portion of
his loot and attacks (mostly) its enemies' ships. Here are some of
the most legendary Canadian criminals to ever hit the high seas.*

ROBERT CHEVALIER DE BEAUCHÊNE

How he lived: Even before Robert Chevalier de Beauchêne
became a privateer, he lived a storied life. Whether the stories
were true is another matter—Chevalier had a reputation of exaggerating.
In 1693, at the age of seven, Chevalier ran away from his home near
Montreal (or maybe was kidnapped…no one knows for sure) and was
adopted by an Iroquois tribe. His parents retrieved him a year or two later,
but Chevalier had already gotten a taste of adventure. He soon ran away
again, this time attaching himself to a band of Algonquins who had sided
with French colonists fighting British invaders. While helping to defend
the settlement of Louisbourg, Nova Scotia, Chevalier met up with a
group of Acadian privateers. He was so dazzled by their tales of life on the
high seas that he joined their crew. After an apprenticeship spent pillag-
ing English colonies along the North American coast, he got a ship and
crew and struck out on his own.

What became of him: Canada remained his home port, but Chevalier
died in France in 1731 while dueling for a woman's affections.

PETER EASTON

How he lived: Not all pirates start out bad. Peter Easton was a naval officer from a distinguished military family. In 1602, Queen Elizabeth I gave
him three warships and sent him to Newfoundland to protect its fishing
fleet from pirates and the encroachments of the Spanish. Easton had a
great year in Newfoundland piloting his ship, the *Happy Adventure*,
through a series of lucrative encounters. Unfortunately, the next year
something terrible happened: peace broke out. When James I succeeded

Elizabeth, he promptly negotiated a treaty with Spain and canceled all privateer commissions. Easton, suddenly out of a job, decided to ignore his new orders. Over the next few years, he bought more ships and "recruited" large crews. (Actually, he press-ganged Newfoundland fishermen to work on his ships.) He continued to attack Spanish vessels, but also decided to diversify, demanding protection money from English ships as well. He even blockaded the busy Bristol Channel in southwestern England, demanding tolls from any ship that wanted to pass through. Eventually, Easton became one of the most successful pirates of the 17th century.

What became of him: Sometimes crime *does* pay. Around 1610, after several years of pirating, Easton retired to Savoy in southern France with about 2 million pounds' worth of gold. There, he married a noblewoman, attained the title of Marquis of Savoy, and lived for at least another 10 years before apparently dying peacefully.

JOHN NUTT

How he lived: John Nutt became a pirate without going through the legal pretense of first being a privateer. Born in England, Nutt visited Newfoundland as a gunner on a ship in 1620. He loved the town of Torbay and resettled his family there before embarking on a life of piracy in the Gulf of Saint Lawrence and the Irish Sea. Nutt was an equal-opportunist who offered protection to English and French settlements alike...for a price. He also recruited sailors by offering regular wages and commissions, a pay and benefit package that lured many men away from the Royal Navy.

What became of him: We don't know. He almost died by hanging in 1623, but George Calvert, an English politician who had been one of Nutt's protection clients, intervened and had him released. Nutt was still pirating as of 1632, but after that, he disappeared.

PIERRE LE MOYNE D'IBERVILLE

How he lived: He was born in Montreal, but had family ties to France. As a sailor and privateer, d'Iberville became renowned for siding with the French to drive English settlers out of Newfoundland. Despite a 1687 "live-and-let-fish" treaty, which allowed the English and French to coexist and fish in the Grand Banks, d'Iberville led raiding parties that terrorized towns along the coast. Over four months in the winter of 1696–97, d'Iberville and his men destroyed 36 settlements. For his splendid work, the French government sent him to the area that's now Louisiana so he could set up a garrison to ward off English ships. Then in 1706, d'Iberville captured the English-held Caribbean island of Nevis and made plans to attack the Carolina colony on the North American mainland. He traveled to Havana, Cuba, to recruit Spanish aid for that venture.

What became of him: In Havana, he caught yellow fever and died. Colonists up and down the North American coast breathed a sigh of relief.

JOSEPH BAKER

How he lived: Some pirates weren't worthy of waving the Jolly Roger. Take Canadian-born Joseph Baker. In 1800, he signed on to the merchant schooner *Eliza*. With two other crewman he'd recruited for his plot, Baker attacked the first mate during a night watch and tossed him overboard. Then the men went after the captain, William Wheland, wounding him in a brief skirmish and taking him hostage. But during a discussion of where to sell the ship's cargo, the mutineers realized that none of them actually knew how to navigate the ship. Sensing an opportunity, Wheland offered to sail them anywhere they wanted…if they spared his life. Baker agreed, but he wasn't an honorable man. When Wheland learned that Baker intended to murder him as soon as they sighted land, he locked the other conspirators in the hold, caught Baker by surprise, and chased him up the mainmast.

What became of him: Wheland kept Baker up there, lashed to the mast, until they landed on St. Kitts in the West Indies, and then turned him over to the authorities. After a four-day trial in April 1800, Baker and his pals were hanged.

HONORABLE MENTION: THE SALADIN MUTINEERS

How they lived: During the mid-1800s, Peruvian guano (excrement from seabirds) was a valuable commodity for manufacturing fertilizer and gunpowder. In 1844, the *Saladin*, a three-masted British ship, sailed from the coast of Peru carrying a huge load of guano and a small fortune in silver. Onboard were a man named George Fielding and his 12-year-old son.

Handwriting analysis was used to detect forgery in ancient Rome.

The elder Fielding, it turned out, was a guano smuggler on the run from Peruvian authorities. He convinced a half-dozen crewmen to take control of the ship and kill the captain and five others. Later, though, the mutineers became suspicious of Fielding and threw both him and his son overboard. Near Country Harbour in Nova Scotia, they decided to run the ship aground and make off with the cargo.

What became of them: Soon after, Canadian authorities caught the six men and put them on trial. Four were found guilty and hanged, but two others were acquitted—the jury believed they'd only joined the mutiny out of fear that they'd be killed.

*   *   *

CANADIANS ON THE ROCK

The prisoner who spent the most time in the notorious prison on San Francisco's Alcatraz Island was Canadian. Alvin "Old Creepy" Karpis was born (without the nickname and with Karpowicz as his last name) in Montreal in 1908. By his 10th birthday, he'd fallen in with a bad crowd that corrupted his morals and shortened his last name. First arrested for burglary in 1926, Old Creepy got hired into an entry-level position in the murderous Barker Gang and quickly worked his way up the ladder to an upper management position, increasing gang profits by innovating a successful strategy of kidnapping industrialists for ransom. Victims included William Hamm Jr. of the Hamm's Brewing Company (netting $100,000, the equivalent of $1.5 million in modern money) and Edward Bremer, president of a Minnesota bank ($200,000/$3 million). As proof of his commitment to the organization, Karpis had his fingerprints surgically removed so he couldn't be traced easily.

Unfortunately, United States bureaucrats caught him anyway and arrested him in 1936, sending him briefly to Leavenworth prison in Kansas, and finally to Alcatraz. When Alcatraz closed in 1962, Karpis was transferred to McNeil Island Penitentiary in Washington where he taught a young Charles Manson (whom Karpis called "lazy and shifless") how to play guitar. In 1969 he was deported to Canada. He died in 1979.

America's last train robbery took place in the BRI's home town of Ashland, Oregon (1923).

MODERN PIRACY

*The Somali pirates that we see on the news are a far cry from the peg-legged,
parrot-shouldered, arrrr-sayin' marauders of yesteryear. Instead of
swords and periscopes, these new pirates carry assault rifles
and satellite phones. And, as twisted as it may seem,
they've become folk heroes to a nation in turmoil.*

THE MOST DANGEROUS PLACE ON EARTH

Few countries are more unstable and chaotic than Somalia. Located on the Horn of Africa, the continent's eastern-most point, Somalia lies right next to the Gulf of Aden and its busy shipping lanes, carrying passengers and cargo from all over the world.

In 1991 Somalia's government collapsed, leaving its nine million citizens to endure two decades of insurgencies, civil war, genocide, famine, drought, corruption, and crime. In 2008 more than 1,800 civilians were killed in violent clashes, and by the next year, more than 1.3 million people were displaced within Somalia and another 330,000 had fled to neighboring countries. Thousands more died from starvation and disease. Although there's now a U.N.-backed government in power, it's spending most of its resources fighting a fringe Islamic insurgency. And with no navy patrolling Somalia's waters, other nations have taken the opportunity to overfish the waters and dump their toxic waste there. But it's in those same waters that many Somalis see their salvation.

SEEKING NEW OPPORTUNITIES

With little hope at home and few prospects if they flee, some young Somali men have taken to a life of piracy. It's not much more dangerous than trying to survive on the war-torn streets, and the pay is a lot better: A pirate can make $10,000 for a successful raid. (Somalia's average wage is below $650 per year.)

Attacking from speedboats and armed with AK-47 assault rifles and rocket-propelled grenades, pirates stop ships and rob them of cash and equipment. The real prize, however, comes from taking hostages and collecting ransom for their release. The practice has become so profitable that at any given time, there are at least 200 hostages being held in the

---

$127 billion per year of Italy's GDP (about 7%) is attributed to organized crime.

Gulf of Aden by Somali pirates. "They have a great business model," according to Admiral Rick Gurnon, head of the Massachusetts Maritime Academy. "See ships, take ransom, and make millions." Says one young pirate, "Foreign navies can do nothing to stop piracy."

DAVID VS. GOLIATH

Just how brash *are* Somali pirates? No ship is too big to take on, and no ransom demand is too high. But that doesn't mean they don't sometimes bite off more than they can chew:

• In 2005 the U.S. cruise ship *Seabourn Spirit* was carrying 311 crew and passengers through the Gulf of Aden. Two speedboats carrying 10 pirates raced up and started firing machine guns and grenades at the liner. The *Spirit's* security team blasted the pirates with a high-pressure water cannon and then pierced their eardrums with an LRAD, or Long Range Acoustic Device, which emits a debilitating sound wave. The confrontation ended when the massive cruise ship simply ran over one of the speedboats.

• In 2006 two U.S. Navy warships spotted a suspicious vessel towing two fishing boats 25 miles off Somalia's coast. This is a standard tactic for pirates: One medium-size "mothership" tows two smaller boats, which carry out the raids. The warships tailed the pirates through the night, and at dawn the Navy sent two boats to investigate. The pirates opened fire on the boarding party. It was the first attack on a U.S. Navy ship in the 21st century. The destroyers easily disabled the fishing boats.

• Seven Somali pirates spotted what appeared to be a commercial tanker on the horizon in March 2009. They approached it and started firing at its hull. But it wasn't a commercial ship…and it wasn't alone. Belonging to the German navy, the heavily armed tanker was participating in "Operation Atalanta"—a military operation designed to combat piracy. The pirates turned around and fled, but by then they'd attracted the attention of an international fleet that included two Greek warships, a Dutch frigate, a Spanish warship, a U.S. Navy amphibious assault ship, several Spanish fighter planes, and two U.S. Marine Cobra helicopters. The armada easily captured the pirates.

• On November 29, 2009, about 800 miles off Somalia's coast, pirates closed in on the *Maran Centaurus*, a Greek vessel carrying a crew of 28 people…and two million barrels of crude oil, worth $150 million. The pirates boarded the ship and captured the crew—who didn't dare fight back because a single shot could have ignited the oil and blown up the ship. What followed was a month-and-a-half-long standoff, which lasted until the ship's owner agreed to the ransom demands on January 18, 2010. But shortly before delivery, a rival group of pirates sped up to the ship, firing their weapons, determined to grab the ransom for themselves. The pirates onboard the *Maran Centaurus*, knowing how combustible the cargo was, actually radioed an anti-piracy task force for help. A nearby warship dispatched two helicopters to protect the ship *and* the pirates. A short time later, a plane flew over and dropped a package containing $9 million—the largest haul in the history of Somali piracy. The hostages, all unharmed, were released. And the pirates took their loot back home.

BIG BUSINESS

As violent as these pirates are, they're fairly tame compared to other crime syndicates. According to Steve Rosenbush of Portfolio.com, "For their part, at a time when terrorists and global drug cartels from Mexico to Brazil have pushed violence to mind-numbing levels, the Somali pirates seem positively businesslike, avoiding unnecessary gunplay and raising capital in an orderly fashion on a small stock exchange." Stock exchange? Yes—in Somalia investors can buy shares of pirate operations and collect dividends after ransom money is delivered. This is the new face of piracy: well-organized plunderers who employ accountants…and even publicists to make statements to the media. And the well-insured shipping companies have come to expect piracy as a cost of doing business in the Gulf of Aden, so they're likely to quietly give in to the demands rather than risk losing a crew, passengers, or cargo. The emboldened Somali pirates have even started patrolling their shores as a makeshift coast guard, running off fishing trawlers and capturing boats that dump their waste.

And much of the hundreds of millions of dollars made by Somali pirates each year goes straight back into the country's tattered economy. As a result, poor coastal towns are starting to thrive again…and the pirates are looked upon as heroes in a country that has had little to cheer about for decades.

Since 1973 U.S. airline security has detected more than 15,000 firearms being smuggled onto planes.

BENCHED!

*Remember the saying "Judge not, lest ye be judged?" These
men in black would have done well to follow that advice.*

THE HONORABLE A. HITLER PRESIDING

Douglas County judge Richard Jones was suspended by the Nebraska Supreme Court after an investigation into 17 complaints concerning his conduct, both on and off the bench. Among the findings:
Judge Jones had taken to signing court documents with names like A.
Hitler and Snow White (he says he did it to keep court personnel on
their toes), and setting bail amounts in the form of "a gazillion pengoes"
and other imaginary currencies (he says it's "a matter of opinion" whether
the fines are nonsensical or not). He was also accused of urinating on
courthouse carpets, making an anonymous death threat against another
judge (he says it was a "prank that went wrong"), and throwing firecrackers into the same judge's office. Judge Jones contested a number of the
charges but admitted he threw the firecrackers. "I was venting," he
explained.

GARDEN-VARIETY CRIMINALS

In August 1998, a Missouri judicial commission found Associate Circuit
judge John A. Clark guilty of misconduct. The charge "most likely to be
remembered," according to the *National Law Journal:* sentencing defendants to community service...and then allowing them to "do their time"
by working in his yard.

WHERE'S YOUR LAWYER?

Dogged by a California state investigation into claims that he was
abusive to defendants who appeared in his court without an attorney,
San Bernardino County judge Fred Heene announced in 1999 that he
would not seek reelection. The commission later concluded he had
indeed been abusive.

An example of Judge Heene's conduct: A woman convicted of a traffic violation asked for more time to complete her community service
because she'd been bedridden—on doctor's orders—during the final weeks

of her pregnancy. The judge denied her request and then sentenced her to 44 days in jail. When she protested that she had a seven-day-old baby at home, the judge replied, "Ma'am, you should have thought about that a long time ago."

TAKING A BITE OUT OF CRIME

In 1997 Judge Joseph Troisi spent five days in jail after he bit defendant William Witten on the nose hard enough to make it bleed. The incident came about when Troisi—until then a "highly regarded member" of the West Virginia bench and former member of the state committee that investigates judicial misconduct—denied Witten's bail request, prompting Witten to mutter an insult under his breath. Troisi then "stepped down from the bench, removed his robe, and there was a confrontation," said state police captain Terry Snodgrass. Judge Troisi pled no contest to criminal battery, served his five days, and then resigned from the bench. He also agreed to seek counseling for "impulse control."

TO TELL THE TRUTH

In 1995 the Texas state bar reprimanded newly elected criminal appeals court judge Steven Mansfield for lying about his personal background during his campaign for office. Mansfield claimed he was born in Texas—a big plus for voters in the Lone Star State—when he was actually born in Massachusetts. He also presented himself as a political newcomer when in fact he'd run for Congress twice in New Hampshire (he lost both times). He claimed to have handled more than 100 criminal cases, but about the only case he'd really handled was his own—when he was charged in Florida for practicing law without a license. (He lost, and had to pay a $100 fine.)

Amazingly, Mansfield managed to hang onto his job in Texas's highest criminal court and kept a low profile until 1999, when he was caught trying to scalp complimentary tickets to a Texas A&M football game and received six months' probation. He left office in 2000 but announced the following year that he wanted to come back because the judiciary was becoming too liberal without him. "I feel that I can be a more effective and more consistent conservative vote on the court," he explained. (He lost.)

REEL CRIME

From the vaults of "Uncle John's Video Treasures," here are some crime capers to consider the next time you want to rent a movie.

THE STUNT MAN (1980) *Mystery/Suspense*

Review: "Nothing is ever quite what it seems in this fast-paced, superbly crafted film. It's a Chinese puzzle of a movie and, therefore, may not please all viewers. Nevertheless, this directorial tour de force by Richard Rush has ample thrills, chills, suspense, and surprises for those with a taste for something different." (*Video Movie Guide*) **Stars:** Peter O'Toole, Steve Railsback, Barbara Hershey

THINGS CHANGE (1988) *Comedy*

Review: "Director David Mamet and co-writer Shel Silverstein have fashioned a marvelously subtle and witty comedy about an inept, low-level gangster. He goes against orders to take an old shoe-shine 'boy' on one last fling before the latter goes to prison for a crime he didn't commit." (*Video Movie Guide 2001*) **Stars:** Joe Mantegna, Don Ameche

LITTLE CAESAR (1931) *Drama*

Review: "Small-time hood becomes underworld big-shot; Robinson as Caesar Enrico Bandello gives a star-making performance in this classic gangster film that's still exciting today." (*Leonard Maltin's Movie Guide*) **Stars:** Edward G. Robinson, Douglas Fairbanks Jr.

NIGHT MOVES (1975) *Mystery*

Review: "While trying to deal with his sour private life, a P.I. is hired by a fading Hollywood star to track down her reckless daughter, involving him in art smuggling, murder, and sex on Florida's Gulf Coast. This incisive psychological drama manages to be both intelligent and entertaining." (*Seen That, Now What?*) **Stars:** Gene Hackman, Jennifer Warren

GET CARTER (1971) *Drama*

Review: "British gangster film set in the 1970s. The inspiration is Hollywood in the 1940s. Michael Caine is a cheap hood who returns home to

---

29% of Americans surveyed admit they've intentionally stolen something from a store.

investigate his brother's death. One of his finest performances." (*Movies on TV*) **Stars:** Michael Caine, Ian Hendry, Britt Ekland

THE KILLER (1989) *Foreign/Action*

Review: "John Woo's best film features an honorable assassin trying to get out of the business. Impeccable pacing and incredible action choreography create an operatic intensity that leaves you feeling giddy. Available both dubbed and in Cantonese with English subtitles." (*Video Movie Guide 2001*) **Stars:** Chow Yun-Fat, Danny Lee

THE TAKING OF PELHAM ONE TWO THREE (1974) *Suspense*

Review: "A ruthless crook named Blue and three cohorts hijack a New York City subway train and hold passengers for one million in cash—to be delivered *in one hour!* Outstanding thriller, laced with cynical comedy, bursts with heart-stopping excitement, terrific performances, and first-rate editing." (*Leonard Maltin's 2001 Movie & Video Guide*) **Stars:** Robert Shaw, Walter Matthau

BIG DEAL ON MADONNA STREET (1958) *Comedy/Foreign*

Review: "A charming Italian comedy. A robbery meticulously planned by a sadsack mix of washed-up pros in which it all goes hilariously wrong." (*TimeOut Film Guide*) **Stars:** Marcello Mastroianni, Vittorio Gassman

A PERFECT WORLD (1993) *Drama*

Review: "This film, directed by Clint Eastwood, features a father-son relationship that develops between an escaped convict and the seven-year-old boy he takes as a hostage. A very American mix of male bonding, road movie, and thriller that reveals a few signs of originality." (*Halliwell's Film and Video Guide*) **Stars:** Kevin Costner, Laura Dern

HEAVENLY CREATURES (1994) *Drama/Fantasy*

Review: "In this Peter Jackson film, two New Zealand schoolgirls conspire to murder one girl's mother when parental concerns about their obsessive friendship threaten to separate them forever. Surreal scenes featuring unicorns, giant butterlies, castles, and claymation knights express the teens' emotional slide into chilling actions." (*Video Movie Guide*) **Stars:** Kate Winslett, Melanie Lynskey

---

The term "racketeering" was coined in 1927 to describe the Mafia's criminal operations.

THE MAD BOMBER, PART I

*From our Dustbin of History files, the story of a city,
a criminal psychiatrist, and a psycho with a grudge.*

SPECIAL DELIVERY

On November 16, 1940, an unexploded bomb was found on a window ledge of the Consolidated Edison Building in Manhattan. It was wrapped in a very neatly hand-written note that read,

CON EDISON CROOKS—THIS IS FOR YOU.

The police were baffled: surely whoever delivered the bomb would know that the note would be destroyed if the bomb detonated. Was the bomb not meant to go off? Was the person stupid…or was he just sending a message?

No discernable fingerprints were found on the device and a brief search of company records brought no leads, so the police treated the case as an isolated incident by a crackpot, possibly someone who had a grievance with "Con Ed"—the huge company that provided New York City with all of its gas and electric power.

WAKE-UP CALL

Nearly a year later, another unexploded bomb was found lying in the street a few blocks from the Con Ed building, this one with an alarm clock fusing mechanism that had not been wound. Again the police had no leads and again they filed the case away—there were larger problems at hand: the war in Europe was escalating and U.S. involvement seemed imminent. Sure enough, three months later, the Japanese attacked Pearl Harbor, triggering America's entry into World War II.

Shortly thereafter a strange, neatly written letter arrived at police headquarters in Manhattan:

I WILL MAKE NO MORE BOMB UNITS FOR THE DURATION OF THE WAR—MY PATRIOTIC FEELINGS HAVE MADE ME DECIDE THIS—I WILL BRING THE CON EDISON TO JUSTICE—THEY WILL PAY FOR THEIR DASTARDLY DEEDS…F. P.

True to his (or her) words, no more bombs showed up during the war, or for five years after that. But in that time at least 16 threat letters, all from

---

In 1994 a man escaped from a West Virginia prison using a rope made of dental floss.

"F. P.", were delivered to Con Ed, as well as to movie theaters, the police, and even private individuals. Still, there were no bombs…until March 29, 1950.

CITY UNDER SIEGE

That day, a third unexploded bomb much more advanced than the previous two was found on the lower level of Grand Central Station. "F. P." seemed to be sending the message that he (or she) had been honing his (or her) bomb-building skills over the last decade. Still, so far none of them had exploded. And police wondered: were these all just empty threats? That question was answered a month later when a bomb tore apart a phone booth at the New York Public Library. Over the next two years, four more bombs exploded around New York City. And try as they might to downplay the threat, the police couldn't keep the press from running with the story. "The Mad Bomber" started to dominate headlines.

More bombs were found, and more angry letters—some neatly written, others created from block letters clipped from magazines—promised to continue the terror until Con Edison was "BROUGHT TO JUSTICE."

Heading up the case was Police Inspector Howard E. Finney. He and his detectives had used every conventional police method they knew of, but the Mad Bomber was too smart for them. In December 1956, after a powerful explosion injured six people in Brooklyn's Paramount Theater, Inspector Finney decided to do something unconventional.

PSYCH-OUT

Finney called in Dr. James A. Brussel, a brilliant psychiatrist who had worked with the military and the FBI. Brussel had an uncanny understanding of the criminal mind, and like everyone else in New York, this eloquent, pipe-smoking psychiatrist was curious about what made the Mad Bomber tick. But because none of the letters had been released to the press, Brussel knew very little about the case. That all changed when police handed him the evidence they had gathered since 1941.

The pressure was on: citizens were growing more panicked with each new bomb, and more impatient with the cops' inability to catch the Mad Bomber. After poring through letters, phone call transcripts and police reports, and studying the unexploded bombs, Dr. Brussel presented this profile to Inspector Finney:

On the show *CSI*, all of the equipment in the lab is fully functional.

It's a man. Paranoiac. He's middle-aged, forty to fifty years old, intro-
vert. Well proportioned in build. He's single. A loner, perhaps living
with an older female relative. He is very neat, tidy, and clean-shaven.
Good education, but of foreign extraction. Skilled mechanic, neat with
tools. Not interested in women. He's a Slav. Religious. Might flare up
violently at work when criticized. Possible motive: discharge or repri-
mand. Feels superior to his critics. Resentment keeps growing. His letters are posted from Westchester, and he wouldn't be stupid enough to
post them from where he lives. He probably mails the letter between
his home and New York City. One of the biggest concentration of
Poles is in Bridgeport, Connecticut, and to get from there to New York
you have to pass through Westchester. He has had a bad disease—possibly heart trouble.

GOING PUBLIC

Finney was impressed…but skeptical. His team had drawn some of the
same conclusions, but even so, there had to be thousands of middle-aged
men who fit that profile. What good would it do?

"I think you ought to publicize the description I've given you," suggested Dr. Brussel. "Publicize the whole Bomber investigation, in fact.
Spread it in the newspapers, on radio and television." Finney disagreed. It
was standard procedure to keep details of investigations away from the
press. But Brussel maintained that if they handled the case correctly, the
Mad Bomber would do most of the work for them. He said that, uncon-
sciously, "he wants to be found out." Finney finally agreed. And as he left
the office, Brussel added one more thing: "When you catch him, he'll be
wearing a double-breasted suit, and it will be buttoned."

So the papers published the profile and the chase went into high gear.
As Finney predicted, "a million crackpots" came out of the woodwork, all
claiming to be the Mad Bomber, but none of them had the Mad Bomber's
skill or his distinctively neat handwriting. A slew of legitimate leads came
from concerned citizens about their odd neighbors, yet nothing solid surfaced. Still, Brussel was confident that the real Bomber's arrogance would
be his undoing.

*Did Brussel's strategy work? Turn to
Part II on page 250 to find out.*

Flamethrowers are legal in 40 US states.

MADOFF WITH THE GOODS

Here's a news item from the future: "June 29, 2159: 231-year-old former stockbroker Bernard Madoff was released today after his 150-year prison sentence ended. His first words to reporters: 'I want my stuff back.'"

EVERYTHING MUST GO

Over a career of more than two decades, stockbroker—and scam artist—Bernie Madoff bilked thousands of investors out of nearly $20 billion in what is considered the biggest Ponzi scheme in history. He was arrested in December 2008, and pleaded guilty to securities fraud, mail fraud, money laundering, perjury, theft, and six other charges four months later. In November 2009, while Madoff was beginning a 150-year prison term, the U.S. Marshals Service attempted to return some of that money to his victims by holding a series of auctions. The first one was held at the Sheraton Hotel in New York City. Purses, ashtrays, dishes, jewelry, golf clubs, stationery, duck decoys, and a Wayne Gretzky action figure were among the 200 items stacked on folding tables or leaned against walls, ready to go to the highest bidder. What did these things all have in common? They belonged to Madoff and his family, and were seized from their Manhattan penthouse and Montauk, Long Island, vacation home.

As collectors from around the world queued up to bid on the items from the New York sale, the auctioneers estimated they'd fetch about $500,000. Turns out they grossly underestimated just how crazy some people will go for anything (no matter how seemingly insignificant) that has "celebrity" status.

HEY BIDDER, BIDDER...SWWWING, BIDDER!

Auction item: A blue satin New York Mets baseball team jacket with "Madoff" stitched on the back in orange. (Ironically, team owner Fred Wilpon was one of Madoff's victims.)
Estimated value: $720
Sold for: $14,500

Longest sentence: An Alabama judge gave Dudley Kyzer 10,000 years for killing his wife.

Auction items: A Lady Hermes brown suede handbag that belonged to Madoff's wife, Ruth, plus two other purses.

Estimated value: $210

Sold for: $1,900

Auction items: Three boogie boards, one with "Madoff" written on it with a black marker.

Estimated value: $80

Sold for: $1,000

Auction item: A set of Madoff's personalized golf clubs (irons only).

Estimated value: $350

Sold for: $3,600

Auction item: A pair of Ruth Madoff's diamond Victorian dangle earrings.

Estimated value: $20,000

Sold for: $70,000

Auction item: A 1960 Hofstra University ring engraved with "BM."

Estimated value: $360

Sold for: $6,000

Auction item: A black leather Mont Blanc wallet embossed with "BM."

Estimated value: $100

Sold for: $2,200

EVERYTHING ELSE MUST GO

At later auctions, Madoff's 61-foot yacht, *Bull*, fetched nearly $1 million; his 38-foot-long boat, *Sitting Bull*, sold for $320,000; and his 21-foot-long *Little Bull* brought in $21,000. Some other Madoff items that collectors made off with: hockey trading cards, a "Bernard Madoff Investment Securities" pen, a Tiffany silver key ring monogrammed "BLM," and the Madoffs' Christofle flatware engraved "RMB." And then there was Madoff's 18-carat-gold Rolex "Prisoner Watch," inspired by the steel watches given to Allied prisoners of war in Germany during World War II. The Prisoner

Q: Why is London's Metro police station known as "Scotland Yard"?...

Watch sold for $65,000 (or about the cost of two years' worth of room-and-board to imprison Madoff).

In the end, the auctions earned about $3 million for the victims—a tiny fraction of what Madoff had stolen from them.

SWINDLER'S TWIST

Following on the heels of the official Bernie Madoff auctions, several *unofficial* "Bernie Madoff Auctions" took place around the country…in much less posh hotels and community centers. Each of these auctions promised bidders a piece of the Madoff pie. The only problem: None of them offered any items that had actually belonged to Madoff. Atlanta-based Southern Star Auctioneers—which held a sale in Syracuse, New York—said they never claimed to be selling Madoff's personal items, just stuff that belonged to his *victims*. But an investigation by the U.S. Marshals discovered that the items didn't even belong to the victims. In some of the other bogus auctions, organizers forged the stockbroker's name on the items: They sold $20 fountain pens for hundreds, even thousands of dollars…proving that even though he's behind bars, Bernie Madoff is still able to part people from their money.

*　　　*　　　*

IF YOU DON'T COUGH, YOU MIGHT GET OFF

Cardiff, Wales: "When a juror coughed, defendant Alan Rashid had a right to feel sick. The cough came at the precise moment that the jury foreman announced a verdict of 'not guilty' in Rashid's trial on a charge of threatening homicide. The cough coincided with the word 'not,' and Judge Michael Gibbon only heard 'guilty.' He sentenced Rashid to two years in prison. As the jury left the court, one inquisitive member of the panel asked an usher why Rashid was going to jail after being found not guilty. So the jurors were herded back into their box, Rashid was brought back to court, and the jury members confirmed their 'not guilty' verdict. Judge Gibbon told the defendant he was free to go. 'I am very relieved, as you would imagine,' Rashid said."

—**Associated Press**

…A: The entrance was once located on Great Scotland Yard Street.

ATTACK OF THE KISSING BANDIT!

*Of all the crimes in this book, those committed by Morganna Roberts
may be the lightest. But she did break the law—and in doing so,
she stole the hearts of sports fans all over the United States.*

ON A BET
One summer afternoon in 1971, a 17-year-old woman named
Morganna Roberts went to Riverfront Stadium to see a Cincinnati Reds game with a friend. The game was pretty uneventful until Roberts's friend "dirty double-dared" her to run out onto the field and give Pete Rose a kiss. Why not? Roberts climbed over the railing, ran across the field, and gave the startled but welcoming Rose a big smooch as fans roared their approval.

Roberts must have enjoyed the experience, because a few games later she ran out onto the field to kiss another player…and then another…and another. Blonde, with a top-heavy Dolly Parton build (she claimed measurements of 60-24-39), Roberts got *a lot* of attention. Her profile rose with each pucker and she soon found her way into the newspapers, where a Cincinnati sportswriter dubbed her "The Kissing Bandit."

SOMETHING TO SEE

If you ever got a chance to see the Kissing Bandit at work, you probably never forgot it. Fans aren't allowed on the field for security reasons, no matter how famous they are, so Morganna typically had to sneak into the baseball park incognito, her ample attributes concealed beneath a bulky jacket or some other loose-fitting garment. Then, at the opportune moment, she'd throw off her disguise and jump down to the playing field wearing a tight T-shirt and short shorts and bound across the field to the object of that day's affection.

Roberts parlayed her fame into a career as an exotic dancer, and, thanks to bookings in nightclubs and strip joints all over the country, she was able to visit nearly every ballpark in Major League Baseball. Over the years she kissed everyone from Johnny Bench and Don Mattingly to

---

Even the quickest DNA testing method takes 48 hours to produce a result.

Nolan Ryan and Cal Ripken Jr. Why stop at baseball? Morganna also snuck into pro basketball games to kiss Kareem Abdul-Jabbar, Charles Barkley, and other greats.

Stadium officials weren't crazy about her breaking the rules, but the players liked her, and many grew to see her as a good luck charm. After she kissed George Brett of the Kansas City Royals in the mid-1980s, his team went on to win the next 22 of 23 games. In 1988 she tried to kiss Ryne Sandberg of the Chicago Cubs but failed when she was blocked by an umpire. Sandberg hit the next pitch out of the park. (Maybe the umpire shouldn't have gotten involved—the Cubs still lost the game.)

BUST-ED

Roberts's antics got her arrested more than once over the years. In 1985 she was charged with criminal trespassing after she ran onto the field during the Houston Astros season opener to kiss pitcher Nolan Ryan. Her attorney claimed that she was a victim of physics—when she leaned over the railing "the laws of gravity took over," he explained. "She ran out onto the field and saw police chasing her, so where would she run but to the safety of the pitcher?" Roberts managed to beat that rap, but when she was arrested in 1988 during the Baltimore Orioles "Fantastic Fan Night," she spent a night in jail before the prosecutor set aside the charges as long as she stayed off the field at Memorial Stadium.

GAME OVER

Roberts was a part of baseball for nearly 30 years, from her late teens into her late forties. But in 1999, she decided to hang it up. She never formally announced her retirement, she just dropped out of sight and stopped giving interviews. When the Seattle *Post-Intelligencer* ran a profile on her in 2001, she again refused to participate, but after the story ran she called the newspaper at 4 a.m. and left a message explaining that she had retired to a "dream life" with her husband and three dogs, in a house alongside a creek and a running trail in the suburbs of Columbus, Ohio. "I just got sick of talking about myself and always being the center of attention," she said in her message. "I had a great time. All the fans were wonderful. All the players were wonderful. But I just had enough."

The average American company loses about 6% of its revenue to fraud each year.

ELEMENTARY, MY DEAR SHERLOCK

*Here are a few of the more interesting comments that author
Arthur Conan Doyle had Sherlock Holmes make.*

"Eliminate all other factors, and the one which remains must be the truth."

"I never guess. It is a shocking habit—destructive to the logical faculty."

"You can never foretell what any one man will do, but you can say with precision what an average number will be up to."

"As a rule, the more bizarre a thing is, the less mysterious it proves to be."

"Life is infinitely stranger than anything which the mind of man could invent."

"There is nothing more deceptive than an obvious fact."

"You know my method. It is founded on the observance of trifles."

"It is always dangerous to reason from insufficient data."

"Crime is common. Logic is rare."

"Any truth is better than indefinite doubt."

"I cannot agree with those who rank modesty among the virtues."

"It is stupidity rather than courage to refuse to recognize danger when it is close upon you."

"Mediocrity knows nothing higher than itself; but talent instantly recognizes genius."

"I can discover facts, Watson, but I cannot change them."

"A man always finds it hard to realize that he may have finally lost a woman's love, however badly he may have treated her."

"The most difficult crime to track is the one which is purposeless."

Companies that specialize in cleaning up crime scenes charge around $600 per hour.

SHANGHAIED!

*Here's a look at one of the strangest crime waves in
American history—one that terrorized even the toughest
characters in town—as city officials, the police,
and even the public looked the other way.*

OUT TO SEA

One evening in the early 1900s, 19-year-old Max DeVeer and a friend were living it up in a San Francisco honky tonk called the Barbary Coast. There they met a man who asked them if they'd like to meet some girls.

"Well, naturally at that age we were raring to go anywhere—females were few and far between," DeVeer told an interviewer half a century later. On the promise of meeting women, he and his friend went to the man's room, where he served them drinks.

"That was the last that I remember," DeVeer said. "The results of it was we woke up on a three-mast ship going through the Golden Gate....Besides my partner and myself, there were three other guys. One of them was a city fireman, and one was a store clerk and the other one was a wino, I guess."

DeVeer and company had all been "shanghaied"—drugged, kidnapped, and sold for as little as $50 a head to the captain of a sailing ship headed for the high seas. When they might make it back to San Francisco was anyone's guess; people who had been shanghaied might remain at sea, working as little more than slaves, for years at a time.

DeVeer's experience wasn't unique. For more than half a century it had been a common practice in San Francisco, Seattle, Portland, and other West Coast ports for men known as "crimps" to shanghai thousands of men every year. Shanghai, China, was a distant port of call, so when someone of seafaring age disappeared from city streets without a trace, people said they'd been "sent to Shanghai" or "shanghaied."

CANVAS AND GOLD

Two events led to the heyday of shanghaiing in the late 1840s. The first was the invention of the clipper ship, a sleek and very fast sailing ship that got its speed from more than 30 sails that were mounted on three giant masts. Lots of sails required lots of sailors to manage them, which increased the demand for sailors.

The second was the California gold rush of 1849, which caused men to abandon the low-paying, dangerous life of a sailor to seek their fortune as "Forty-Niners." There were always plenty of sailors willing to go *to* San Francisco; the problem was that as soon as a ship dropped anchor in San Francisco Bay, the crew abandoned ship and headed for the gold fields. By the end of 1849 more than 700 abandoned ships lay at anchor in the bay in need of crews to sail them back out again.

For San Francisco's merchants and city fathers, the situation was intolerable. If the city was going to grow, the port had to function normally—San Franciscans had to be able to import the supplies they needed and export the goods they produced, and ship owners had to feel confident that if they sent a ship to San Francisco, they'd eventually get it back again. So when ship captains began offering $50 per head to anyone who could find them sailors to get their ships back out of port, crimps with colorful nicknames like Scab Johnny, Chloroform Kate and the Shanghai Chicken set to work meeting the demand. Business leaders, City Hall, and even the police turned a blind eye.

THE WORST PORT IN THE WORLD

Shanghaiing was a common practice in just about every port city on the West Coast. But San Francisco's reputation paled in comparison to Portland, Oregon, which was known as the "Unheavenly City," the "Forbidden City," and "The Worst Port in the World." If the sophistication of the city's shanghai network was any measure, the nicknames were well deserved.

Portland's waterfront was one of the seediest parts of town. The neighborhood was filled with saloons, pool halls, brothels, and even opium dens that served not only sailors on shore leave, but also any loggers, ranch hands, river workers, and other laborers who might be in town looking for a good time. Even when these establishments weren't owned outright by crimp gangs, they were usually in cahoots with them.

Some business owners trapped their victims just by letting nature take its course—when a customer passed out drunk in a bar or became incapacitated in an opium den, the saloon keeper left them to the mercy of the crimp gangs. If two drunks got in a bar fight, the crimps waited for it

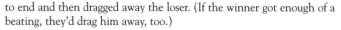

to end and then dragged away the loser. (If the winner got enough of a beating, they'd drag him away, too.)

Other proprietors took a more active approach: They served up punches made of beer mixed with schnapps and laced with laudanum or other drugs, or gave their customers "Shanghai smokes" —cigars laced with opium. Some businesses even had trap doors in the floor that sent unsuspecting victims plunging to the cellar, into the arms of waiting crimps. In Portland alone, 1,500 people were shanghaied in a typical year. In the busiest years the number climbed as high as 3,000—more than eight victims a day.

THE SHANGHAI TUNNELS

Nearly everyone who was shanghaied in Portland ended up in a cellar below street level. In the neighborhoods near the waterfront, all the buildings' cellars were connected to a network of tunnels and alleyways that ran all the way to the water's edge. This elaborate maze of underground passages, infamously known as the "Shanghai Tunnels," are what set Portland apart from other West Coast cities.

In other towns crimp gangs only shanghaied sailors as the need arose. If a ship pulled into port and the captain let it be known that he needed seven men to fill out his crew, the crimp gangs went out and kidnapped seven men. But Portland's crimp gangs outfitted the Shanghai Tunnels with makeshift prison cells, which allowed the gangs to kidnap people, then hold them captive underground for weeks at a time. Then, when a ship needing men sailed into port, the crimp gangs were ready. They slipped drugs into their victims' food and dragged them through the tunnels to the waiting ship. By the time the drugs wore off, the victims were out to sea with no hope of escape. They had only two choices: work or get thrown overboard.

Some captains paid their shanghaied sailors nothing; others paid a nominal wage but then charged the victims for their food and necessities and even deducted the crimp gang's kidnapping fee from their pay. Either way the result was the same: After everything was totaled up, the sailors were essentially working for free.

NOBODY'S PERFECT

Crimp gangs and sea captains weren't the only ones who benefited from the shanghai system; that was why it lasted as long as it did. Kidnapping waterfront riffraff and sending them off to sea lowered the crime rate (excluding kidnapping, of course). If you had lent someone money and they refused to pay it back, you could arrange to have them shanghaied. Likewise, if *you* owed someone money and didn't want to pay it back, you could have the lender shanghaied, too. Not many people concerned themselves with the plight of shanghaied sailors or even noticed when they disappeared—most were transients with few ties to the community.

The crimp gangs protected their interests by being active in the political machines that dominated government in cities such as Portland and San Francisco. In California, two crimps named Joseph "Frenchy" Franklin and George Lewis even managed to get themselves elected to the state legislature, where they succeeded in blocking laws that attempted to outlaw shanghaiing.

PULLING INTO PORT

In the end it wasn't a legal or moral crusade that ended the cruel shanghai system, it was steam: Steamships didn't have sails, and could get by with less than half the crew of a sailing ship. By the time Max DeVeer and his friend woke up on their sailing ship as it was headed out of the Golden Gate, steamships were already overtaking sailing ships and the age of shanghaiing was drawing to a close.

*   *   *

SEEING IS BELIEVING

Even though the age of shanghaiing may be over, Portland's Shanghai Tunnels are still in existence, and parts of them are even open for public tours. Want to check them out yourself? You can find the information online, or contact the city's tourist bureau for details. Reservations are required, and it's a good idea to book well in advance—the tours are popular and frequently sell out. Just make sure you tell your loved ones where you're going first, because if you don't come back, the oceans are a mighty big place to search for you.

Largest diamond heist: The 2003 Antwerp Diamond Center job. It netted $100 million.

THE KILLER VS. THE KING

*When you've been around as long as Uncle John has,
you'll probably start to assume you've heard every
story there is about pop music. Wrong! Here's
one that was new to all of us.*

OLD FRIENDS

Elvis Presley was the "King of Rock 'n' Roll"; Jerry Lee Lewis was the first person to be inducted into the Rock and Roll Hall of Fame. They were both hugely influential in formulating the sound of rock 'n' roll music—both were raised singing gospel music in the Pentecostal church, and they both got their start at Sam Phillips's famous Sun Studios in Memphis, Tennessee. Presley and Lewis were good friends early in their careers, and were even known to go on motorcycle rides and double dates together.

During one of Lewis's recording sessions in late 1956, Presley, who had moved on to record for RCA, stopped by to see his old friends at Sun. Rockabilly pioneer Carl Perkins was also hanging around, and a jam session broke out with the three. Sam Phillips quickly called his other big star, Johnny Cash, to join in, and the star-packed session became known as the "Million Dollar Quartet." As Presley's and Lewis's careers took different paths, double dates and motorcycle rides gave way to gold records and international tours. They never again had the same day-to-day friendship they had during the Sun Studio years, but their relationship was still amicable.

"THE KILLER" IS COINED

In 1957, while Presley was selling millions of records and starring in movies, Lewis made the headlines by marrying his 13-year-old third cousin (and the daughter of his bass player), a move that virtually ended his rock 'n' roll career. In 1973 he rose from the ashes to become a successful country music performer, but bad publicity from his erratic behavior continued to dog him.

During Prohibition, half of all federal prison inmates were in jail for violating liquor laws.

"The Killer" was a nickname that Lewis lived up to—thanks to both his aggressive piano style and a number of highly publicized violent incidents. In 1958 on Alan Freed's *Big Beat Show*, a dispute broke out between Lewis and Chuck Berry over who would close the show. When promoters decided that Berry would be the closer, Lewis protested by pouring a Coke bottle full of gasoline on the piano and lighting it ablaze after his finale—"Great Balls of Fire." In 1976 at his 41st birthday party, he accidentally shot his bass player in the chest, later claiming that he didn't know the gun was loaded. More tragedy: Lewis's fourth wife drowned in a swimming pool in 1982, and the following year his fifth wife died shortly after their wedding from a drug overdose. But Lewis's strangest incident of violence was aimed at his old friend, Elvis Presley.

GUNPLAY AT GRACELAND

At 2:50 a.m. on November 22, 1976, Jerry Lee Lewis unexpectedly pulled up to the front gate of Graceland in a brand-new Silver Shadow Rolls-Royce and asked to see Presley. The King's cousin, Harold Loyd, was working the guard's booth and told Lewis that Presley was sleeping. Lewis thanked Loyd and drove away, leaving Loyd puzzled by the event. Later that morning, Lewis was arrested for driving without a license, driving while intoxicated, and reckless driving after rolling his Rolls-Royce while rounding a corner in the Memphis suburb of Collierville. (Drunk and reckless driving must have been popular in the Lewis family—when Lewis was arrested and taken to Hernando Jail, his father Elmo was there on similar charges.)

RETURN ENGAGEMENT

Ten hours later, Lewis was out on bail and at it again. He was drinking at a popular Memphis nightspot called the Vapors when, for reasons that are still disputed between the King's and the Killer's camps, he left the bar and decided to make his way back to Graceland. He got there at 2:50 a.m., almost the exact time he'd arrived the night before, but this time he was driving a brand-new Lincoln Continental…and he was in a different mood.

"He was outta his mind, man. He was screamin', hollerin', and cussin'," Loyd recalled. Lewis was angry, drunk, and armed with a Derringer pistol. "Get on the @#$%&* phone!" Lewis yelled at Loyd, waving the pistol. "I know you got an intercom system. Call up there and tell

Elvis I wanna visit with him! Who in the hell does he think he is? Tell him the Killer's here to see him!"

LITTLE SISTER

Lewis's sister, Linda Gail, recalled that "Jerry was really havin' one big party at the time," that he admitted he'd been "partyin' and drinkin'," and that he was out of it. But Gail swears that Lewis just wanted to visit with Presley. Cousin Harold read the situation differently.

He went into the guard booth and called up to the main house. He was told to call the cops, which he did immediately. Then the King himself called down to the guard booth. Loyd remembered the conversation exactly, including how badly Presley would stutter when he was nervous. " Wh-wh-what the hell's goin' on down there, Harold? Wh-wh-what's that @#$%&* guy want? I-I-I don't wanna talk to that crazy sonofab#$@%. Hell no, I don't wanna talk to him. I'll come down there and kill him! You call the cops, Harold. When they get there, tell 'em to lock his butt up and throw the key away. Okay? Thank you, Harold."

JAILHOUSE ROCK

When Officer Billy J. Kirkpatrick arrived, he ordered Lewis out of the car, but the Killer wouldn't comply. "[Kirkpatrick] had to pull him out of the car," Loyd recalled. "He told him to keep his hands on the steering wheel where he could see 'em. Jerry said he just wanted to see Elvis, but Kirkpatrick told him to shut up. Now Jerry, he had tried to hide his pistol by puttin' it in between his knee and the door. When Kirkpatrick opened the door, the damn gun fell out onto the floorboard. Kirkpatrick picked up the gun, and it was cocked and loaded!"

Kirkpatrick also found that the front passenger window of Lewis's car was smashed out and that Lewis had a deep gash on his nose, which he concluded was due to "broken glass resulting from [Lewis] attempting to jettison an empty champagne bottle thru the closed window of his '76 Lincoln." Kirkpatrick and four other policemen arrested Lewis and took him to jail, ironically, just as Lewis's father, Elmo Lewis, was being bailed out. The elder Lewis arrived at Graceland just as the wrecker arrived to tow away Lewis's Lincoln. "Ha! Ain't this some crap, man?" Loyd remembered Elmo saying when he arrived on the scene. "I just got word that they've taken my son to jail. I just got me outta the Hernando Jail, and Jerry done gone ahead."

The Latin *capere* means "one who catches." That's where the term "cop" comes from.

SUSPICIOUS MINDS

Word soon got out that "the Killer" was trying to kill "the King," but Lewis's sister Linda Gail believes that Presley called Lewis at the Vapors and invited him to come to Graceland, that Harold Loyd never told Presley that Lewis was there, and that Lewis became belligerent because he thought Presley would get mad at him if he didn't take the invitation seriously. "I believe, really and truly, that the people who were associated with Elvis at that time were trying to manipulate him," Gail says. "He was supporting all of them financially, and it was in their best interest to keep him isolated. If him and Elvis had started runnin' the roads together, can you imagine what that would have been like? It probably would have been more than Memphis could handle."

LAST MAN STANDING

After the incident, the Killer and the King's friendship was never the same. When Elvis Presley died in 1977, Lewis said, "I'm glad. Just another one outta the way. What the @#%* did Presley ever do except take dope I couldn't get ahold of?" Then after Johnny Cash died in 2003, the 71-year-old Lewis televised an all-star tribute concert called *Last Man Standing*, a reference to his being the last surviving member of the "Million Dollar Quartet."

*   *   *

SMART CROOKS (for a change)

How do you make sure the police won't interrupt your burglary? Fix it so they can't even leave their headquarters. That's what happened in 2001 in the Dutch town of Stadskanaal. Thieves simply padlocked the front gates of the high fence that surrounds the police compound, then robbed a nearby electronics store. That set off a burglar alarm in the police station, but there was nothing police could do about it—they were all locked in. As the crooks made off with TVs and camcorders, Stadskanaal cops had to sit and wait for reinforcements to arrive from the next town. A police spokesman said, "It's a pity all our officers were at that moment in the police station. Normally most of them are on patrol." They've since taken precautions to make certain it never happens again.

According to the FBI, 75% of bank robbers use the stolen money to buy drugs.

THE KING SHOOTS THE PRESIDENT

In the history of the United States, thirteen people have tried to assassinate the president. Here's the story of the first one.

JUST A SHOT AWAY

On the rainy morning of January 30, 1835, Richard Lawrence sat on a chest in a shop in Washington, D.C., clutching a book and laughing maniacally to himself. Suddenly he stood up, dropped the book, and said, "I'll be damned if I *don't* do it!" Lawrence grabbed two pistols, put them in his coat pocket, and headed for the U.S. Capitol. There, he waited behind a pillar for President Andrew Jackson to emerge from the funeral of Congressman Warren Davis. After a few minutes, the 68-year-old president hobbled into view, leaning on the arm of the U.S. treasury secretary. Lawrence leaped from behind the pillar, pointed a pistol at Jackson, and pulled the trigger.

The gun misfired.

Undeterred, Lawrence pulled out the second pistol and fired one more time at point-blank range.

That gun also misfired.

Enraged, Jackson struggled to get away...from his companions who were holding him back. The elderly president swung his cane wildly at Lawrence, shouting, "Let me alone! Let me alone! I know where this man came from!" Jackson had assumed that his would-be assassin had been sent by one of his political opponents. Jackson assumed incorrectly.

NUTTY AS A FRUITCAKE

Born in England in 1800, Richard Lawrence moved to the U.S. when he was 12 years old and lived an uneventful life as a house painter in Washington, D.C. But then something changed. In 1832 Lawrence suddenly decided to go to England, but only got as far as Philadelphia. When he returned to D.C., he complained that all the newspapers in Philly had attacked his character. As he raved on and on, his family was shocked. That was, by all accounts, Lawrence's first psychotic episode.

California penal code bans the scattering of "cremains" from the Golden Gate Bridge.

THE KING AND I

In the months and years that followed, Lawrence drifted further into madness. He developed an extravagant sense of fashion. Decked out in exorbitantly expensive finery, Lawrence took to standing completely still in his doorway for hours on end so passersby could "bask in my presence." He was no longer Richard Lawrence, he told people, but "King Richard III of England" (who reigned for two years in the 1480s). Lawrence quit his job painting houses; he assured his concerned friends and family that he would become wealthy as soon as the American government awarded him the money he was owed. (He claimed he owned two lavish estates.)

But the money never came. And who was to blame? President Andrew Jackson. Because he publicly opposed the national bank, Jackson was single-handedly preventing this transfer of funds. Lawrence came to the "natural conclusion": Remove Jackson, and get the money he was owed. It made perfect sense, at least to Lawrence. That's what led him to try to kill the president on that January day in 1835.

DEPOSED

Lawrence was defiant in his innocence. At one point during his trial, he angrily stood and announced, "It is for me, gentlemen, to pass judgment upon *you*, and not you upon *me*!" The prosecuting attorney, Francis Scott Key (the man who wrote "The Star-Spangled Banner"), pointed out that the only reason Jackson wasn't killed was because the bullets and powder had fallen out of both guns in Lawrence's pocket. (It was a humid day, and the shoddy pistols were affected by the moisture.) After that, Key didn't have to work very hard to convince the jury that "King Richard" was mad. It took them only five minutes to deliberate. The verdict: Guilty by reason of insanity. (Historians theorize that the chemicals in Lawrence's paints were what ultimately drove him to suffer from paranoid schizophrenic delusions.)

Lawrence lived out the rest of his life in the Government Hospital for the Insane in Washington, D.C., where he died in 1861.

*   *   *

Police Blotter: "A woman reported Thursday that someone broke into her home on Summer Street and switched hardware in her computer with identical hardware that does not work. There are no leads."

Step back, smartmouth: A cop can TASER you from 15 feet away.

COPS GONE CRAZY

*We respect the police for keeping us somewhat
safe in this crazy world. But as these stories
prove, cops are only human.*

ARE Wii HAVING FUN YET?
In September 2009, narcotics investigators in Polk County, Florida, searched the home of a known drug trafficker. While removing weapons, drugs, and stolen goods, several officers passed the time by taking part in a video bowling tournament on the suspect's Wii videogame system. The cops competed fiercely, stopping their search when their turn came up. Little did they know their activities were being recorded by a wireless security camera that the drug dealer had set up to watch for intruders. A local TV station got hold of the footage and aired clips of the cops giving each other high-fives and distracting their fellow bowlers with lewd gestures. "Obviously, this is not the kind of behavior we condone," Lakeland Police Chief Roger Boatner said. The impromptu tournament might even jeopardize the case against the career criminal, whose lawyer called the search improper. "Investigations are not for entertainment," he said.

BETWEEN A GUN AND A HARD PLACE

MRI machines are huge, complex magnets; even the tiniest metal object can severely damage one. In 2009 Joy Smith, an off-duty deputy from Jacksonville, Florida, took her mother to get an MRI... and forgot that she was still carrying her police-issue Glock handgun. Smith walked into the MRI room and her gun was pulled from its holster; she tried to hang onto it, but her hand became stuck between the pistol and the machine—which made a horrible nose before shutting off. Smith sustained only minor injuries. The MRI center didn't fare as well: Between repairs to the machine and a day's lost revenue, the cost to the center topped $150,000.

GUILT BY ASSOCIATION

In September 2009, Dutch police officers raided a farm near Wageningen University in the Netherlands and destroyed an entire crop of what they called "some 47,000 illicit cannabis plants" with a street value of $6.45 million. However, according to university officials who cried foul, the plants were *not* psychotropic marijuana—which is illegal to grow—but hemp-fiber plants—which are perfectly legal to grow, and for which they had a permit. The plants had been part of a multiyear study to test hemp as a sustainable source of fiber. The project has been postponed while the school attempts to recoup the costs from the police department. "The street value from a drug point of view," said a disappointed university official, "is less than zero."

TAKE A BITE OUT OF A CRIMEFIGHTER

Two employees of the Police Officer Standards and Training Council in Meriden, Connecticut, had, according to reports, a "spirited" relationship—analyst Rochelle Wyler and training coordinator Francis "Woody" Woodruff, a former police chief, regularly taunted and insulted each other. One day in April 2009, Woodruff jokingly referred to Wyler as a "clerk." She responded, "Whatever, Woody. Bite me." So Woodruff grabbed her left arm and bit her, leaving tooth marks and a bruise. Woodruff claimed he was just "horsing around," but Wyler reported the incident, and Woodruff was arrested and charged with assault.

SNOWBALLISTICS

One snowy afternoon in December 2009, about 200 office workers took part in a snowball fight on 14th Street in Washington, D.C. Everyone was having a good time...until someone threw a snowball at a Hummer SUV driving down the road. The Hummer slid to a halt; a large, imposing man got out. "Who threw that damn snowball?" he shouted. When no one answered, the man pulled out a pistol, sending people running for cover. A few tense moments later, a uniformed police officer arrived and ordered the man to drop his weapon. That's when the gunman identified himself as Detective Mike Baylor. With the danger passed, the crowd started chanting: "You don't bring a gun to a snowball fight." At first, the D.C. police department denied that the detective, a 28-year veteran, pulled out his gun. But the incident was caught on several cell phone cameras and soon made the rounds on YouTube...and then the local news. D.C. police chief Cathy Lanier called Baylor's actions "totally inappropriate." He was placed on desk duty.

In Charleston, South Carolina, prisoners may be charged $1 for the ride to jail.

HARD-BOILED HAMMETT, PART I

Here's the story of Dashiell Hammett, king of the crime novel.

Samuel **Spade's** jaw was long and bony, his chin a jutting v under the more flexible v of his mouth. His nostrils curved back to make another, smaller, v. His yellow-grey eyes were horizontal. The v motif was picked up again by thickish brows rising outward from twin creases above a hooked nose, and his pale brown hair grew down—from high flat temples—in a point on his forehead. He looked rather pleasantly like a blond satan.

He said to Effie Perine: "Yes, sweetheart?"

She was a lanky sunburned girl whose tan dress of thin woolen stuff clung to her with an effect of dampness. Her eyes were brown and playful in a shiny boyish face. She finished shutting the door behind her, leaned against it, and said: "There's a girl wants to see you. Her name's Wonderly."

"A customer?"

"I guess so. You'll want to see her anyway: she's a knockout."

"Shoo her in, darling," said Spade. "Shoo her in."

Those are the opening lines from *The Maltese Falcon*, Dashiell Hammett's 1930 novel, voted one of the 100 best novels in the English language by the Modern Library, and the one for which he's most famous. Hammett's looks were a far cry from Sam Spade's: he was thin—and his short white hair and little black mustache made him look anything but tough. But like the rugged antiheroes in his detective stories, Hammett lived a hard life, drank heavily, and preferred to work alone. And his character showed in the stories he wrote for *Black Mask* magazine during the 1920s, which established him as the king of the hard-boiled mystery writers and the father of the film noir movie classics that followed. Although Hammett didn't invent crime fiction, he wrote with such skill that his influence

---

The insanity defense is used in less than 1% of all court cases.

dominated it, elevating the genre to an art form. But that's not how it started out.

PULP FICTION

Cheap adventure stories published in pocket-sized paperback books first appeared the mid-1800s. Publishing firms saved money by printing them on the cheapest paper available, made from pure wood pulp without any rag fiber (hence the term "pulp fiction"). The earliest were Western stories that featured frontier heroes, but as the Wild West was tamed, the cowboy's urban counterpart began to emerge in the form of the streetwise detective. By the 1870s, the detective story had established itself as a genre. Serialized adventures of characters like Old Cap Collier, Broadway Billy, Jack Harkaway, and the mysterious Old Sleuth, Master of Disguise, helped to develop the style. These were hard-fisted, tough-guy heroes who inhabited a dark, urban underworld where violence seemed to be the only means of establishing order.

Crime fiction magazines and dime novels grew steadily in popularity through the end of the 19th century and into the 20th. By the 1920s, there were more than 20,000 magazines in circulation in the United States. Pulp titles like *The Nick Carter Weekly*, *Detective Stories*, *Girl's Detective*, *Doctor Death*, *Argosy*, and *Police Gazette* dominated newsstands during Prohibition, giving rise to a class of working writers who earned about a penny a word, some using several pseudonyms so they could publish more than a million words per year. Hammett wanted to be a part of it.

In late 1923 he arrived at *Black Mask* magazine, which printed "Stories of Detection, Mystery, Adventure, Romance, and Spiritualism." Earlier that year, the magazine had published a story by Carroll John Daly called "Three Gun Terry," considered the first authentic "hard-boiled" detective story. Yet although he didn't invent the style, Hammett quickly dominated it. Over the next seven years he wrote more than 50 stories for *Black Mask*, becoming its premier writer, and helping it become *the* premier magazine of hard-boiled fiction. Hammett's influence was such that other writers accused the magazine's editors of forcing them to copy him.

DASHIELL HAMMETT, P.I.

So how was Hammett able to bring such an impressive realism to his characters? Experience. Before becoming a writer, he had been a detective—he was an operative with the Pinkerton Agency from 1915 to 1922.

Hammett had had many jobs before that: newsboy, freight clerk, laborer, and rail yard messenger, but it was all just to help support his parents and his two brothers.

SMART KID

Born in 1894, Samuel Dashiell Hammett grew up between Baltimore and Philadelphia. He learned a love of reading from his mother, who was a nurse, and street smarts from his father, who was a farmer, gambler, occasional politician, and notorious womanizer. Although he never finished high school, young Hammett was a voracious reader. And after spending time on the road with his father, he was also streetwise. So when Hammett arrived at the Pinkerton office in Baltimore to take a clerk job, his bosses soon recognized that this 21-year-old kid would make a great field operative. They placed him under the wing of one of their best private eyes, James Wright, who taught Hammett the ins and outs of "tailing a perp and bringing him in." Wright was the inspiration for the Continental Op, the hero of Hammett's early stories.

Little is known about Hammett's days as a Pinkerton operative. Most biographers agree that he embellished his tales to help create a mystique about himself. In his book *Shadow Man*, author Richard Layman says that Hammett "in a half self-serving, half playful manner, characteristically amplified his stories, rewriting, revising, even inventing accounts of his experiences." What *is* known, however, is that Hammett was a master at tailing suspects. According to one colleague, Dash (as he was known to friends) once followed a man through six small towns without ever being detected. He was quickly rising through the agency ranks, primed to become one of Pinkerton's best. Everything changed when he chose to fight in World War I.

A LIFELONG CONTRACT

Hammett enlisted in the army in 1919 and served as a sergeant in the ambulance corps, but was discharged a year later when he contracted first tuberculosis and then the Spanish flu. The diseases would plague him for the rest of his life, not only putting a halt to his detective and military careers, but also affecting his relationships with women. (While recovering, he married a nurse named Josephine Dolan, but because TB is contagious, in 1926 she was advised by doctors to take their two daughters and leave him.)

Hammett did go back to Pinkerton after he recovered, but he grew

Miguel de Cervantes wrote *Don Quixote* while in prison.

disillusioned with the Pinkerton style of law enforcement after an incident in Montana. The story goes that he was offered $5,000 to kill Frank Little, a labor boss who was organizing miners. Hammett refused, but Little was ultimately captured by five men—allegedly Pinkerton *ops* (short for "operatives")—and hanged from a railroad trestle in Butte. Hammett biographer Diane Johnson writes:

> Perhaps at the moment he was asked to murder Frank Little, or perhaps at the moment that he learned that Little had been killed, possibly by other Pinkerton men, Hammett saw that he himself was on the fringe…and was expected to be, according to a kind of oath of fealty that he and other Pinkerton men took. He also learned something of the lives of poor miners, whose wretched strikes the Pinkerton people were hired to prevent, and about the lies of mine owners. Those things were to sit in the back of his mind.

Not only was Hammett at odds with his Pinkerton bosses because of his idealism and growing distrust of authority, but his chronic TB made it impossible for him to endure assignments that often took place on long, cold nights. He left the agency in 1922 to find something that required less physical effort.

PEN IN HAND

Unemployed and disabled, Hammett took a job as an ad writer for a San Francisco jewelry store but found the work unfulfilling. He wanted to write about something that he knew, that he was passionate about. Being a fan of detective stories—but disappointed by their lack of authenticity—Dashiell Hammett decided to create the detective that he was never able to be in real life. "Your private detective does not," he said, "want to be an erudite solver of riddles in the Sherlock Holmes manner, he wants to be a hard and shifty fellow, able to take care of himself in any situation, able to get the best of anybody he comes in contact with, whether criminal, innocent bystander, or client." So Hammett started pounding out the dark characters and vigilante justice that expressed his cynical views of the world of crime and punishment. Just as he had impressed the Pinkertons with his skill and wit a few years before, he equally impressed the editors at *Black Mask* with his descriptive prose and tight storytelling.

Hammett's adventure was just getting started. To read about his meteoric rise and tragic demise, hoof it on over to page 280.

To be a lawyer, you must pass the Bar, but there are no formal qualifications to be a federal judge.

THE GODMOTHERS

In 1990 the Italian police started rounding up underworld leaders all over Italy. But once the men were gone, the women took over… and proved that queenpins can be just as ruthless as kingpins.

ALL IN THE FAMILY. In June 1999, police in Sicily arrested Concetta Scalisi, the Godmother of an area known as the "Triangle of Death." She had ruled over her crime family's dealings in heroin, extortion, and violence in three towns on Mount Etna in Sicily after the death of her father. She was personally wanted for three murders.

SHE'LL NEVER CHANGE HER SPOTS. In December 2000, police arrested Erminia Giuliano, of the Camorra, Naples' version of La Cosa Nostra. "The Godmother" had inherited the job when the last of her five brothers was arrested. Police claim she had ruthlessly and casually ordered numerous executions of rivals, and was ranked one of Italy's 30 most dangerous criminals. When arrested, the 45-year-old made a special request of the police—she wanted to go to the hairdresser and be allowed to wear a leopard-skin outfit to prison.

MOB BOSS MADAM. Erminia Guiliano's rival in Naples was Maria Licciardi, who took over her family after her husband's arrest. She built the family's business by forging alliances with several other Camorra clans and by adding prostitution—regarded by old-school Mafia as an "immoral" business—to heroin trade and extortion. The alliances eventually broke down and between 1997 and 1998 she dragged her family through gang wars that killed more than 100 people. She was arrested on June 14, 2001.

BAD HAIR DAY. On May 5, 2002, there was an argument in a Naples hair salon between Clarissa Cava and Alba Graziano. The Cavas and the Grazianos had been bloody rivals for 30 years. Several days later, Graziano and her two daughters, aged 21 and 22, drove up to the car occupied by Cava, 21, her two aunts and and her sister—and machine-gunned them. Cava and her two aunts were killed. The Graziano's were later heard laughing and toasting the killings on police surveillance tapes.

SONS OF GUNS

We aimed for this page to be a high-caliber bulletin loaded with surefire origins of some famous "peacemakers." Bull's-eye!

ELIPHALET REMINGTON II (1793–1861)

The story goes that in 1816 young Remington needed a new rifle—so he made one at his father's forge at Ilion Gulch, in upstate New York. That fall he entered a shooting contest with his new flintlock. He won only second place, but the gun was so good (and so good-looking) that before the day was over, Remington had taken orders for several more rifles. Suddenly he was in the gun business. By 1839 E. Remington & Sons was a booming company in Ilion. Though it's no longer a family business, Remington still manufactures world-renowned rifles on the same site. (They also made typewriters and electric shavers.)

SAMUEL COLT (1814–1862)

At age 15, Colt left his father's textile mill in Connecticut for a sailor's life. Legend says he was at the ship's wheel when he got his big idea—a pistol with a revolving cylinder. Colt received a European patent for the invention in 1835 and took it to the United States the following year. His fortune was assured when the U.S. army began supplying its officers with Colt revolvers during the Mexican War from 1846 to 1848. The Colt .45 Peacemaker became—and still is—a symbol of the American West.

GEORG LUGER (1849–1923)

The real name of Luger's gun is "Pistole Parabellum." Americans know it as the "Luger" because the U.S. importer in the 1920s, AF Stoeger & Co., marketed it under the German gun designer's name. Georg Luger made the first Luger-type pistol for a German weapons manufacturer in 1898. The German military started buying them in the early 1900s; during World War II they were the official sidearm of the Nazis. The sleekly designed guns are prized by collectors today and are still used in competitions because of their accuracy. Why "Parabellum"? It comes from the Latin phrase *Si vis pacem, para bellum*—"If you want peace, prepare for war."

The FBI & the National Bureau of Standards started the world's first...

HORACE SMITH (1808–93) & DANIEL WESSON (1825–1906)

Smith was a Springfield, Massachusetts, toolmaker; Wesson was a gunsmith from nearby Northborough. They joined forces in 1852, introducing a groundbreaking invention: the self-contained, waterproof "cartridge," or bullet. Before that, all the ingredients—gunpowder, ball, and primer—had to be mixed by hand. In 1869 they introduced the Smith & Wesson "Model 3 American" pistol. Customers ranging from the Russian army to Annie Oakley helped make it one of the most popular handguns in the world. Other Smith & Wesson notables: the .357 Magnum and the .44 Magnum, made famous by Clint Eastwood in the *Dirty Harry* movies.

DR. RICHARD J. GATLING (1818–1903)

Gatling was an inventor during the mid-1800s. Most of his inventions were agriculture-based, but in 1861 he came up with the fearsome Gatling Gun, a hand-cranked machine gun that fired 200 bullets a minute. A medical doctor, Gatling thought his gun's super firepower would require fewer soldiers on the battlefield, resulting in fewer casualties. He was wrong; it just made soldiers more effective killing machines. After improvements were made in 1866, it became a weapon of choice for armies worldwide for the next 40 years.

HIRAM MAXIM (1840–1916)

Legend has it that Maxim, an American expatriate, visited the 1881 Paris Electrical Exhibition, where he heard someone say, "If you want to make a lot of money, invent something that will enable Europeans to cut each other's throats with greater facility." Shortly thereafter, Maxim invented the first "automatic" machine gun—it reloaded itself automatically, firing more than 500 bullets per minute. The British bought it in 1889 (the United States turned it down), and by 1905 more than 20 armies and navies around the world were using the Maxim Machine Gun. Other Maxim inventions: the gun silencer and cordite (smokeless gunpowder). Knighted by the British in 1901, Sir Hiram died in 1916.

JOHN CANTIUS GARAND (1888–1974)

In 1934 Garand, a Canadian-born employee of the United States Armory in Springfield, Massachusetts, designed what would become the mainstay of the American military, the M-1 Garand rifle. It was "gas operated,"

...computerized fingerprint database in the 1960s.

meaning that gas buildup behind an exiting bullet was routed to drive a piston that put the next bullet into place—very quickly. That made it semiautomatic, a huge advantage over Japanese and German rifles, which were still bolt-action at the start of World War II. Almost four million M-1 rifles were made during the war, and Garand didn't make a cent off them—he worked for the Armory for 36 years and never received more than his standard pay.

MIKHAIL TIMOFEEVICH KALASHNIKOV (B. 1919)

Kalashnikov was a Russian tank driver during World War II. After being badly injured in 1941, he turned to weapon design and produced the light, inexpensive, and extremely durable AK-47. The "AK" stands for Automatic Kalashnikov; the "47" comes from 1947, the year the new rifle was introduced. The gun became standard issue for the Soviet army in 1949 and was soon being used by communist armies and insurgents all over the world. It's estimated that there are more Kalashnikovs world-wide—perhaps as many as 100 million—than any other gun in use today.

UZIEL GAL (1923–2002)

Gal was a young Israeli army officer who submitted a design for a new submachine gun to the military in 1951, shortly after the founding of Israel. The "Uzi," as it came to be known, was small, powerful, cheap to manufacture, and easy to maintain. The most innovative part of Gal's design: putting the magazine inside the pistol grip, making it easy for soldiers to reload in the dark. Today Uzis are used by military and police in more than 90 countries; the gun has made the Israeli munitions industry more than $2 billion. Gal died in 2002, and the Israeli military officially stopped using the Uzi a year later. Ironically, he asked that his name not be used for the gun. (The request was ignored.)

*　　　*　　　*

YOUR TAX DOLLARS AT WORK

In 1996 Redwood City, California, installed eight microphones around town to identify possible drive-by-shootings. Number of Redwood City drive-bys before the installation: 0. Number after: 0.

What is the #1 cause of wrongful convictions? Eyewitness mis-identification.

STRANGE PRISONER LAWSUITS

We noticed that a lot of the most bizarre legal battles we've reported on over the years have come from behind bars.

THE PLAINTIFF: Frederick Newhall Woods IV, serving a life sentence for the infamous Chowchilla, California, school bus kidnapping

THE DEFENDANT: The American Broadcasting Company

THE LAWSUIT: In 1976 Woods and two accomplices kidnapped a bus driver and 26 elementary school students and buried them underground. When ABC aired a TV movie docudrama about the kidnapping in 1994, Woods was offended. He sued the network, claiming that the TV show "portrayed (him) as being callous, vicious, hardened, wild-eyed, diabolical, and uncaring."

THE VERDICT: Case dismissed.

THE PLAINTIFF: Kenneth Parker

THE DEFENDANT: Nevada State Prison

THE LAWSUIT: Parker was an inmate, serving 15 years for robbery. He wanted to buy two jars of chunky peanut butter from the prison canteen. (Cost: $5.) But the canteen had only one jar of chunky peanut butter. When they had to substitute a jar of creamy for the second one, Parker sued for "mental and emotional pain," asking for $5,500 and the imprisonment of a prison official.

THE VERDICT: The case went on for two years before it was ultimately dismissed.

THE PLAINTIFF: Richard Loritz

THE DEFENDANT: San Diego County

THE LAWSUIT: Loritz was imprisoned for three months in 1995. During that time, he says, he asked for dental floss and was refused. As a result, he developed four cavities. He sued for $2,000 in dental expenses.

THE VERDICT: The case was thrown out of court.

Congress creates an average of 56 new federal crimes each year.

THE PLAINTIFF: Scott Gomez Jr.

THE DEFENDANT: Pueblo County Jail, Colorado

THE LAWSUIT: In 2007 Gomez tried to escape—he melted the ceiling tiles of his cell with a homemade candle, climbed out to the roof, and attempted to scale down the outside wall. Instead, he fell 40 feet to the pavement and was severely injured. Gomez sued, arguing that the prison was responsible because they "failed to provide ceiling tiles that could not be removed by melting them with a homemade candle" and ignored his "propensity to escape" (he'd tried to escape twice before).

THE VERDICT: Lawyers for the prison pointed out a Colorado state law that prevented citizens from suing for damages sustained while committing a felony...such as escaping from prison. Case dismissed.

THE PLAINTIFF: Chad Gabriel DeKoven

THE DEFENDANT: Michigan Prison System

THE LAWSUIT: DeKoven, a convicted armed robber who goes by the name "Messiah-God," sued the prison system, demanding damages that included thousands of trees, tons of precious metals, peace in the Middle East, and "return of all U.S. military personnel to the United States within 90 days."

THE VERDICT: Case dismissed. While noting that all claims must be taken seriously, the judge ultimately dismissed the suit as frivolous. DeKoven, the judge said, "has no Constitutional right to be treated as the 'Messiah-God' or any other holy, extra-worldly, or supernatural being."

THE PLAINTIFF: Robert Paul Rice

THE DEFENDANT: Utah State Prison

THE LAWSUIT: Rice sued the prison for violating his religious freedom, claiming that he listed "the Vampire Order" as his religion and should have his religious needs provided for. According to the suit, prison officials failed to provide a "vampire diet" (only grains and vegetables—no meat) or a "vampress" with whom he could partake in "the vampiric sacrament." Lawyers for the prison argued that it provides five diets to choose from and "vampire" isn't one of them. And a "vampress?" Sorry, prisons in Utah do not allow conjugal visits.

THE VERDICT: Rice lost. The court ruled that the case "raised questions that are so insubstantial as not to merit consideration."

NO ONE IS INNOCENT: THE RONNIE BIGGS STORY

From small-time crook to family man to the world's most famous punk-rocking, beach-basking fugitive, this brash Brit captured the heart of a nation…and drew the ire of Scotland Yard.

ANARCHY IN THE U.K.

The greatest train robbery in British history was not orchestrated by Ronnie Biggs, nor did he have a big part in the heist. In fact, shortly before it took place—coincidentally on the night of Biggs's 34th birthday in August 1963—he had all but given up a life of crime.

Born in 1929 to a poor family living in a poor section of South London, Ronald Arthur Biggs had been in trouble with the law since he was a teenager. Prone to stealing anything that wasn't nailed down—pencils, pills, cars—he was caught as often as he was not, and spent much of his early adulthood behind bars. It was there that Biggs learned a trade, house-painting, and by his 30s, he had decided to go legit. Biggs married, had two sons, and tried to make an honest living as a painter. It turned out that he wasn't a very good painter, either, and he was having trouble paying the bills. So he phoned a friend.

AN OFFER HE COULDN'T REFUSE

When Biggs called Bruce Reynolds, an old prison buddy, in 1963 to ask for a loan of £500 to "tide him over," Reynolds offered Biggs something better—a job. And not just any job, but a role in a train robbery the likes of which had never been seen in the U.K. Biggs's answer: No. He couldn't risk losing his family to more prison time. But Reynolds pressed on, promising Biggs a payday of at least £40,000 for one night's work. And Biggs wouldn't even have to do the actual thieving. All he had to do was recruit a friend of his who could operate a train and then keep the actual train driver quiet while more experienced criminals did the hard stuff. Reluctantly, Biggs signed on. He told his wife he had an out-of-town painting job that would take a few weeks. Then he and Reynolds headed for the English countryside to meet up with the rest of the gang.

Moby Dick author Herman Melville was once imprisoned in Tahiti. His crime: mutiny.

TRAINSPOTTING

There were 16 men in on the job, a joint venture of two South London gangs. Some were responsible for obtaining vehicles, others for arranging hideouts, one to follow train schedules, and Biggs's friend to drive the train. The plan: Stop the Glasgow-to-London mail train in remote Buckinghamshire in the middle of the night, break in, drive the locomotive and the money car to a bridge, and then steal the load of used bills that were on their way to London to be destroyed.

Working from a rented farmhouse, and relying on information provided by British mobsters, the job went down at 3:30 a.m. on August 8. One of the men tampered with a signal to stop the train. Then the strongarms, posing as rail workers, overtook the mail crew, beating the driver senseless. One problem: Biggs's friend couldn't get the train to start back up, and it needed to get to a bridge where a truck was waiting. So they revived the injured driver and made him do it. Then the men formed a human chain to carry the 120 bags of money to the truck. It wasn't pretty, but the job was over in 40 minutes. When the gang got back to the farm, they realized their haul was *huge*: £2.6 million ($3.8 million U.S.). It was Biggs's 34th birthday, and a happy one at that.

PRINTS OF DARKNESS

But their celebration was short-lived. Although the job was successful, they weren't too adept at covering their tracks. The initial plan was to burn down the farmhouse and with it all of the evidence—money bags and everything else they touched, including beer bottles and Monopoly game pieces. But the investigation by Scotland Yard was unprecedented in its size and scope, and within a day, the gang learned that the police were honing in on the farm, so they abandoned it, not wanting to start a big summer fire and give away their position. Reynolds hired a man to clean up the incriminating evidence, but instead the "cleaner" took his payment and ran, making it easy for the cops to lift fingerprints and track down most of the 16 train robbers, including Biggs. Little of the money was recovered. Biggs had hidden his share, a whopping £147,000.

The press coverage—like the loot—was also bigger than they had expected. Their names were plastered over papers worldwide, and Biggs, though he played only a small part, became famous. Wanting to make an example of Biggs, the judge sentenced him to 30 years at Wandsworth Prison in London. The day he arrived, Biggs started planning his escape.

Until President Kennedy was killed, it wasn't a federal crime to assassinate the President.

RUN, RONNIE, RUN

In 1965, after barely a year and a half in prison, Biggs and six other inmates used a homemade rope to climb a wall and jump into a waiting lorry. While Biggs fled to the countryside, the embarrassed British police force launched a massive manhunt all over the U.K. But Biggs was gone. He made it to Paris, where he received a painful round of reconstructive surgery. With a false identity and altered face, one "Terrence Furminger" quietly boarded a flight bound for Australia.

There, Biggs met up with his wife and two sons in Melbourne, and they were able to live quietly for a few years under the radar. But as the other escapees were rounded up, Biggs became the only member of Britain's Great Train Robbery still on the lam. That made him among the most wanted men in the world. When tipsters steered the police to Australia, Biggs knew he had to run again. He said good-bye to his family and caught a flight for South America, first landing in Bolivia and then spending time in Argentina and Venezuela. By this point, however, his loot had all but run out and he was once again making an honest living as a construction worker. He was careful not to break the law for fear of extradition back to England, where a maximum-security cell was waiting for him. With a decade gone by since the Great Train Robbery and his daring escape, Biggs faded out of the public eye…for a while.

THE UNABASHED BANDIT

In 1974, through a ruse by London's *Daily Express* offering Biggs £50,000 for an exclusive interview, British police tracked him down in Rio de Janeiro. Word of the capture got out, and Biggs's name once again made headlines. Scotland Yard officials, patting themselves on the back for a job well done, were preparing to extradite him back to Britain. But then Biggs caught a huge break: He'd taken a mistress in Rio (one of several, actually), and she was pregnant with his baby. According to Brazilian law, he could not be deported if he was the sole source of income for his family. And just like that, Ronnie Biggs got to stay in Rio.

His status as antihero skyrocketed in England. Not only was he part of the fabled Great Train Robbery, but he escaped from prison *and* outsmarted Britain's top cops. But the real kicker was that Biggs was allowed to live in paradise…in plain sight. That's about as big as an "up yours" as anyone could give to Scotland Yard, and rowdy British youth took notice.

John Dillinger was known to offer cab fare home to his hostages when he released them.

CRIME DOES PAY

In 1978, after Johnny Rotten left the Sex Pistols, the remaining two members of the seminal punk rock band went to Rio and tracked down Biggs. They set up a recording studio in a church, procured a lot of booze, and Biggs—wrinkled and gray—belted out the lead vocals on the Sex Pistols' single "No One Is Innocent." Here's a verse:

God save politicians! God save our friends the pigs!
God save Idi Amin and God save Ronald Biggs!
God save all us sinners! God save your blackest sheep!
God save the Good Samaritan and God save the worthless creep!

Biggs was more than a fugitive, he was a hero—and a tourist attraction to boot. Not allowed to take a real job in Brazil because of his legal status, he took to charging tourists to spend time with him. "If you can't live off the money you stole," he said, "at least live off your reputation as a thief." For $60, visitors could indulge in "The Ronnie Biggs Experience" at his small villa. They'd enjoy a pleasant meal, a poolside party, and the star attraction: listening to Ronnie Biggs make fun of the Scotland Yard detectives who couldn't have him. However, he was trying to support *two* families, so he wrote a book telling his version of events called *Odd Man Out*. (The Rio tourist industry made out okay as well, selling Ronnie Biggs T-shirts and coffee mugs in souvenir shops.)

But the Brits kept the pressure on. In 1981 he was actually kidnapped by bounty hunters and loaded into a sack on a yacht bound for England. He was freed in Barbados and went straight back to Rio.

LONDON CALLING

By 2000, Biggs was 71 years old and wanted to go home to England. He hoped his age and poor health would keep him out of prison, but officers were waiting when his plane landed at Heathrow Airport, and they took him straight to his prison cell. Biggs's fans were incensed at the inhumane treatment; his critics wanted him to rot in there. After several rejected appeals, Biggs was finally freed in 2009 after a stroke had left him unable to move or speak. But the old man, reputed to be "dead within days," thumbed his nose one more time at Scotland Yard. How? He got better. As of 2011, Ronnie Biggs, 82, is still kicking. "There's a difference between criminals and crooks," he says. "Crooks steal. Criminals blow some bloke's brains out. I was a crook."

The last stagecoach robbery in America took place in Nevada (1916).

THE YAKUZA LIFE

Our introduction to this Japanese crime syndicate (page 116) gave you an overview of what they're all about. Now we take you on the inside.

JOINING UP

• Becoming a Yakuza member can be as easy as walking into one of their offices and asking for an application. Because it's not illegal to be Yakuza, they're quite open about their existence—each office has a wooden sign out front that displays the name of the family. Members even carry business cards. Some families publish their own magazines, advertise, march in parades, and send recruiters to schools and prisons.

• There are no requirements to become a member—well, except one: You must be male. The only woman recognized by a Yakuza family is the boss's wife, the *ane-san*, which means "older sister." Though she does not participate in criminal activity, all members must show her the same respect they show the boss.

• Yakuza families adopt young men from all walks of life, but most are the disenfranchised: orphans, small-time criminals, and refugees. Because of a law passed in 1992, leaders are legally responsible for the criminal actions of their recruits. Therefore, an entrant may be required to pass a written exam to prove his knowledge of the Yakuza and the law. Once he passes the test, the *obun* is assigned to his *oyabun*, his new father.

SHEDDING THE PAST

• In an initiation ceremony, the obun and oyabun share cups of *sake* (rice wine) mixed with salt and fish scales, and the obun promises his unquestioning loyalty to the Yakuza family.

• Next he begins work on his full-body tattoo, which will depict clan symbols and traditional Japanese scenes such as samurai warriors. A member will wear these tattoos as symbols of a Yakuza's outsider status and his lifelong pledge to the clan.

ASCENDING THE RUNGS

• The Yakuza offer many exciting criminal opportunities, including gambling, smuggling, money laundering, extortion, narcotics, prostitution, and gunrunning. Like any pyramid scheme, those at the top make the

---

While she was serving time in prison in 2005, Martha Stewart became a billionaire.

most money. One way to move up is to recruit more "children," essentially building your own gang, until you become a local boss. One can also advance by making money for the family.

• The most profitable and least dangerous way to do this is via corporate extortion; simply find some dirt on an executive and threaten to expose it unless the company offers a payoff. In Japan, embarrassment and shame are often feared as much as physical pain, so the demands are usually met.

• Japan is a society where directness is considered rude, and even gangsters make their threats in a polite manner. One way to make a threat: Pose as a magazine publisher and then promise to print a favorable review about the company in exchange for shares. Then, as a shareholder, the company can be extorted from the inside.

• However, these kinds of tasks are reserved for experienced members. The most common lament of the young Yakuza is boredom. New recruits typically spend their first few years training and performing menial tasks like answering phones, serving guests, cooking, and cleaning.

YAKUZA AND THE LAW

• In the United States, the Racketeer Influenced and Corrupt Organizations Act (RICO) makes it illegal to belong to an ongoing criminal organization. There are no similar laws in Japan, allowing criminals to legally form large, well-structured gangs. So, while members can be arrested for crimes, they cannot be arrested simply because they are a Yakuza

• There are no statutes in Japan that prohibit money laundering, making the Yakuza very financially successful. And with financial success comes power. As such, organized crime has been influencing politics in Japan since World War II. Even now, several prominent politicians have family members who bear Yakuza tattoos.

• Relations between Japanese authorities and the Yakuza are complex. Some of the police admire the Yakuza's code of chivalry. As long as the gangsters are not too disruptive, the police mostly leave them alone. In return, the mobsters occasionally turn in a member of a gang to help the cops "solve" a case. At the same time, however, the Yakuza are indeed criminals, and always try to stay one step ahead of the law.

YAKUZA AND THE PEOPLE

• For the most part, the Japanese public tolerates the Yakuza. Some people have even come to appreciate them. For example, after a car accident, instead of hiring lawyers, one party might hire a Yakuza member called a *jiken-ya* (incident specialist) to propose a settlement. Usually an agreement is made without threats or violence.

• The Yakuza also try to play up their image as champions of the downtrodden and the outcast, providing havens for *burakumin* (a segregated group of "untouchables"). They also provide a home for high-school dropouts unable to succeed in Japan's highly competitive educational system. By "adopting" the rougher elements of society, the Yakuza help to discipline criminals and minimize violent acts against ordinary people. Ironically, the Yakuza have helped to keep Japan's crime rate one of the lowest in the world.

• Yakuza members are often employed by the community as fund raisers, bodyguards, and campaign workers. Every so often, these "Robin Hoods" do good deeds: After the devastating earthquake and tsunami in March 2011, many Yakuza families provided food, shelter, and trucks to clean up the debris. A few months later, however, Japanese officials complained that the gangsters had bullied their way into being awarded contracts to finish the cleanup effort. They are outlaws, after all, and because of that, the Yakuza are shunned by mainstream Japanese society.

BAD BOYS

• A crop of younger, more violent criminals are changing the way the Japanese view the Yakuza. Street gangs are taking over. In a recent case in Nagoya, police arrested 19 teenagers for nearly 100 muggings. In another, two of Tokyo's largest teen gangs went head-to-head in a turf war, and a passerby was stabbed and beaten to death.

• Aging Yakuza members have grown quite dismayed with the decline of moral values and the rise in violence, especially gun-related violence. Many are leaving the organization and snitching on their fellow members. If they can escape, awaiting them are legitimate Japanese employers who openly offer jobs and rehabilitation programs for Yakuza members who wish to renounce their lives of crime.

• The most powerful Yakuza families have started acting less like the Mafia and more like legitimate corporations, moving into mainstream high finance. What does all this mean? The future of the world's largest crime syndicate is uncertain.

"If your boss says the passing crow is white, you must agree." —Yakuza proverb

DOUBLE TROUBLE

Having an identical twin isn't always twice as nice.

TWINS: John and Glen Winslow, 38

DOUBLE TROUBLE: When John Winslow was pulled over in Council Bluffs, Nebraska, in July 2004, he didn't have his license with him, and he knew he had a misdemeanor warrant for damaging property. So rather than admit who he was, John identified himself as Glen Winslow. What John didn't know at the time was that his twin brother Glen was also wanted by the police—for first-degree sexual assault. When John identified himself as Glen, the police immediately slapped the cuffs on him and hauled him off to jail.

OUTCOME: John confessed to lying to the police, but they weren't taking any chances. They held him until a fingerprint check confirmed that he really was John. Then he spent 10 days in jail for the original property damage charge, for not having a driver's license, and for providing false information to police. A new arrest warrant was issued for Glen; he was taken into custody in Omaha five days later.

TWINS: Angela and Sharon Statton, 19

DOUBLE TROUBLE: In April 1997, Angela got into a heated argument with her boyfriend and called the police. When they arrived, the boyfriend lied and said Angela wasn't Angela, but her sister Sharon... who had a warrant for failure to appear on shoplifting charge. Angela insisted she really *was* Angela, and to prove it she pleaded with the police to drive her to her mother's house to talk to the real Sharon. Even after talking to the real Sharon, the officers weren't convinced. They wanted to arrest both sisters but couldn't because they only had one warrant. In the end, they arrested Angela on Sharon's warrant.

OUTCOME: Angela spent four nights in jail before she got her day in court. Then she and Sharon appeared together and convinced the judge that Angela really was who she said she was. "I kept telling people, 'My name is not Sharon, it's *Angela*!'" said Angela (we think). "They thought I was playing with them, but I wasn't. I sat in jail for nothing. I'm just glad I'm out." Sharon was ordered to reappear at a later date to answer the shoplifting charges, but no word on which of them showed up.

Elvis Presley's prisoner number in *Jailhouse Rock*: 6239.

THE GREAT BRINKS ROBBERY

*It was the perfect crime—so well planned and executed
that all the gang members needed to do to was lie low
until the heat cooled down. But could they?*

IN AND OUT

The year was 1950. It was a cold January in Boston. At around 7 p.m. on the 17th, a green 1949 Ford truck pulled up in front of the Prince Street entrance of the Brinks Armored Car garage. Millions of dollars in cash, checks, and money orders were stored inside the building. Seven men emerged from the back of the Ford and walked swiftly to the front door. Each man wore a Navy peacoat, gloves, rubber-soled shoes, and a chauffeur's cap.

After a series of blinking flashlight signals from a nearby rooftop, one of the men pulled out a key and unlocked the front door. Once inside, each man donned a Captain Marvel Halloween mask and went to work. They walked up the stairs and encountered a second locked door. Another key was produced, and they entered a room where five surprised Brinks employees were counting money. The gang pulled out handguns and quickly subdued the stunned Brinks men. Once their captives were bound and gagged, the masked men began collecting the loot.

With clockwork precision and very little talking, the gang filled their bags with money. Fifteen minutes after their arrival, the robbers—each carrying two full bags—left the building. Six of them got back into the truck and one got into a Ford sedan parked nearby. As they made their getaway, the employees managed to free themselves and call the police. When it was over, $1.2 million in cash and $1.5 million in checks, money orders, and securities were missing. It was the single largest robbery in U.S. history.

URBAN HEROES

The daring crime made front-page news all over the country. And the public was sympathetic with the robbers almost as soon as they heard about it.

About 6,000 American banks are robbed every year.

Their nonviolent methods and their audacity to take on a company as huge as Brinks made them cult heroes. Comedians and cartoonists joked about it, mocking the huge security company's apparent lack of security. On his weekly TV variety show, Ed Sullivan announced that he had some very special guests: the Brinks robbers themselves. Seven men wearing Captain Marvel masks walked onstage to thunderous applause. It became more than a passing fad—the press dubbed it the "Crime of the Century."

COPS…

The Boston police and Brinks were humiliated. How could seven men so easily walk off with more than $2.7 million? The FBI took over the case and immediately found some good news: word on the street was that the caper had been in the works for months, and informants were naming names. Among the prime suspects: some of Boston's most notorious petty criminals, such as Anthony Pino, Joseph McGinnis, Stanley Gusciora, and "Specs" O'Keefe—all men known for pulling off similar crimes, although nothing nearly as big. The bad news: they all had alibis. But when a green Ford truck matching witnesses' descriptions was found in pieces at a dump near where O'Keefe and Gusciora lived, the investigators knew they were hot on the trail. They just needed proof.

…AND ROBBERS

The Feds' instincts were correct: O'Keefe and Gusciora were two of the key men behind the Brinks job. But what they didn't know was that it was Anthony Pino, an illegal alien from Italy, who first came up with the idea…back in 1947.

Pino had the savvy to do the job, but he couldn't do it alone. So he'd called a meeting of some members of the Boston underworld and put together a gang. By the time they were ready to go, there were 11 members: Pino; his associate, liquor store owner Joseph McGinnis; strong-arms O'Keefe and Gusciora, both experienced criminals with reputations for keeping their cool and handling weapons; Pino's brother-in-law, Vincent Costa, the lookout; Adolph "Jazz" Maffie; Henry Baker; Michael Vincent Geagan; Thomas "Sandy" Richardson; James Faherty; and Joseph Banfield.

It would be the heist of a lifetime, and the gang spent the next two years preparing for it. Pino cased the Brinks building from nearby rooftops, and was amazed at how lax the security was. Still, they would

DeBeers spends millions per week buying stolen diamonds back so they don't flood the market.

take no chances: They broke in after hours on several different occasions and took the lock cylinders from five doors, had keys made to fit them, and returned the cylinders. And while inside, they obtained the Brinks shipment schedules. It took discipline to not steal anything on those smaller break-ins, but they knew the real score would be on the big break-in, planned for a time when the day's receipts were being counted and the vault was open. They were willing to wait.

By December 1949, Costa, the lookout man, could tell exactly how many employees were in the building and what they were doing by observing which lights were on. After about a dozen dress rehearsals, the gang made their move. The job went down without a hitch.

THE LONG GOODBYE

The robbery was the easy part. Now each gang member had to keep quiet, not spend money like crazy, and lay low for six long years, after which the statute of limitations would run out. If they could do that, they would all be scot-free...and very rich.

A small portion of the loot was split up among the gang members, but most of it was hidden in various places. O'Keefe and Gusciora put their share ($100,000 each) in the trunk of O'Keefe's car, parked in a garage on Blue Hill Avenue in Boston—with the agreement that the money was not to be touched until 1956.

Even though they were careful to destroy any physical evidence tying them to the crime, they were known criminals and couldn't evade suspicion. Many were picked up and questioned by the FBI. All denied involvement; all provided alibis (though more than a few were shaky); and all of their homes and businesses turned up nothing in searches. Still, investigators knew there was something fishy going on. Their best approach would be to get one of the men to sing; they just had to watch closely and wait for someone to slip up.

SOMEONE SLIPS UP

Less than six months after the Brinks job, O'Keefe and Gusciora were nabbed for robbing an Army-Navy store in Pennsylvania. Police found a pile of cash in the car, but none of it could be tied to the Brinks job. O'Keefe was sentenced to three years in the Bradford County jail; Gusciora was sentenced to five years.

In 1658 the Virginia legislature passed a law outlawing lawyers.

O'Keefe wanted to appeal but had no money for legal bills, so he talked Banfield into retrieving his share of the money from the car. It was delivered a few weeks later (minus $2,000). But O'Keefe couldn't keep it behind bars, so he sought out another gang member, the only one left on the outside that he thought he could trust—Jazz Maffie. Bad move: Maffie took O'Keefe's money, disappeared, then reappeared claiming it had been stolen. Then Maffie said he had spent the money on O'Keefe's legal bills. O'Keefe, meanwhile, was stuck in jail and getting angrier.

The Feds worked this angle, trying to create a wedge between O'Keefe and the rest of the gang. They told O'Keefe that the gang had ratted him out for the Brinks job. But O'Keefe stuck to his guns and kept denying any involvement.

THE TENSION MOUNTS

Prior to committing the robbery, the 11 men had agreed that if any one of them "muffed" (acted carelessly), he would be "taken care of" (killed). Sitting in jail, O'Keefe convinced himself that the other members of the gang had "muffed." And he vowed he would get his share of the loot… one way or another.

After he was paroled in the spring of 1954, O'Keefe returned to Boston to ask McGinnis for enough money from the loot to hire a lawyer for his pending burglary charge. But McGinnis wouldn't budge. So O'Keefe kidnapped McGinnis's brother-in-law, Costa, demanding his share as ransom. He only got some of it but still released the hostage. Pino and McGinnis, in the meantime, decided that O'Keefe needed to be "taken care of."

BULLET-PROOF

That June, O'Keefe was driving through Dorchester, Massachusetts, when a car pulled up next to him and sprayed his car with bullets. O'Keefe escaped unharmed. Days later, fellow gang member Henry Baker shot at him, but O'Keefe escaped again. Fearing retribution, Pino brought in a professional hit man named Elmer "Trigger" Burke. When Burke found his target and shot him in the chest and wrist with a machine gun, Specs O'Keefe lived up to his reputation as one of the toughest crooks in the Boston underworld by surviving. By this point, he was extremely angry.

The term "serial killer" was coined by FBI agent Robert Ressler in the 1970s.

O'Keefe immediately went to the cops and fingered Burke, who was arrested and convicted for attempted murder. But the plan backfired. While he was talking to police, they discovered that O'Keefe was carrying a concealed weapon, a violation of his parole. He was arrested and sentenced to 27 months in prison. Knowing that there was a contract on O'Keefe's life, the FBI stepped up their interrogations. But he still wouldn't confess.

THE HEAT IS ON

Time was starting to run out. It had been more than five years since the crime, and the deadline for the statute of limitations was getting closer and closer. Thousands of hours had gone into identifying the suspects, but the FBI still had no hard evidence. As the case remained in the public eye, each passing day without an arrest was an embarrassment.

Through all of it, the Feds knew that O'Keefe was the key, so they kept chipping away at him. When they informed him that a huge portion of the loot had been recovered, he finally gave in. On January 6, 1956, Specs O'Keefe called a meeting with the Feds and said, "All right, what do you want to know?" It was 11 days before the six-year statute of limitations would take effect.

O'Keefe spelled out every detail to the police—except where the rest of the money was hidden. He had no idea. (Neither did the police—they had exaggerated the loot-recovery story as a ruse to get O'Keefe to talk.)

TRIED AND CONVICTED

Police rounded up all of the remaining members. They were arrested and tried amid a media circus. More than 1,000 prospective jurors had to be excused because they admitted they were sympathetic to the robbers. In the end, a jury found all of them guilty. Each man was sentenced to life in prison. Some died there—others were later released on parole.

For turning state's evidence, O'Keefe was given a reduced sentence. After prison, he changed his name, moved to California, and reportedly worked as Cary Grant's chauffeur.

The Brinks gang stole $2.7 million in cash and securities. The government spent *$29 million* trying to catch them and bring them to justice. But in the end, only 0.2% of the loot—$51,906—was recovered. What happened to the remaining 99.8% is a mystery.

Police-issued TASERS have a 5-second recharge time; civilian ones take 30 seconds to recharge.

BELLE WAS A STARR

"When the legend becomes fact, print the legend."
—The Man Who Shot Liberty Valence (1962)

FOXY LADY

The Wild West had its share of lawless legends, but the overwhelming majority of them were men. Perhaps that's why in 1889—shortly after her death—tales of Belle Starr and her outlaw ways entranced the nation. Reporter Richard Fox published *Belle Starr, the Bandit Queen, or the Female Jesse James*, which chronicled the gunslingin', horse-rustlin', man-eatin' adventures of the roughest, toughest, shootingest lady that ever did live!

One problem: Fox made most of it up. Yes, there was a Belle Starr, and yes, she did spend some time on the shady side of the law. She even served nine months in prison for rustling horses. But when it comes right down to it, most of her adventures—from saloon shootouts to bank robberies to all the men she was supposed to have "known"—were nothing more than the inventions of a pulp writer looking to thrill his readers.

So which parts of the Belle Starr legend are true, and which are false?

SHIRLEY YOU CAN'T BE SERIOUS

Before she called herself Belle, she was born Myra Maybelle Shirley in 1848 to well-to-do parents in Missouri. They tried to raise her as a proper young woman, but Belle's biggest influence was her older brother Bud, who showed her how to ride a horse and shoot a gun. During the Civil War, the Shirleys sided with the Confederacy. Bud partnered up with a band of young guns, including future outlaws Frank and Jesse James and Cole Younger. Belle passed on information collected at social gatherings to her brother during these times. Bud was killed by Union troops in 1864, and sme accounts have Belle taking to her guns to avenge Bud's death. Historians find that unlikely.

Another part of the legend pairs Belle with Cole Younger. Not only were the two an item, she had his love child. Younger denied this; he did meet Belle in 1864 but didn't see her see her again for four years. By then she'd married another man and was pregnant with *his* child.

REED BETWEEN THE LINES

Which is the truth? Historians speculate that after the Civil War, the Shirleys had moved to Texas, where Belle met her first husband, Jim Reed. Legend has it that Belle's parents objected to their pairing, so the lovebirds ran away and got married on horseback, with the rites performed by a member of Reed's gang. In reality, the elder Shirleys were fine with the match and the couple had normal nuptials.

But their lives didn't stay normal. Reed tried farming. He didn't like that. He wasn't much of a salesman, either, so he took to thieving. Reed hooked up with the gang of Tom Starr, a Cherokee outlaw of some infamy. During this spell with Starr, Reed shot a man and then took Belle and their daughter Pearl to California in 1869 until things cooled off in Texas.

But Reed ran into trouble in California for counterfeiting. With the law hot on his tail, he moved his family back to Texas after the birth of their son in 1871. Reed continued his life of crime, but there's little record that Belle was interested in joining him. She left Reed, who died in 1874, shot while trying to escape arrest.

A STARR IS BORN

Not much is known about the six years between Reed's death and Belle's second marriage in 1880. Hence, this is the period where Belle's "biographers" peppered her history with wild tales of her life of crime. She burned down buildings, eloped with a deputy in order to spring herself from jail, busted up poker games with gunplay, and rewarded members of her gang with her…favors. The real explanation is probably much more pedestrian; she more likely spent time with her mother and the Reed family in Texas.

In 1880 Belle married Tom Starr's son Sam, who was nearly a decade younger than Belle. The couple settled in the Indian Territory near Arkansas in a place they called Younger's Bend.

HORSEPLAY

One of Belle's first verified events of lawful malfeasance occurred in 1882 when she and Sam were both charged with larceny for stealing horses. They were convicted and sentenced to a year in the pokey. The two were out in nine months, partially due to Belle's "good behavior" with the warden. Another legend? Perhaps not.

Over the next few years, Belle and Sam were suspected in a string of horse thefts and other robberies, but Belle usually managed to beat the rap. Sam Starr started spending a lot of time away from home. Lucky for Belle, she met John Middleton, with whom it is very likely she had an affair. Middleton died not long after Belle purchased a horse for him—which, it turned out—had been stolen. Belle was charged with larceny again, but the evidence wasn't strong enough to convict her.

FOR WHOM THE BELLE TOLLS

Legends aside, the real story of Belle Starr was tragic. She lost Sam at a Christmas party in 1886 after he drew a gun on an old enemy and was shot to death. Still grieving, Belle had a brief dalliance with an outlaw named Jack Spaniard, who would soon be swinging from a gallows. Belle married her third and last husband: Bill July, the adopted son of Tom Starr and thereby, her late second husband's brother. This marriage was not especially happy; rumor had it that Belle's new husband had found a young Cherokee woman on the side.

Belle's children were none too fond of her, either. Her daughter Pearl became pregnant out of wedlock, causing Belle to boot her out of the house and break up her romance. Belle's son Ed hated Bill July. Belle also wasn't making friends with neighbors—she reneged on an agreement to let Edgar Watson rent her land for farming. She made the mistake of slipping into their conversation that she knew Watson was wanted for murder in Florida and chided him about what a shame it would be if the authorities found out.

In 1889, while she was riding her horse home after visiting some friends, a shotgun blast rang out. Belle Starr was killed. Implicated in the murder were Watson, Bill July, and even her own son and daughter. The prime suspect was Watson, who had motive and opportunity (the shooting occurred near his home) and had done this sort of thing before. But officially the murder was never solved.

In the end, there was no denying that Starr's life was eventful, just not as eventful as the pulp writers made it sound. Given the choice, which life would Belle Starr have preferred to live? A quote she once made pretty much answers that question: "I am a friend to any brave and gallant outlaw."

"COP KILLER"

*Ice-T pioneered the genre of gangsta rap—graphically
violent and politically charged songs about life in the
ghetto. But one of his songs in particular has
become synonymous with controversy.*

ORIGINAL GANGSTER

Ice-T (real name: Tracy Marrow) grew up in the tough South Central neighborhood of Los Angeles, was a member of the notorious Crips gang as a teenager, and even worked as a pimp. In 1984 he decided to channel his stories of street life into music. Albums like *6 in the Morning* (1987) and *O.G.: Original Gangster* (1991) made him one of the bestselling and best known West Coast rappers.

In 1990 Ice-T wrote a song called "Cop Killer." Inspired by the 1977 Talking Heads hit "Psycho Killer" (a first-person narrative from the perspective of a murderer), the song is a young black man's account of being so fed up with racially motivated police brutality that he murders a police officer. Sample lyrics: "I'm 'bout to bust some shots off / I'm bout to dust some cops off / cop killer, better you than me."

A METALLIC TASTE

The song was so aggressive that Ice-T decided it wouldn't make a good rap song, but was perfect for his heavy-metal band side project, Body Count. Based on Ice-T's star power, the group signed with Sire Records (a division of Warner Bros.) and released their self-titled debut album in March 1992. The first single: "Cop Killer."

While the song didn't get much radio or MTV play (neither thrash metal nor hardcore rap generally do), it was a single by a major artist at the peak of his career, so Warner Bros. did a fair amount of promotion for *Body Count*, including selling the CD in tiny body bags instead of the usual long cardboard boxes CDs came in at the time.

But what really got "Cop Killer" noticed was its timing. In 1991 African-American motorist Rodney King had been severely beaten by several white L.A. police officers (and the incident was caught on videotape) and at the time of "Cop Killer's" release, those officers were on trial for the incident. In late April 1992, the four policemen were acquitted, enraging the African-American community. Los Angeles endured three days of riots, fires, and looting.

PROTEST

As pundits weighed in on the riots' causes, some blamed the song. The Dallas Police Association actually lobbied to get "Cop Killer" banned—it organized a boycott of all Time Warner products in an effort to force Warner Bros. to withdraw the album from stores because it "promoted violence" toward police. Decency crusader Tipper Gore publicly denounced the song, as did President George Bush and Vice President Dan Quayle (who also spoke out against the immorality of *Murphy Brown*, a TV sitcom about a single mother). Warner executives even reported receiving death threats.

On the other side, one major police organization, the National Black Police Association, supported "Cop Killer," arguing that the song accurately identified police brutality as the cause of the rise in anti-police sentiment. Other people said the song was blamed unjustly in the emotional aftermath of the riots. Criminologist Mark S. Hamm of Indiana State University pointed out that there was no controversy surrounding the Talking Heads' "Psycho Killer" or Eric Clapton's "I Shot the Sheriff," which was a #1 hit in 1974.

COUNTERPROTEST

Body Count was never actually banned or pulled from store shelves, but there were a few isolated incidents:

• A small record store in Greensboro, North Carolina, stopped selling it after local police told them they would no longer respond to emergency calls at the store if it continued to stock the album.

• When Body Count was scheduled to open for Metallica at a concert in San Diego, California Governor Pete Wilson demanded the band be dropped from the bill. As a compromise, the group was allowed to play under the promise that they wouldn't perform "Cop Killer." They took the stage…and played the song anyway.

Ice-T thought the controversy was absurd, because "Cop Killer" was entirely a work of fiction. "I ain't never killed no cop," he said. "I felt like it a lot of times. But I never did it. If you believe that I'm a cop killer, you believe David Bowie is an astronaut" (in reference to Bowie's "Space Oddity").

A FORCED HAND

In late 1992, Ice-T asked Warner Bros. to pull *Body Count* from stores and re-release it—without "Cop Killer." Warner agreed, but not before it flooded stores with over half a million copies of the intact version of *Body Count*, ensuring there were plenty to meet demand for the "banned" album. Ultimately, it was one of the bestselling albums of Ice-T's career.

So why did Ice-T voluntarily recall "Cop Killer"? Strangely, it was out of respect for his record label. As he explained in his autobiography *The Ice Opinion*, "Warner never censored us. But when the cops moved on Body Count, they issued pressure on the corporate division. So even when you're in a business with somebody who might not want to censor you, economically people can put restraints on them."

Nevertheless, in 1993 Warner's corporate division tried to make the music division censor songs and artwork on Ice-T's next album, *Home Invasion*. In response to the pressure, Ice-T left Warner Bros. and signed with Priority Records, a small hardcore rap label. Body Count moved to Virgin Records.

AFTERMATH

The original 1992 recording of "Cop Killer" is no longer commercially available, although there is a version on a 2005 Body Count live album. And Ice-T has only recorded two albums in the last 10 years (along with two Body Count albums). Following an appearance in the hit movie *New Jack City* in 1991, he took on more and more acting roles. In 2000 he joined the cast of *Law and Order: Special Victims Unit*. The characters in both projects are, ironically, cops.

*   *   *

"The gangster and the artist are the same in the eyes of the masses. They are both admired and hero-worshipped, but there is always present an underlying desire to see them destroyed at the peak of their glory."

—**Stanley Kubrick**

Only 12% of those arrested for murder are female.

DUMBERER CROOKS

*Our favorite crooks are the ones who do something
dumb, and then do something even dumber.*

EMPTY YOUR BRAINS IN THIS TRAY

"Clyde Lamar Pace II made two mistakes. The first, Polk County sheriff's deputies say, was when he emptied his pockets to pass through a courthouse metal detector and apparently forgot about the small bag of marijuana. He threw it in a baggie without realizing it, and the person working the security post said, 'Hey, what's this?' Chief Deputy Bill Vaughn said. 'He gave that old "uh-oh, I've-been-caught" look, and the chase was on.' The second mistake was when he ran away from deputies, directly into a locked revolving door. Pace, 18, was arrested for drug possession and resisting arrest."

—*The Des Moines Register*

THANKS, MOM

"Trilane A. Ludwig, 24, of Vancouver, was arrested after a traffic stop early New Year's Day. At 5:30 a.m. he called his mother, Angela Beckham, and asked her to bail him out with the money in his wallet. She handed $500 to a clerk, who suspected the money was phony and called police. The police report described the counterfeit bills as bad copies that were the wrong size. Beckham said she wasn't going to shell out any real cash to bail him out. The case has been referred to the Secret Service."

—*Kansas City Star*

THEY'LL NEVER FIND ME HERE...OR HERE

"In December 1999, Christopher S. Newsome broke into the Delaware County Courthouse in Muncie, Indiana, and stole $25 from the receptionist's desk. He then hid in a closet, where a janitor found him. When the janitor went to call authorities, Newsome sprinted out of the courthouse, through a parking lot, and toward a nearby building. Unfortunately for Newsome, that building was the county jail. Moments later, the 26-year-old was in handcuffs."

—*Realpolice.net*

Country with the most prisoners per captia: the US (1 per 143). Least: India 1 per 3,940.

HOW'D YOU GUYS FIND ME?

"Police didn't have much trouble finding Joshua W. Kochell, 27, who they say robbed two Lafayette, Indiana, gas stations. They tracked him through the monitoring device he was ordered to wear on a 2001 sentence for theft and habitual offense. Kochell was being held in Tippecanoe County Jail on $60,000 bond."

—**Associated Press**

GUILTY AND GUILTIER

"A New York woman who was given probation for robbery faces four years in jail after punching a juror outside the court. Octavia Williams came face-to-face with juror Geraldine Goldring just after Goldring and the other jurors found her guilty of stealing $160 from a woman in Times Square. Williams ran off after the assault but was caught and returned to the courtroom, where she was charged with assault and contempt of court for ignoring the judge's instructions to report to probation immediately after the verdict."

—*New York Daily News*

NOTE TO SELF...

"Police in Hillsborough, North Carolina, responded to a call from a bank about a man who was acting suspiciously. Capt. Dexter Davis confronted the man and asked if he had a weapon. 'He pulled his book bag off his shoulders, opened the bag up and held it open to me to show he didn't have a gun,' Davis said. When Davis looked inside, there was a note in clear view. It read, 'I want $10,000 in $100 bills. Don't push no buttons, or I'll shot [sic] you.' Davis laughed out loud, and then arrested Christopher Fields (who also was carrying a 10-inch knife) and turned him over to the FBI."

—*Durham Herald-Sun*

CRASH TEST DUMMY

"In Springfield, Illinois, Zachary Holloway, 20, and a pal were arrested and charged with breaking into one car and stealing, among other things, a motorcycle helmet, then attempting to break into another car. To try to get into the second car, Holloway put on the helmet, stood back from the car and charged into it, head-butting a window, unsuccessfully, twice."

—*"The Edge," The Oregonian*

In the US, bounty hunters catch about 30,000 bail jumpers per year—a 90% success rate.

HOLLYWOOD SCANDAL, PART II

*When we last left Silver Screen star Fatty Arbuckle
(page 141), he was preparing to stand trial for a
murder he didn't commit. Now back to the case.*

EXTRA!
Much like the Menendez brothers trials and the O. J. Simpson trials of the 1990s, the media—which in the 1920s consisted mostly of newspapers—had a field day with the Arbuckle trial. Unlike the Simpson trial, however, the lack of evidence in the Arbuckle trial led most newspapers to conclude that Arbuckle was innocent. Most papers, that is, except for those owned by media baron William Randolph Hearst. His papers loudly attacked Arbuckle's character, insinuated his guilt, and ran as many as six special editions per day to keep readers up to date on the latest developments in the case.

The Hearst papers published the most lurid accounts of the crime and the trial, and even stooped to publicizing totally unsubstantiated rumors about the case—the most famous of which was that Arbuckle, supposedly too impotent from booze to rape Rappé himself, had used a Coke bottle (some accounts said it was a champagne bottle) instead, causing her bladder to rupture. "Nowhere in any testimony in the court transcripts, police reports, or personal interviews did this story appear," Andy Edmonds writes in *Frame Up! The Untold Story of Roscoe "Fatty" Arbuckle.* "Everyone connected with the case vehemently denied it, yet it is the most popular story, and one of the most ugly lies, still connected with the ordeal. The fabrication haunted Roscoe throughout the remainder of his life."

GOING TO COURT
As Brady prepared his case, one of the first things he did was see to it that Maude Delmont would not be able to testify. He knew that the other witnesses would prove she had lied in her police statement. Furthermore, Delmont had changed her story so many times that Brady knew she

would be caught in her own lies during cross-examination. Rather than let that happen, Brady had her arrested on an outstanding charge of bigamy. Delmont—the only person who claimed that Arbuckle had committed a crime—spent the next several months in jail, where Arbuckle's attorneys could not get at her.

THE TRIAL

The People v. Arbuckle lasted from November 14 to December 4, 1921. More than 60 witnesses were called to the stand, including 18 doctors. According to Bernard Ryan in *Great American Trials*,

> Through defense witnesses, lawyer Gavin McNab revealed Virginia Rappé's moral as well as medical history: As a young teenager, she had had five abortions in three years, at 16, she had borne an illegitimate child; since 1907, she had had a series of bladder inflammations and chronic cystitis; she liked to strip naked when she drank; the doctor who attended her in the several days before she died concluded that she had gonorrhea; when she met Arbuckle for the first time on Monday, she was pregnant and that afternoon had asked him to pay for an abortion; on Wednesday, she had asked her nurse to find an abortionist….Medical testimony proved that Virginia Rappé's bladder was cystic—one of the causes of rupture of the bladder.

Arbuckle Takes the Stand

The climax of the trial came on Monday, November 28, when Arbuckle testified in his own defense. He recounted how he had found Rappé in his bathroom vomiting into the toilet, and how he had helped her into the next room when she asked to lie down. Arbuckle testified that he spent less than 10 minutes alone with Rappé before summoning Maude Delmont, who took over and asked him to leave the room. He stood up well under cross-examination; and the final testimony, in which expert witnesses testified that the rupture of Ms. Rappé's bladder was not caused by external force, seemed to cinch the case for Arbuckle.

THE VERDICT

As the case went to the jury, both sides appeared confident of victory. But on December 4th, after 44 hours of deliberation, the jury announced that it was hopelessly deadlocked, and the judge declared a mistrial.

One juror, a woman named Helen Hubbard—whose husband was a

lawyer who did business with the D.A.'s office—held out for a conviction throughout the entire deliberations.

The Second Trial

The case went to trial a second time, beginning on January 11 and lasting until February 3. The second trial was much like the first, only this time the defense introduced even more evidence concerning Ms. Rappé's shady past. But Arbuckle's lawyers, confident they would win handily, did not have Arbuckle take the stand in his defense. That was a huge mistake— this time the jury deadlocked 9–3 in favor of *conviction*.

The Third Trial

The case went to trial a third time on March 13. This time, Arbuckle's defense left nothing to chance: it provided still more evidence questioning both Rappé's physical health and her moral character, and it brought Arbuckle back to the stand to testify on his own behalf.

FINAL VERDICT

The case went to the jury on April 12, 1922. They deliberated for less than 5 minutes, then returned to court and read the following statement:

> We the jury find Roscoe Arbuckle not guilty of manslaughter.
>
> Acquittal is not enough for Roscoe Arbuckle. We feel that a great injustice has been done him. We feel also that it was only our plain duty to give him this exoneration, under the evidence, for there was not the slightest proof adduced to connect him in any way with the commission of a crime.
>
> He was manly throughout the case, and told a straightforward story on the witness stand, which we all believed.
>
> The happening at the hotel was an unfortunate affair for which Arbuckle, so the evidence shows, was in no way responsible.
>
> We wish him success....Roscoe Arbuckle is entirely innocent and free from all blame.

THE AFTERMATH

Roscoe Arbuckle was a free man, but his life was in tatters. The trials had cost him more than $750,000, wiping out nearly his entire life savings (the $3 million Paramount contract had fallen through when the scandal broke). As if that wasn't bad enough, the IRS went after him a few months later, when it seized the remainder of his estate to collect more than $100,000 in back taxes. It also obtained a court order to attach whatever wages he earned in the future until the entire tax debt was paid back.

THE HAYS OFFICE

Things got even worse for Arbuckle. Largely because of the scandal, 12 of Hollywood's top studio moguls hired William Hays, chairman of the Republican National Committee and a former postmaster general, to become America's "movie czar." His job: Keep Hollywood's image clean. His first task: Deal with Arbuckle.

Hatchet Job

Six days after Arbuckle was acquitted, the "Hays Office" (as it came to be known) banned him from the screen. The public was led to believe it was a moral issue. Actually, Hays was doing the bidding of Paramount heads Adolph Zukor and Jesse Lasky, who no longer wanted to work with Arbuckle, out of fear that he was box office poison. But they didn't take any chances; rather than risk losing Arbuckle to a competing studio, they lobbied the Hays Office to ban him from the film industry entirely.

COMEBACK

The ban was lifted eight months later, but the taint remained and Arbuckle had trouble finding work. He began work on a short subject film called *Handy Andy*, but was so hounded by reporters that he gave up on the project.

Over the next decade he appeared in stage shows, ran a Hollywood nightclub, and directed a number of films under the pseudonym William B. Goodrich (Will B. Good). But it wasn't until 1932—more than 10 years after the trials—that he had a chance to return to the screen. Studio head Jack Warner hired him to act in a film called *Hey, Pop!* It was a box office success, and Arbuckle was signed for six more films. He only completed three—*Buzzin' Around*, *Tamalio*, and *In the Dough*. The evening *In the Dough* finished shooting, Arbuckle celebrated at dinner with his wife and went home to bed. He died in his sleep at about 2:30 a.m., leaving an estate valued at less than $2,000.

Between 1934 and 1955, there was not a single bank robbery in Hawaii.

HOW TO MAKE PRISON WINE

The bad news: You're in jail. The good news: You can still enjoy one of the finer things in life—wine. You just have to make it yourself. In the toilet.

WHAT YOU'LL NEED: several thick black garbage bags; a few slices of bread or rolls; some warm water; a straw; sugar packets or cubes; and something fruity with sugar in it, such as fruit juice, tomatoes, or Kool-Aid packets.

DIRECTIONS

Step 1. You'll start by making a double- or triple-thick brewing chamber. Do this with a plastic trash bag stuck inside another trash bag stuck inside another trash bag.

Step 2. Pour in a gallon of warm water.

Step 3. Add as much fruity material as you can muster. This can be anything from leftover fruit juice to orange rinds, raisins, tomatoes, Kool-Aid, even ketchup packets…or a little bit of each—whatever you can salvage from the limited offerings of the prison cafeteria. The fermentation process turns sugar into alcohol, so the more sugar or sugar-rich foods and liquids you have, the stronger the wine will be. Throw in about 50 sugar packets or sugar cubes, and add a new one every other day or so.

Step 4. Fermentation is triggered by the addition of yeast. Since yeast packets aren't readily available in prison, you'll have to get creative. Bread has yeast in it, but what really has a large concentration of yeast is bread *mold*. So snag some bread from the cafeteria when it's still fresh and moist and put it on a shelf for a few days until it starts to get moldy. When the mold forms, the bread is ready to go into the wine bag. Think ahead: The moldy bread should go into the chamber at the same time as the fruity material.

Step 5. Seal the bag by knotting it tightly. Run it under hot tap water every day for about 15 minutes and wrap it in a blanket to keep it warm.

A single hair can reveal a person's sex, age, and race. (Good thing Uncle John is bald.)

Step 6. As the yeast in the bread mold ferments the sugar into alcohol, it creates carbon dioxide as a by-product, and that has to have some way to escape. So ventilate the chamber by cutting a tiny hole in the garbage bags and inserting a straw.

Step 7. Hide it. (Is there a prison anywhere in the world that lets inmates make their own liquor?) Three days will produce a slightly alcoholic wine, but wait a week and the wine will ferment into a strong—but horrible-tasting—brew of about 13 percent alcohol, the higher end of commercially available wine's alcoholic content.

Step 8. When the week is up, wait. You can't drink it quite yet. You have to "shock" the wine to stop the fermentation process. Here's how: Place the bag (careful of the straw and straw-hole) in the toilet bowl. Flush the toilet every few minutes for about an hour to allow the cold water to wash over the outside of the bag, cooling the wine and ending fermentation.

Step 9. Enjoy. (And try not to get caught.)

*   *   *

REPORTEDLY SAID BY COPS TO SUSPECTS...

• "Take your hands off the car, and I'll make your birth certificate a worthless document."

• "If you run, you'll only go to jail tired."

• "Can you run faster than 1,200 feet per second? In case you didn't know, that is the speed of a nine-millimeter bullet fired from my gun."

• "So you don't know how fast you were going. I guess that means I can write anything I want on the ticket."

• "Warning? You want a warning? Okay, I'm warning you not to do that again or I will give you *another* ticket."

• "Yeah, we have a quota. Two more tickets and my wife will get a toaster oven."

• "Just how big *were* those two beers?"

In 1986 a guard in an armored car was killed when $50,000 worth of quarters fell on him.

WEIRD SENTENCES

*These sentences may have made sense at the time
they were handed down...but we doubt it.*

• Leah Marie Fairbanks of Duluth, Minnesota, pleaded guilty to first-degree assault charges and was sentenced to 14 months probation...plus she had to read seven classic novels and the Declaration of Independence and then write reports on each one.

• Anna Mae Leach of Castle Shannon, Pennsylvania, was jailed for a week for not returning three videotapes. (The charges turned out to be false.)

• Gloria Cisternas of Santiago, Chile, was sentenced to seven days in jail for failing to pay a $63 (U.S.) fine. She had been fined for failing to keep her lawn green.

• *USA Today* reported that Utah's Tom Green had been convicted for polygamy and criminal nonsupport. Sentence: "0–5 years in prison."

• Tony and Angelica Flores spent a night in jail after failing to appear for their court date. Criminal charges had been filed against them in Peoria, Arizona, for keeping their Christmas lights up too long.

• In Louisville, Kentucky, Luther Crawford, father of 12 kids by 11 different women, was $33,000 behind on child support payments. He avoided going to prison by accepting the judge's offer that he refrain from sex until he has paid up.

• A wealthy Finnish man was fined $103,000—for a speeding ticket. In Finland, traffic fines are levied in proportion to the driver's income.

• Four Swedish teenagers were convicted of high treason for their plot against King Carl Gustaf. Their plot: to throw a strawberry cream pie at him.

13 American prisons banned the TV show *Prison Break*.

THE DISAPPEARANCE OF THE *MARY CELESTE*

One of the most famous unexplained disappearances ever recorded is the case of the Mary Celeste. *In 1872 the ship was found drifting aimlessly in the Atlantic, in seaworthy condition and fully provisioned. But the entire crew had vanished without a trace, and the presence of blood stains found on the empty vessel has fueled rumors that a grave crime was committed on board. But what really happened? To this day, no one knows.*

BACKGROUND

On November 5, 1872, the *Mary Celeste* set off from New York carrying a cargo of l,701 barrels of commercial alcohol. Her captain was Benjamin Spooner Briggs, a well-known seaman who allowed no drinking on his ship and regularly read the Bible to his men. The crew had been carefully chosen for their character and seamanship, especially because the captain had brought along his wife and two-year-old daughter. He was looking forward to a safe and pleasant voyage.

DISAPPEARANCE

One month later, on December 5, Captain Morehouse of the *Dei Gratia*—another cargo ship bound for Gibraltar—noticed a vessel on the horizon. It looked like it was in trouble, so he changed course to see if he could be of assistance. After calling out to the ship and getting no reply, Morehouse lowered a boat and sent two men to board. It was immediately evident that the ship, which turned out to be the *Mary Celeste*, was deserted. The men looked for underwater damage, but the vessel was not leaking, and was in no danger of sinking. There was evidence that the *Mary Celeste* had encountered bad weather, but on the whole she was in perfectly good condition and should have had no problem continuing her journey.

Stranger yet, there were six months' worth of provisions aboard and plenty of fresh water. All of the crew's personal possessions were intact—even the ship's strongbox. In fact, absolutely nothing was missing except some of the ship's papers and the ship's lifeboat. Captain Briggs, his family, and the crew had obviously abandoned the ship in a hurry...but why? What could have frightened them so much that they'd desert a seaworthy vessel for an overcrowded yawl and take their chances in the stormy Atlantic?

INVESTIGATION

Still puzzled by the disappearance of the crew, Captain Morehouse decided to claim the *Mary Celeste* as salvage. He put three men aboard her and proceeded with both ships to Gibraltar.

Officials in Gibraltar were suspicious of Morehouse when he showed up with a "salvage" ship in such good condition, still carrying valuable cargo. They investigated and discovered that:

• The *Mary Celeste*'s hull was perfectly sound, indicating she had not been in a collision. Nor was there any evidence of explosion or fire.

• The cargo of commercial alcohol seemed to be intact and complete.

• A phial of sewing machine oil was standing upright, spare panes of glass were found unbroken, and the furniture in the captain's cabin was in its proper place—all indications that the ship hadn't endured particularly rough weather.

• The fact that the crew had left behind all their possessions— even their tobacco—indicated that they had left the ship in a panic, afraid for their lives, but the investigators could see no reason for this.

• The most mysterious item aboard was a sword found under the captain's bed. It seemed to be smeared with blood, then wiped. Blood was also found on the railing, and both bows of the ship had strange cuts in them which could not be explained.

THE OFFICIAL WORD

Solly Flood, attorney general for Gibraltar, found the bloodstains suspicious and was convinced there had been violence aboard the *Mary Celeste*. However, the Vice Admiralty Court issued a verdict clearing Morehouse and his crew of any suspicion. After the ship's owners paid Morehouse a reward, the *Mary Celeste* was given a new crew, and went on to Italy, where her cargo was delivered. She continued to sail for 12 years but was known as a "hoodoo ship," so most seamen refused to set foot on her.

It is a crime in Parkersburg, West Virginia, to sneak up on policeman and shout "Boo!"

WHAT HAPPENED?

The mysterious disappearance of the *Mary Celeste*'s crew had people all over the world imagining possible scenarios.

• Some believed a mutiny had occurred—the crew murdered the captain and his family, then took the ship. But if that were true, why did they abandon their prize?

• There was the possibility that pirates attacked the ship and killed everyone on it. But that made no sense because nothing was stolen.

• Perhaps an outbreak of disease panicked those left alive. But why would they subject themselves to the close quarters of the smaller boat, where the crowding would *guarantee* that everyone caught the disease?

• The most outrageous explanation offered was that the ship had been attacked by a giant squid several times, until everyone was killed. But a squid wouldn't have been interested in the ship's papers. And a squid wouldn't need the ship's lifeboat.

Because the story of the *Mary Celeste* got so much publicity, phony survivors started popping up and selling their stories to newspapers and magazines. But they all checked out false—no one who claimed to have been on board had their facts straight.

ONLY ONE EXPLANATION?

The mystery of the *Mary Celeste* has puzzled people for over a century. In all that time, say experts, only one feasible explanation has been proposed. This postulates that four things happened, in succession:

1. The captain died of natural causes while the ship was caught in bad weather.

2. A crew member misread the depth of the water in the hold, and everyone panicked, thinking the ship was going down.

3. They abandoned ship in such a hurry that they took no food or water.

4. Everyone in the lifeboat either starved or drowned.

Is that what happened? No one will ever know.

In 1876 the lawless town of Deadwood, South Dakota, averaged one murder per day.

FALSELY ACCUSED

*You're just living your life, doing your thing, and then—boom!—someone
accuses you of a crime you didn't commit. Everything goes topsy-turvy
and nothing is ever the same again. It happened to these people.
(Warning: Some of the allegations are disturbing.)*

THE ACCUSED: A.J. and Lisa Demaree, of Peoria, Arizona

BACKGROUND: In 2008, after the Demarees and their three daughters, aged 5, 4, and 1, returned from a trip, A.J. took his camera's memory card to Walmart to have prints made.

STORY: A few of the 144 photos showed the girls playing at bathtime. "They're typical pictures that 99% of families have," A.J. said. A Walmart employee, however, thought the photos were pornography and called the cops. Result: Child Protection Services went to the Demarees' home and took the girls away. A.J. and Lisa were questioned by police, who wouldn't even let them see their kids. No criminal charges were filed and the parents were granted supervised visitation rights, but the girls were remanded to the state until an investigation was completed. After officials interviewed the couple's friends and coworkers, Lisa was suspended from her teaching job, and both parents were put on a list of sex offenders. A month later they still didn't have their children, so they asked that a judge review the case. He looked at the pictures and determined that they were *not* pornographic, and ruled the kids be returned immediately. But the investigation dragged on for a year.

OUTCOME: The Demarees are suing Walmart for not displaying its "unsuitable print policy." They're also suing the state of Arizona, who they claim slandered them by telling their friends and co-workers that the couple were "child pornographers." In all, the family is seeking $8.4 million for "emotional stress, headaches, nightmares, shock to their nervous system, grief, and depression."

THE ACCUSED: Francis Evelyn, 58, a custodian at Brooklyn's Public School 91 in New York City

BACKGROUND: Having spent nearly 20 years in the job, Evelyn was well respected at work and in his neighborhood. The native Trinidadian

---

During Prohibition, the jury in one bootlegging case was arrested after they drank the evidence.

described himself as "happy-go-lucky," had no criminal record, and was less than two years from retirement.

STORY: On March 19, 2007, police officers arrived at P.S. 91, arrested Evelyn, cuffed him, and took him away for questioning. Police commissioner Raymond Kelly announced that Evelyn was accused of the "heinous rape of an eight-year-old student on multiple occasions." Detectives told Evelyn that if he didn't confess, they'd make sure he got a life sentence in the "worst kind" of prison, where he'd likely be raped and possibly killed. If Evelyn did confess, they said, he'd get a lesser sentence. They even said they had DNA evidence against him. "How?" replied Evelyn. "I didn't *do* anything!" Then the police took the unorthodox step of locking him up in Rikers Island Prison with actual murderers and rapists.

OUTCOME: Three days later, police finally interviewed the accuser. It turned out that she was known as a "troubled child" who had lied about being abused on previous occasions. (The principal knew this, but failed to tell the police.) Worse still, the girl described her attacker as a bald, white man, yet cops arrested Evelyn, who is black. The charges were dropped immediately, and Evelyn was free. But the story had already gained worldwide attention. "On the bus home," Evelyn said, "a woman was reading the paper with my picture on the cover. The headline said 'The Rapist.'" He couldn't walk down the street without people pointing at him or insulting him. He was given his job back, but was unable to go near the school for months because he'd "start shaking." At last report, Evelyn was suing the city of New York for $10 million. "They ruined my life. I don't want those charges just to be sealed," he said. "I want them to be washed away!"

THE ACCUSED: Richard Jewell, a security guard at the 1996 Olympic Summer Games in Atlanta, Georgia

STORY: Jewell was patrolling Centennial Park, the "town square" of the Olympics, at 1:00 a.m. when he noticed a suspicious bag under a bench, only a few feet away from where thousands of people were enjoying a concert. Inside the bag were three pipe bombs surrounded by a bunch of nails. Jewell called the bomb squad and immediately started evacuating people. A few minutes later, the bombs exploded. Although two people were killed and dozens more were injured, it could have been much, much worse.

The press called Jewell a hero as the manhunt for the bomber began. President Bill Clinton announced: "We will spare no effort to find out who was responsible for this murderous act. We will track them down. We will bring them to justice." Suddenly, the FBI was under a lot of pressure, which may be why they leaked a "lone bomber" criminal profile, with a note that Jewell was a "person of interest." The next day, *The Atlanta Journal Constitution* ran this headline: "FBI suspects hero guard may have planted bomb." For the rest of the summer, the FBI and the press followed Jewell wherever he went. Editorials called him a "failed cop" who planted the bomb and then called it in just so people would think he was a hero. News cameras were there when the FBI searched his apartment and special reports broke into regular programming to broadcast the searches live.

OUTCOME: In October 1996, the FBI announced that they had no evidence linking Jewell to the bombings and that he was no longer a suspect. So did he return to being regarded as a hero? No. "No one wanted anything to do with him," said his lawyer. Jewell sued four news outlets for libel (but not the FBI). "This isn't about the money," he said in 2006. "It's about clearing my name." CNN, NBC, and the *New York Post* all agreed to settle their lawsuits, but the *Atlanta Journal Constitution* would not. That case was dismissed a few months after Jewell died in 2007 of heart failure at age 44.

SO WHO DID IT? In 2003 the FBI arrested Eric Rudolph, who had also bombed an abortion clinic and a lesbian nightclub in Atlanta. Investigators were able to link him to the Olympic bombing because of similarities among the three bombs.

THE ACCUSED: Abu Bakker Qassim, a Chinese citizen

BACKGROUND: Qassim is a Uighur Muslim (pronounced WEE-gur) living in northwestern China. Uighurs are a Turkic ethnic group that the Chinese government considers terrorists, so they are persecuted and also highly taxed. With little possibility of work and his wife pregnant with twins, Qassim fled the country in 1999, hoping to join a Uighur community in Turkey, make some money, and then send for his family. He never made it.

STORY: His journey led him to the wrong place at the wrong time: Afghanistan in September 2001. When the United States retaliated for the 9-11 attacks, the village where Qassim was staying was bombed. Along with several other people, he hid in caves in the Tora Bora mountains. Known as a terrorist stronghold, the caves were bombed relentlessly. Qassim wasn't a terrorist, but he'd learned how to use a machine gun at a Uighur village. He escaped to Pakistan in late 2001, where his group met some people who promised to take them to the city. But instead they were led into a trap. The people were bounty hunters, receiving $5,000 from the American government for every terrorist they turned over. Because Qassim had received weapons training, he was considered an enemy combatant. He was incarcerated in Afghanistan, and six months later, along with several other Uighers, he was transported to the U.S. military prison at Guantanamo Bay.

OUTCOME: Three and a half years after their arrival, Qassim and four of his countrymen were listed as "NLEC"—No Longer Enemy Combatants. A federal judge ruled that the men be set free. But they weren't. They spent another year in Guantanamo—not because the U.S. wanted to keep them, but because no other country would take them. "After four years at Guantanamo Bay," he explained, "you earn the title 'terrorist.' And the Chinese strongly believe it." Had Qassim been returned to China, he said, he would be tortured. American officials agreed, but also denied him entry to the United States. The governments of Canada and several European countries rejected him as well. Only one country opened its borders to him: Albania. Even though there were no other Uighurs there and he didn't speak Albanian, he went there and worked hard to make a life. Six years after he left his wife, he was finally able to phone her for the first time. At last report, Qassim was working at an Italian restaurant in Albania and was close to raising enough money to retrieve his wife and the 10-year-old twins he's never met. He's also petitioning the U.S. government to release 16 other Uighurs who are still being held at Guantanamo, all of whom he says are innocent.

THE ACCUSED: Eric Nordmark, 35, a homeless man in Garden Grove, California

STORY: In May 2003, Nordmark was walking down the street when two police officers told him to sit down on the curb. Nordmark explained that he was an "army vet looking for work." A few minutes later, the cops brought him to the station and took his mug shot. Then he was released. A few days later, he found a job setting up rides at a carnival. After his first day, he went to a store to buy some beer and cigarettes. When he walked out, the police were waiting for him. They cuffed him and arrested him. The charge: the assault of three 11-year-old girls. A few days earlier, the girls had claimed they were attacked by a homeless man on the way home from school, and escaped when one of them kicked the man in the groin. Nordmark's disheveled appearance matched their description, and two of the three girls identified him in a photo lineup. Bail was set at $50,000, but Nordmark didn't even have $50, so he was forced to remain in jail until his trial began…eight months later. Although Nordmark repeatedly denied attacking or even ever meeting the girls, several witnesses were set to testify that the local kids were afraid of him. On the second day of the trial, one of the accusers took the stand. "He started choking me," she testified. "And then I turned purple…I couldn't breathe, and I felt like I was going to black out." That night, Nordmark told his lawyer that if he was convicted, he'd kill himself before he ever got to prison—he'd heard how child molesters are treated in jail.

OUTCOME: The following day, Nordmark was brought back into the courtroom. Only the lawyers, the judge, and one of the girls were there. The judge told him, "All charges have been dismissed. You're free to go." The girl apologized and explained that they made up the story because they got home late from school that day and didn't want to get in trouble. The following week, all three girls were arrested at their school for the false accusation and led away in handcuffs. Two were given 30 days in detention. The girl who committed perjury got 45 days. Nordmark told reporters he wasn't really angry with the accusers. "Kids are kids. They do bonehead things." What upset him most was that the police didn't perform a thorough investigation at the beginning. All they had to do, he said, was interview the girls individually and the truth would have come out. But they interviewed them as a group, and Nordmark ended up spending eight months in jail for a crime he didn't commit.

*   *   *

COP-BOT

The city of Perm, Russia, spent a fortune on a crime-fighting robot designed to patrol streets and beam video to police stations, alerting officers to crimes in progress. After just three hours on the job, the six-foot-tall, egg-shaped robot broke down. Reason: It was raining, which shorted out the robot's electrical system.

Ew! The 3-acre University of Tennessee Body Farm has about 40 corpses decomposing at a time.

THE NIGERIAN SCAM

When Uncle John checked his e-mail this morning, he found one from someone claiming to need help moving millions of dollars out of their country. Sound familiar? Here's some background info on one of the most popular Internet scams of all time.

YOU'VE GOT MAIL

To: TRUSTWORTHY AMERICAN
From: MIRIAM_ABACHA@NIGERIA.GOV
Subject: URGENT BUSINESS PROPOSAL

DEAR SIR, SINCE MY HUSBAND THE FORMER PRESIDENT DIED THE NIGERIAN GOVERNMENT HAS FROZEN OUR FAMILY BANK ACCOUNT IN SWITZERLAND (US$22,000,000).

PLEASE HELP US TRANSFER THIS MONEY INTO YOUR COUNTRY. IF YOU ALLOW US TO DEPOSIT THE FUNDS IN YOUR BANK ACCOUNT TEMPORARILY, WE WILL GIVE YOU 20%, OR $4,400,000.

THIS TRANSACTION IS 100% SAFE. THIS MATTER IS STRICTLY CONFIDENTIAL. THANK YOU.

MRS. MIRIAM ABACHA

If you're online, there's a very good chance that an e-mail similar to this one may be sitting in your in-box right now. Requests for help moving large sums of money out of third world countries are believed to be the second-most common type of spam (after sales pitches for male virility drugs). And as you've probably already guessed, the offer *is* too good to be true—it's a classic scam.

OUT OF AFRICA

Cons like these are called "Nigerian scams," because when they first started circulating in the 1970s, many came from the west African nation of Nigeria. They're also known as "419 scams," after the section of the Nigerian criminal code that deals with e-mail crime. Today they can originate from any number of countries. Since the fall of Saddam Hussein, they've even come from people claiming to have connections to the former dictator or his dead sons, Uday and Qusay. But Nigeria is still considered to be the capital of these scams, so the nickname has stuck.

THE BASIC SCAM

• Collecting $4.4 million for doing almost nothing is a pretty attractive come-on and, for many, too powerful to resist. If you do reply, the scammer will promise the money again—but this time, he'll also ask you to send a small sum up front, $1,000 or more, to help in transferring the funds out of Nigeria and into your bank account. Maybe they'll claim they need it to bribe an official, or to pay a fee or tax that's holding up the millions that will soon be yours. But sending $1,000 or even $5,000 to secure a payoff of $4.4 million seems like a bargain, doesn't it?

• What happens if you wire the $1,000 to Nigeria? One thing is certain: You won't get $4.4 million. The scammer will invent new obstacles to explain why the money is being held up and will ask you for more money to clear up the red tape. No matter how many times you send more money, some new problem will always arise, requiring still more money to help sort it out.

ADVANCED SCAMS

Bank Account Clean Out: Why settle for stealing your money in installments? The e-mailer may ask you for your bank account number(s), as well as your business cards and blank sheets of letterhead. If you send them the numbers and the materials, they'll use them to empty all your bank accounts in one fell swoop.

The Travel Plan: Some scammers even invite victims to travel to Nigeria, where they pose as bank or government officials, meeting in borrowed offices in a bank or government building. While there, you'll be asked for even more money. If you don't have it, or refuse to hand it over, you can be beaten, held for ransom, or even killed. The U.S. State Department estimates that at least 15 people have been murdered after being lured to Nigeria as part of a 419 scam.

Foreign Lottery: Have you ever received an e-mail telling you that you've won millions in a foreign lottery? Or that you've inherited a fortune from a relative you've never heard of? Any time you're promised a fortune but are asked to pay money up front, it's a version of a 419 scam.

Infamous stagecoach robber "Black Bart" was actually Charles Bolton, a shy, quiet bank clerk.

eBay Car Purchase: There's even a version of the scam that targets people selling cars on eBay. The scammer will buy your car and ask you to ship it to Nigeria, but will explain that a friend in the United States who owes them money will pay for it. If the car sells for $5,000, the friend will send you a cashier's check for $10,000—the amount they supposedly owe to the buyer—and arrange for you to wire the difference to the buyer. By the time the issuing bank notifies you that the cashier's check is a fake, you've already sent your $5,000 (and perhaps even your car) to Nigeria.

HISTORY

The Nigerian scam started in the 1970s. In those days, scammers sent airmail letters to names and addresses pulled out of old phone books and business directories. Sending letters was expensive, so the scammers usually targeted businesses instead of individuals, since businesses were likely to have more money.

And the volume of mail sent was miniscule by today's electronic standards: At the peak of the snail mail phase in the early 1980s, it's estimated that 250,000 Nigerian scam letters were sent to the United States every year. When fax machines caught on, the scam became cheaper than ever. But what really revolutionized it was, of course, the Internet. Who needs stamps or long-distance fax charges? Computers made it possible to send thousands or even millions of scam e-mails with a single keystroke. Costs dropped so low that scammers could afford to target individuals instead of businesses, and they set their sights on pulling lots of little scams instead of a few big ones.

A lot of people have gotten rich off the scams, and in addition to buying mansions and luxury cars, many of Nigeria's newest millionaires invested their ill-gotten gains in Internet cafés—from which even more Nigerian scam e-mails could be sent.

SCAM FACTS

• No one knows for sure just how much money Nigerian scammers fleece from their victims each year because many victims are too embarrassed to come forward. The U.S. Secret Service estimates that Americans lose as much as $100 million a year.

• For years the Nigerian government ignored the problem, but now they're taking steps to fight it—taking out ads in major American newspapers, allowing the U.S. Secret Service to open offices in Nigeria, and even warning westerners as they arrive at Murtala Mohammed International Airport in Lagos. But nothing seems to stem the flow of victims.

BIG FISH

The National Consumers League calculates that the average loss to 419 scams in 2001 was $5,957. Have *you* been conned? Take heart—some of the largest losses have been racked up by people working in law, banking, or finance—people who should have known better. Take these folks, for example:

Graeme Kenneth Rutherford. Rutherford, a star money manager and former Citibank executive in New Zealand, was taken in by scammers who told him they wanted to pay him $300,000 a year to manage $30 million for a Nigerian oil company…but first he had to help them transfer the money out of Nigeria. Rutherford poured $600,000 of his own money into the scam, borrowed more from his father, then talked wealthy friends and business associates out of $7 million more, telling them he was investing their money in safe European investments with "locked-in profits" of at least 70%. He sank every penny into the scam and lost it all.

In July 2000, Rutherford was convicted on 23 counts of forgery and fraud and sentenced to six and a half years in prison. He blames his poor judgment on painkillers he was taking for his sore back. "My resolve was hardened by my absolute conviction that the Nigerian scheme was genuine," he says.

Nelson Sakaguchi. Sakaguchi, a Brazilian, was a director of the Banco Noereste Brazil in the mid-1990s, when scammers claiming to control the Central Bank of Nigeria "awarded" him a million-dollar contract to finance the construction of a new international airport in Nigeria. The airport didn't exist, of course, but that didn't stop Sakaguchi from transferring $250 million of the bank's money to Africa without notifying any of his superiors, making this by far the largest 419 scam to come to light so far.

Why'd he do it? The scammers promised Sakaguchi that they'd give him a $40 million kickback as his share of the deal, which, of course, he never got. Banco Noroeste collapsed in 2001. As of April 2004, Sakaguchi was jailed in Switzerland awaiting trial on embezzlement and bank fraud.

What famous American prison was named for a bird? Alcatraz. It's Spanish for "pelican."

KILLER QUOTES

Here's a glimpse into the minds of serial killers. Be warned: These are as disturbing as they are fascinating. (Number of murders in parentheses.)

"The fantasy that accompanies and generates the anticipation that precedes the crime is always more stimulating than the immediate aftermath of the crime itself."

—Ted Bundy (36+)

"There's been 11 hardback books on me, 31 paperbacks, 2 screenplays, 1 movie, 1 off-Broadway play, 5 songs, and over 5,000 articles. What can I say about it? I have no ego for any of this garbage."

—John Wayne Gacy (33)

"I have noticed that the people who try hardest to impose moral code on others are often the least careful to abide by that moral code themselves."

—Ted Kaczynski (3)

"Have you ever seen the coyote in the desert? Watching, tuned in, completely aware, he hears every sound, smells every smell, sees everything that moves. He's in a state of total paranoia, and total paranoia is total awareness."

—Charles Manson (9)

"If you shoot someone in the head with a .45 every time, it becomes like your fingerprint, see? But if you strangle one, stab another, and one you cut up, and one you don't, then the police don't know what to do. They think you're four different people. What they really want, what makes their job so much easier, is pattern. What they call a *modus operandi*. That's Latin."

—Henry Lee Lucas (convicted of 3, confessed to 3,000)

"We've all got the power in our hands to kill, but most people are afraid to use it. The ones who aren't afraid control life itself."

—Richard Ramirez, the Night Stalker (16+)

"They were sinners. I was doing God's work."

—Eddie Seda, New York City's Zodiac Killer (3)

"If I knew the true, real reasons why all this started, before it ever did, I wouldn't probably have done any of it."

—Jeffrey Dahmer (7)

Estimate: About 90% of the Tiffany & Co. products listed on eBay are counterfeit.

INSTANT JUSTICE

*Sometimes crooks get a dose of instant karma—
and sometimes that's just funny.*

CRIME: In September 2003, two men attempted to break into a bank in Kansas City.
INSTANT JUSTICE: Cops in a police cruiser saw the two thieves running down a street with crowbars in their hands and chased them into a grassy field. When they lost sight of the fleeing suspects, the officers stopped and got out of the car—and then heard moans. It turned out that one of the robbers was hiding in the tall grass and the cops drove over him. The lucky thief suffered only a scrape on his forehead.

CRIME: Wanton Beckwith, 27, stole a car in Monrovia, California, in May 2003. After a high-speed chase by police, he exited the car and ran into a house to hide.
INSTANT JUSTICE: Somebody was home—and that somebody had a samurai sword. He pointed it at the intruder's face, led him back outside and held him—at swords length—until police arrived.

CRIME: In September 2003, 18-year-old Michael Watt walked into a health food store in Uttoxeter, England, pulled out a knife, and demanded money.
INSTANT JUSTICE: The sole employee, 48-year-old Lorraine Avery, refused. "I thought, 'He's not having our money, I've worked hard for it.'" She looked for something to hit the thief with but couldn't find anything. So she grabbed an industrial-sized bottle of salad dressing, pointed it at him, and told him to get out of the store. Watt wouldn't go—so she started squirting him with the dressing. "He kept coming at me with the knife," Avery told reporters, "and I kept squirting him." It worked! The would-be robber left the store, and police were able to track him down… by following the trail of salad dressing.

CRIME: In January 2004, an unknown man grabbed a bag out of a car stopped at a stoplight in Sydney, Australia.
INSTANT JUSTICE: The car belonged to Bradley McDonald, a local

snake catcher. In the bag was the snake he had just caught—a four-foot-long, venomous, red-bellied black snake. "It might teach him a lesson," McDonald said.

CRIME: Roy A. Gendron, 45, broke into a home in rural Alabama.

INSTANT JUSTICE: The homeowner's son, Richard Bussey, caught Gendron loading furniture and other items onto his truck. Bussey had a gun in his car, so he pulled it on Gendron. But he didn't have a telephone and didn't know what to do next, so he made the burglar mow the lawn—with a push mower—while he thought about it. He eventually took Gendron's driver's license, which the police used to track down and arrest the thief a short time later. Assistant D.A. Brian McVeigh told reporters that if he ever found himself in a similar situation, "I'll try to get some yard work out of the guy."

CRIME: An inmate at the county jail in St. Charles, Missouri, attempted to escape.

INSTANT JUSTICE: The escapee ran into the prison's darkened parking garage and headed for an open door marked "Fire Exit." Sensing that freedom was about to be his, he turned around, gave the approaching deputies a salute, and dashed through the door…running smack into the brick wall behind it. Deputies took the unconscious man to a nearby hospital.

CRIME: In July 1996, 37-year-old Willie King snatched a wallet from the coat of an old woman on a street in Greenwich Village, New York City.

INSTANT JUSTICE: The woman was 94-year-old Yolanda Gigante. Who's that? The mother of Vincent "The Chin" Gigante, reputed head of the Genovese crime family, one of the country's most powerful criminal organizations. King was caught a short time later, and as soon as he realized who he'd mugged he agreed to plead guilty to grand larceny. Sentence: 1½ to 3 years in prison. "My client admitted his guilt at the earliest opportunity, because he wants to put this incident behind him," King's lawyer told the judge. "He hopes the Gigante family will, too."

*   *   *

"Make crime pay. Become a lawyer."   **—Will Rogers**

Most common crime in America: Shoplifting. Two million people are arrested for it every year.

THE MAD BOMBER, PART II

*When we left the case of the Mad Bomber (page 176), Dr. James
Brussel, the original "profiler," had just released his theories to
the press, setting the game afoot. Here's how it played out.*

FOUND OUT

The Mad Bomber's response to his case being made public: he took his terror a step further. The bombs kept coming and the letters got more brazen. "F. P." even called Brussel on the telephone and told him to lay off or he would "be sorry." Brussel had him exactly where he wanted him.

The final clue came when police received a letter revealing the date that began the Mad Bomber's misery: September 5, 1931—almost 10 years before the first bomb was found. Brussel immediately ordered a search of Con Ed's personnel files from that era. An office assistant named Alice Kelly found a neatly written letter from a former employee named George Metesky who had promised that Con Edison would pay for their "DASTARDLY DEEDS."

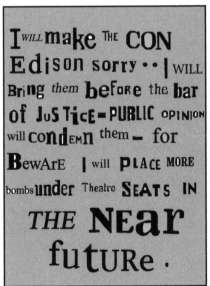

I WILL make THE CON Edison sorry ·· I WILL Bring them beFoRe the bar of JuSTicE=PUBLIC OPINION will conDEMn them — for BewArE I will PLACE MORE bombs under Theatre SEATS IN THE NEar futURe.

The police traced Metesky to what neighborhood children called the "crazy house" on Fourth Street in Waterbury, Connecticut, just beyond Westchester County, New York. When they arrived, George Metesky was wearing…pajamas. He greeted them warmly and freely admitted to being the Mad Bomber. He even showed them his bomb-making workshop in the garage.

Bruce Springsteen got busted trying to climb over the gates of Graceland in 1976.

They told him to get dressed for his trip to the station. He returned wearing…a double-breasted suit, buttoned.

DEDUCTIVE REASONING

So how was Dr. Brussel able to provide such an accurate description?

• It was pretty evident that the Mad Bomber was a man. In those days, very few women would have had the knowledge necessary to make bombs. Bomb-making is, moreover, a classic behavior of paranoid males.

• Because 85% of known paranoids had stocky, muscular builds, Brussel added it to the profile. Metesky had a stocky, muscular build.

• Male paranoiacs have difficulty relating to other people, especially women, and usually live with an older, matriarchal-type woman who will "mother" them. Metesky lived with his two older sisters.

• Another clue to Metesky's sexual inadequacy, Brussel claimed, was his lettering. His script was perfect except for the "W"s—instead of connecting "V"s that would have been consistent with the rest of the letters, Metesky connected two "U"s, which Brussel saw as representing women's breasts.

• Brussel concluded that Metesky was between 40 and 50 years old because paranoia takes years to develop, and based on when the first bomb was found, Metesky had to have already been well down the road. Brussel was close—Metesky was 54.

• What led Brussel to believe that Metesky did not live in New York City was his use of the term "Con Edison"—New Yorkers call it "Con Ed."

• Metesky's language identified him as middle European, too. His use of "dastardly deeds," as well as some other phrases, was a sign of someone with Slavic roots. There was a high concentration of Poles in southern Connecticut, and Brussel connected the dots.

• Paranoids believe that the world conspires against them, so Brussel knew that something traumatic must have happened to Metesky. He was right. On September 5, 1931, Metesky was injured in a boiler explosion at a Con Ed plant. He complained of headaches, but doctors could find no sign of injury. After a year of sick pay and medical benefits, Metesky was fired. A failed lawsuit sent him over the edge, and he began plotting his revenge.

• Brussel also predicted that the Bomber would have a debilitating heart disease. He was close: Metesky suffered from a tubercular lung.

• How did Brussel know what kind of suit Metesky would be wearing when he was arrested? Simple: Paranoids are neat freaks, as was apparent in his letters and bombs. He would wear nothing less than the most impeccable outfit of the day—a double-breasted suit, buttoned.

AFTERMATH

George Metesky proudly explained everything to the police. In all, he had planted more than 30 bombs, but miraculously, no one was killed. Metesky said that that was never his intention. "F. P.", he explained, stood for "Fair Play."

On April 18, 1957, George Metesky was found mentally unfit to stand trial and was committed to the Matteawan Hospital for the Criminally Insane. In 1973 he was deemed cured and was released. Metesky lived out the remainder of his days in his Waterbury home, where he died in 1994 at the age of 90. Dr. Brussel gained celebrity status for his role in the case; today he's considered the father of modern psychological profiling in criminal investigations.

TRAGIC LEGACY

Although Metesky's bombs never killed anybody, it was more because of strange luck than "Fair Play." (Police called it a "miracle" that his theater bombs—planted inside the seats—never took any lives.) Even worse, Metesky may have helped pave the way for others who were more successful in their terrible exploits. According to investigators, both the "Zodiac Killer," who killed at least six people—some with bombs—in the San Francisco area in the 1970s, and Ted "Unabomber" Kaczynski, who killed three people in the 1980s and 1990s with package bombs, were inspired by George Metesky, New York City's Mad Bomber.

*   *   *

"One thing I can't understand is why the newspapers labeled me the Mad Bomber. That was unkind."
—**George Metesky**

In the early 1800s, the Texas Rangers were paid $1.25 per day for their services.

GOING OFF TRACK

On page 207, we told you about Britain's Great Train Robbery of 1963, one of the largest hauls ever taken from a railroad—but it certainly wasn't the only one. Here are five more notable train hiests…some greater than others.

1. THERE'S GOLD IN THAT THAR TRAIN!

When you think of train robberies, you probably think of the Old West. But the most lucrative train robbery of the 19th century took place in England, and it didn't involve horses or blazing six-guns. Instead, the robbery was the culmination of great planning and execution. Edward Agar and William Pierce masterminded the plot, recruiting a couple of railroad employees and others as needed. They knew that, on May 15, 1855, three boxes of gold would be traveling by train across England. For the robbery, they boarded the train and, with keys made from wax impressions, were able to open the railroad safes, remove 200 pounds of gold from sealed boxes, fill the boxes with lead shot as a decoy and seal them up again, and then saunter off the train at the Dover station, making their escape. For a year they remained uncaught and may have gotten away with the crime, except for one problem: Agar had been arrested for writing bad checks and sentenced to serve time in an Australian penal colony. He instructed Pierce to pay the mother of his child £7,000 (almost $750,000 in today's dollars); when she didn't get the money, the woman went to the railroad managers and told them what she knew about the robbery. Agar corroborated her story and turned state's evidence, resulting in long sentences for his co-conspirators. Authorities were able to recover only £2,000 worth of gold. The rest is still missing.

2. JESSE JAMES: THE FIRST ROBBERY

As Confederate guerrillas, brothers Frank and Jesse James engaged in looting, killing Union soldiers and civilians, and destroying property during the Civil War. After the war ended, they formed a gang and turned to bank robbery, sometimes killing bystanders in the process. (In letters sent to sympathetic newspaper editors, they claimed that they were avenging the South's defeat.) In 1873 the gang turned to robbing trains, and their first heist took place near Adair, Iowa. Wearing Ku Klux Klan costumes, they derailed a train, which killed the engineer, and then they terrorized

---

According to a study by Visa, most identity thefts are perpetrated by someone the victim knows.

the dazed and wounded passengers into giving up their valuables. Between that and the train's safe, the gang netted $2,337, which was more than enough to inspire them to try again. Despite cultivating an image as modern-day Robin Hoods, the James brothers kept most of their ill-gotten gains for themselves.

3. WANT A LITTLE MONEY WITH YOUR DYNAMITE?

Butch Cassidy and the Sundance Kid have been a part of American folk-lore for more than a century. The first movie to tell of their exploits was released in 1903, but it was the 1969 movie starring Robert Redford and Paul Newman that immortalized the pair. The real Butch (Robert Leroy Parker) and Sundance (Harry Longabaugh) headed a gang called the Wild Bunch, who robbed banks and trains mostly in Wyoming. They started out in 1896 as small-time hoods, often wearing cloth napkins pilfered from local restaurants. When they discovered the magic of dynamite, they began to use it with increasing regularity to open safes, create shock and awe among train crews, derail trains, and destroy cars and engines. On June 2, 1899, they got a little too explosion-happy after commandeering a Union Pacific train. When mail clerks refused to open the door, the gang blew it open, leaving the clerks too deafened and dazed to remember the combination to the train's safe. So the impatient gang decided to blow open the safe. Unfortunately, they also blew up the walls and ceiling of the train car, launching $20,000 skyward and damaging many of the remaining bills in the $30,000 that they escaped with.

4. AN ACTUAL *TRAIN* ROBBERY

On April 12, 1862, conductor William Fuller and his crew had just sat down for breakfast at a stop called Big Shanty outside Atlanta, Georgia, when he saw his train rolling out of the station. Fuller couldn't send a telegram ahead to stop the train—the little outpost didn't have a telegraph station. It wouldn't have mattered anyway. The thieves were 22 Union army spies led by James Andrews, a Kentucky smuggler who also did espionage work for the North. The men, posing as passengers, had boarded the train in small groups. Their mission was to cut telegraph wires, dynamite bridges, and sabotage tracks to keep the Confederate army from sending reinforcements and supplies as the Union army marched toward Chattanooga, Tennessee.

For more than 80 miles, Andrews and his men did what they could to throw off the chase, but Fuller and his crew switched trains to get around obstacles and followed on foot. Near the end, they barreled along the tracks full speed in a train going in reverse. Andrews and his men ran out of fuel a few miles from Chattanooga, and they scattered into the woods, hoping for escape. Eventually, they were all caught (as were two conspirators who missed the train because they'd overslept). Andrews and seven others were hanged and buried in an unmarked grave, six were traded to the North as prisoners of war, and eight escaped from their prison camp to safety. Secretary of War Edwin M. Stanton awarded Medals of Honor to six of Andrews's men—some of the first such medals ever given out in U.S. history.

5. BEZDANY RAID

"I haven't got money and I must have it for the ends I pursue." So wrote Józef Piłsudski in a letter to a friend on September 26, 1908…right before his team of Polish revolutionaries embarked on a daring train robbery. Their target? A mail train carrying tax money from Warsaw to St. Petersburg, Russia. (Russia, Prussia, and Austria had conquered and divided up Poland in the late 1700s, and Piłsudski was leading a charge to free his people.) That evening, the 16 men and four women boarded the train in two waves. Then at the tiny station in Bezdany, Lithuania, they sprang into action—one group captured the station and cut telecommunications wires; the other assaulted the train with guns and bombs. Using dynamite, they ripped open the fortified mail car and stuffed the money into cloth bags. Then they escaped in different directions and all got away. The haul was a spectacular 200,812 rubles, more than $4 million in today's dollars—a fortune in impoverished Eastern Europe. It kept Piłsudski's paramilitary organization in good stead for many years. In 1918 Poland became one country again, and Piłsudski was its first leader.

*   *   *

MYTH-CONCEPTION

Myth: If you get arrested, you're entitled to make one phone call.

Fact: There's no law anywhere that guarantees this. It's just a courtesy or privilege offered, not a legal right. (Some jurisdictions might even let you make a second phone call.)

Only woman to rob a stagecoach and survive: Pearl Hart, in 1899.

THERE OUGHTA BE A LAW

The syndicated TV show Celebrity Justice *asked a slew of celebrities to finish this sentence: There oughta be a law…*

"…against people who scrape their silverware on plates. I hate that."
—**Rebecca Romijn**

"…against people who get into the '10 items or less' line with more than 10 items and use a credit card where it says 'cash only.'"
—**Samuel L. Jackson**

"…against people who make jokes that aren't jokes. Like when you say, 'Is today Tuesday?' And somebody says, 'All day!' That's not a joke. Not funny. Don't say it."
—**Hank Azaria**

"…that if you are a good driver, and you have a reasonable IQ, you should be able to drive any speed you want."
—**Jenna Elfman**

"…against honking your horn unless it's absolutely necessary. Otherwise you're going to drive everybody crazy, the stress level will come up, people will be fighting in the streets. Don't honk your horn!"
—**Dick Clark**

"…against people coming into a meeting, in close quarters, with bad breath."
—**Coolio**

"…against people that when they give you your change at the cash register, that they put the dollar down first, and then the change."
—**Elizabeth Perkins**

"…that if a guy gets dumped by a woman on national TV, he should get half of everything she owns. I mean that's how it works in the real world."
—**Charlie, *The Bachelorette***

"…and a serious fine for people who don't pick up their dog turd, and I want them to be thrown in jail."
—**Marg Helgenberger, CSI**

"…that the whole world sort of adopts Spain's timetable, where you sort of take the whole day off to relax and have fun."
—**David Arquette**

"…that people smile at at least three people every day."
—**Orlando Bloom**

Arrrgh! More than 70% of the world's pirated goods come from China.

IT'S A WEIRD, WEIRD CRIME

As we near the end of this True Crime collection, Uncle John wanted to make sure we included these folks—some of the oddest lawbreakers of all-time. (Read it or he'll steal your hairpiece.)

TO TELL THE TOOTH

"A toothless man has been arrested for stealing toothbrushes. According to *O Dia* newspaper, 32-year-old Ednor Rodrigues was filmed taking seven toothbrushes from a supermarket in Ribeirao Preto, Brazil. When he was approached by the police, he tried to deny the robbery—even showing the officers his toothless mouth. He finally admitted to the crime: 'I don't know why I did it. I know it was stupid. I have no teeth, what was I thinking?'"

—**Sunday Mail** [Scotland]

SCALPED

"Paul J. Goudy, of Lemoyne, Pennsylvania, was sentenced to 23 months probation after pleading guilty to theft by unlawfully taking a man's hairpiece. Last January, Edward Floyd was sitting at a Harrisburg restaurant when Goudy ripped the hairpiece off Floyd. Restaurant witnesses identified Goudy and when questioned by police he admitted that he'd done it on a dare—a friend had offered him $100 to steal the hairpiece. Dauphin County Judge Richard A. Lewis also fined Goudy $500 and ordered him to write a letter of apology to Floyd."

—**United Press International**

COMPUTERCIDE

"George Doughty of Lafayette, Colorado, won't have any more problems with his computer. He was accused of shooting his Dell laptop four times with a Smith & Wesson revolver in the middle of his Sportsman's Inn Bar and Restaurant. He then allegedly hung the remains of the laptop on the wall 'like a hunting trophy,' said Lt. Rick Bashor of the Lafayette Police Department.

Real Headline: SHOOTING REPORTED AT FIRING RANGE

"Doughty, 48, who owns the establishment, entered the bar from his office and told the two patrons and bartender that he was going to shoot his computer. He then set his laptop on the floor, warned the customers to cover their ears and fired away. Doughty never explained what prompted his actions, but told police that 'it seemed like the right thing to do at the time.'"

—Court TV

KEEP YOUR EYES ON THE PRIZE, NOT THE PIES

"A 280-lb. thief broke into a Romanian bakery and stole $250, but couldn't resist the sweet temptation. He got stuck trying to exit through a window—after stuffing himself full of pies. The 29-year-old man was still stuck there in the morning when the shop owner, Vasile Mandache, arrived for work. He said, 'I saw all the pie wrappers on the floor, and then saw a pair of stubby, fat legs hanging out the window. I just had to call my friends to come and have a look before we called the police, it was so funny.'"

—Short News

A PIG'S RANSOM

"'Raw fruit and vegetables—or else the pigs get it!' That's what a Gallatin, Tennessee, woman read in a ransom note after a pair of concrete swine were swiped from her front yard. The foot-tall plaster porkers, one dressed in farmer's overalls and the other in a pink dress, vanished from in front of Mary Romines' trailer. Other pieces of statuary, including concrete chickens and a few other pigs, were disturbed, but not taken. Tacked to the front gate was a note with a specific demand: two ears of corn and one ripe mango.

"Two days after the piggies, worth about $10 each, flew the coop, Romines got another menacing message—a well-done pork chop attached to a note reading, 'Cooked the Pig.' The next night, another note raised the demands—a potato in addition to the corn and mango. Signed 'The Big Bad Wolf' and accompanied by a bag of pork rinds, the note asked Romines if she was scared. 'They think they have me buffaloed, but now I'm mad,' Romines said. 'They may think it's funny, but they're going to be charged with theft.' Police agreed that the perpetrator will be criminally charged. The case remains under investigation."

—Fox News

TALK TO THE SWORD

On page 34, we told you a bit about the hit of notorious New York mobster Dutch Schultz. But his story didn't end with a bullet. Here's the grisly story of his bizarre last words.

BACKGROUND

On October 23, 1935, 33-year-old Dutch Schultz (real name: Arthur Flegenheimer) was dining at the Palace Chophouse, a restaurant in Newark, New Jersey, that also served as a mob hideout. Schultz was in the bathroom when three Murder, Inc. hit men working for a rival gang burst in—"Charlie the Bug" Workman, Emanuel Weiss, and a third man known only as "Piggy." They went into the back room and shot Schultz's associates Otto Berman, Abe Landau, and Lulu Rosenkrantz. Schultz heard the shots but couldn't stop urinating fast enough to flee.

While he was still peeing, the hit men came into the bathroom. Schultz turned around and they shot him in the stomach. The bullet pierced his liver, colon, and gall bladder, and exited out his back.

Not wanting to be found dead with his pants unzipped in a men's room, Schultz stumbled into the restaurant; Rosenkrantz, still alive, called an ambulance from a phone booth and then collapsed. The police arrived first and loaded Schultz up on brandy to numb the pain. It didn't work. When they finally got to the hospital, Newark police sergeant Luke Conlon interrogated Schultz. In a state of physical agony, high fever, drunkenness, and morphine-induced euphoria, Schultz babbled on for nearly two hours. What follows is an actual transcript of Schultz's talkfest.

LAST WORDS

Schultz: George, don't make no bull moves. What have you done with him? Oh, mama, mama, mama. Oh stop it, stop it; eh, oh, oh. Sure, sure, mama? Has it been in any other newspapers? Now listen, Phil, fun is fun. Aha…please! Papa! What happened to the sixteen? Oh, oh, he done it? Please…please…John, please. Oh, did you buy the hotel? You promised a million sure. Get out. I wish I knew. Please make it quick, fast, and furious. Please. Fast and furious. Please help me get out; I'm getting my wind back, thank God. Please, please, oh please. You will have to please tell him, you got no case? You get ahead with the dot dash system. Didn't I speak that time last night. Whose number is that in your pocketbook, Phil? 13780. Who was

---

Number of shopping carts stolen from Los Angeles stores in 2005: 6.2 million.

it? Oh, please, please. Reserve decision. Police, police, Henny and Frankie. Oh, oh, dog biscuit and when he is happy he doesn't get snappy please, please do this. Henny, Henny, Frankie! You didn't meet him; you didn't even meet me. The glove will fit what I say oh, kayiyi, kayiyi. Sure, who cares? When are you through! How do you know this? How do you know this? Well, then, oh, Cocoa; no...thinks he is a grandpa again and he is jumping around. No Hoboe and Poboe I think mean the same thing.

Conlon: Who shot you?

Schultz: The boss himself.

Conlon: He did?

Schultz: Yes, I don't know.

Conlon: What did he shoot you for?

Schultz: I showed him, boss; did you hear him meet me? An appointment. Appeal stuck. All right, mother.

Conlon: Was it the boss shot you?

Schultz: Who shot me? No one.

Conlon: We will help you.

Schultz: Will you help me up? Okay, I won't be such a big creep. Oh, mama. I can't go through with it, please. Oh, and then he clips me; come on. Cut that out, we don't owe a nickel; fold it; instead, fold it against him; I am a pretty good pretzeler. Winifred—Department of Justice. I even got it from the department. Sir, please stop it. Say listen, the last night.

Conlon: What did they shoot you for?

Schultz: I don't know, sir. Honestly I don't. I don't even know who was with me, honestly. I went to the toilet and when I reached the...the the boy came at me.

Conlon: The big fellow gave it to you?

Schultz: Yes, he gave it to me.

Conlon: Do you know who the big fellow was?

Schultz: No. See, George, if we wanted to break the ring. No, please I get a month. They did it. Come on. *(Unintelligible)* cut me off and says you are not to be the beneficiary of this will. I will be checked and double-checked and please pull for me. Will you pull? How many good ones and how many bad ones? Please! I had nothing with him. He was a cowboy in one of the seven days a week fight. No business; no hangout; no friends; nothing; just what you pick up and what you need. I don't know who shot me. Don't put anyone near this check—you might have—oh, please, please do it for me. Let me get up, sir, heh? In the olden days they waited and they

When New York's Sing Sing prison opened in 1826, it imposed...

waited. Please give me a shot. It is from the factory. Sure, that is a bad. Well, oh good ahead that happens for crying. I don't want harmony. I want harmony. Oh, mama, mama! Who give it to him? Who give it to him? Let me in the district-fire-factory that he was nowhere near. It smoldered. No, no. There are only ten of us and there are ten million fighting somewhere in front of you, so get your onions up and we will throw up the truce flag. Oh, please let me up. Please shift me. Police are here. Communistic...strike... baloney. Please, honestly this is a habit I get; sometimes I give it and sometimes I don't. Oh, I am all in. That settles it. Are you sure? Please let me get in and eat. Let him harass himself to you and then bother you. Please don't ask me to go there. I still don't want to. I still don't want him in the path. It is no need to stage a riot. The sidewalk was in trouble and the bears were in trouble and I broke it up. Please put me in that room. Please keep him in control. My gilt-edged stuff and those dirty rats have tuned in. Please mother, don't tear, don't rip; that is something that shouldn't be spoken about. Please get me up, my friends. Please, look out. The shooting is a bit wild, and that kind of shooting saved a man's life. No pay-rolls. No walls. No coupons. That would be entirely out. Pardon me, I forgot I am a plaintiff and not defendant. Look out. Look out for him. Please. He owes me money; he owes everyone money. Why can't he just pull out and give me control? Please, mother, you pick me up now. Please, you know me. No. Don't you scare me. My friends think I do a better job. Police are looking for you all over. Be instrumental in letting us know. They are Englishmen and they are a type I don't know who is best, they or us. Oh, sir, get the doll a roofing. You can play jacks and girls do that with a softball and do tricks with it. I may take all events into consideration. No. No. And it is no. It is confused and its says no. A boy has never wept nor dashed a thousand kin. Did you hear me?

Conlon: Who shot you?

Schultz: I don't know.

Conlon: How many shots were fired?

Schultz: I don't know. None.

Conlon: How many?

Schultz: Two thousand. Come on, get some money in that treasury. We need it. Come on, please get it. I can't tell you to. That is not what you have in the book. Oh, please warden. What am I going to do for money? Please put me up on my feet at once. You are a hard-boiled man. Did you hear me? I would hear it, the Circuit Court would hear it, and the Supreme Court might hear it. If that ain't the payoff. Please crack down on the Chinaman's friends and Hitler's commander. I am sore and I am going to give you honey if I can. Mother is the best bet and don't let Satan draw you too fast.

...absolute silence on the prisoners, enforced by whipping.

Conlon: What did the big fellow shoot you for?

Schultz: Him? John? Over a million, five million dollars.

Conlon: John shot you, we will take care of John.

Schultz: That is what caused the trouble. Look out. Please get me up. If you do this, you can go on and jump right here in the lake. I know who they are. They are French people. All right. Look out, look out. Oh, my memory is gone. A work relief police. Who gets it? I don't know and I don't want to know, but look out. It can be traced. He changed for the worse. Please look out; my fortunes have changed and come back and went back since that. It was desperate. I am wobbly. You ain't got nothing on him but we got it on his helper.

Conlon: Control yourself.

Schultz: But I am dying.

Conlon: No, you are not.

Schultz: Move on, Mick and mama. All right, dear, you have got to get it.

(Schultz's wife, Francis, arrives.)

Mrs. Schultz: This is Francis.

Schultz: Then pull me out. I am half crazy. They won't let me get up. They dyed my shoes. Open those shoes. Give me something. I am so sick. Give me some water, the only thing that I want. Open this up and break it so I can touch you. Dennie, please get me in the car.

Conlon: Who shot you?

Schultz: I don't know. I didn't even get a look. I don't know who can have done it. Anybody. Kindly take my shoes off. *(They're already off.)* No. There is a handcuff on them. The Baron does these things. I know what I am doing here with my collection of papers. It isn't worth a nickel to two guys like you or me but to a collector it is worth a fortune. It is priceless. I am going to turn it over to—turn you back to me, please Henry. I am so sick now. The police are getting many complaints. Look out. I want that G-note. Look out for Jimmy Valentine for he is an old pal of mine. Come on, Jim, come on. Okay, okay, I am all through. Can't do another thing. Look out mama, look out for her. You can't beat him. Police, mama, Helen, mother, please take me out. I will settle the indictment. Come on, open the soap duckets. The chimney sweeps. Talk to the sword. Shut up, you got a big mouth! Please come help me up, Henry. Max, come over here. French-Canadian bean soup. I want to pay. Let them leave me alone.

Schultz died two hours later, without saying another word.

In Malaysia, drunk drivers are jailed...and so are their spouses.

HEY, I RECOGNIZE THAT BUTT CRACK!

Well, I do. What do you want me to say?

In November 1997, Minneapolis native Tom Tipton, 63, got the thrill of his life when he was invited to sing the national anthem before a Minnesota Vikings football game. Across town, an off-duty sheriff was watching the pregame show—and recognized Tipton's name. Tipton, it turned out, was wanted on two warrants in Minneapolis. He was arrested during the game.

• In 2006 a man in Mill Valley, California, was arrested after he called a bomb threat into a Walgreen's pharmacy. The clerk who answered the phone recognized his voice: The man had just been at the counter to get a prescription filled, and had called in the threat because he thought it was taking too long.

• In 2001 Chicago police arrested 19-year-old Marque Love on bank robbery charges. Love had once worked at the bank, and a teller recognized him—by his distinctive blue suede shoes.

• In 2006 Robert Russel Moore of Prince Frederick, Maryland, was arrested and charged with the robbery of an Arby's restaurant where he was recently employed. At the subsequent trial, four of his former fellow employees testified that, although he was wearing a mask, they recognized Moore in surveillance tapes—especially when he bent over and they recognized his "butt crack" above the top of his pants. A former manager also testified that he had talked to Moore repeatedly about his "butt crack problem." Moore was sentenced to 10 years in prison.

• In 1999 a man wearing a long dark coat and a mask walked into the Royal Casino in Aberdeen, South Dakota, pointed a gun at the clerk, and demanded money. The next day, local man Jerold Nissen, 44, was arrested for the crime. Nissen was a regular at the casino, and the clerk had recognized the distinctively powerful odor of his cologne. He was sentenced to seven years in prison.

In 2005 a Dutch court let a bank robber deduct his gun as a "legitimate business expense."

BELLE GUNNESS: THE TERROR OF LA PORTE

A dark tale from our "Dustbin of Gruesome History" files.

THE DISCOVERY

On the night of April 28, 1908, Joe Maxson, a hired hand on a farm outside of La Porte, Indiana, awoke in his upstairs bedroom to the smell of smoke. The house was on fire. He called out to the farm's owner, Belle Gunness, and her three children. Getting no answer, he jumped from a second-story window, narrowly escaping the flames, and ran for help. But it was too late; the house was destroyed. A search through the wreckage resulted in a grisly discovery: four dead bodies in the basement. Three were Gunness's children, aged 5, 9, and 11. The fourth was a woman, assumed to be Gunness herself, but identification was difficult—the body's head was missing. An investigation ensued, and Ray Lamphere, a recently fired employee, was arrested for arson and murder. Before Lamphere's trial was over, he would be little more than a sidebar in what is still one of the most most horrible crime stories in American history…and an unsolved mystery.

BACKGROUND

Belle Gunness was born Brynhild Paulsdatter Storseth in Selbu, Norway, in 1859. At the age of 22 she emigrated to America and moved in with her older sister in Chicago, where she changed her name to "Belle." In 1884 the 25-year-old married another Norwegian immigrant, Mads Sorenson, and the couple opened a candy shop. A year later the store burned down, the first of what would be several suspicious fires in Belle's life. The couple collected an insurance payout and used the money to buy a house in the Chicago suburbs. Fifteen years later, in 1898, *that* house burned down, and another insurance payment allowed the couple

---

to buy another house. On July 30, 1900, yet another insurance policy was brought into play, but this time it was life insurance: Mads Sorenson had died. A doctor's autopsy said he was murdered, probably by strychnine poisoning, so an inquest was ordered. The coroner's investigation eventually deemed the death to be "of natural causes," and Belle collected $8,000, becoming, for 1900, a wealthy woman. (The average yearly income in 1900 was less than $500.) She used part of the money to buy the farm in La Porte. But there was a lot more death—and insurance money—to come.

MORE SUSPICIONS

In April 1902, Belle married a local butcher named Peter Gunness and became Belle Gunness. One week later, Peter Gunness's infant daughter died while left alone with Belle...and yet another insurance policy was collected on. Just eight months after that, Peter Gunness was dead: He was found in his shed with his skull crushed. Belle, who was 5'8", weighed well over 200 pounds, and was known to be very strong, told the police that a meat grinder had fallen from a high shelf and landed on her husband's head. The coroner said otherwise, ruling the cause of death to be murder. On top of that, a witness claimed to have overheard Belle's 14-year-old daughter, Jennie, saying to a classmate, "My mama killed my papa. She hit him with a meat cleaver and he died."

Belle and Jennie were brought before a coroner's jury and questioned. Jennie denied making the statement; Belle denied killing her husband. The jury found Belle innocent—and she collected another $3,000 in life insurance money. And she was just getting started.

NOT WELL SUITED

Not long after Peter Gunness's death, Belle started putting ads in newspapers around the Midwest. One read:

> Comely widow who owns a large farm in one of the finest districts in La Porte County, Indiana, desires to make the acquaintance of a gentleman equally well provided, with view of joining fortunes. No replies by letter considered unless sender is willing to follow answer with personal visit. Triflers need not apply.

The ads worked, and suitors began to show up at the farm with visions of "joining fortunes" in mind. John Moo arrived from Minnesota in late

1902 with his life savings of $1,000 in hand. He stayed at the farm for about a week…and disappeared. Over the years several more met the same fate: Henry Gurholdt from Wisconsin, who had brought $1,500; Ole B. Budsburg, also from Wisconsin, who brought the deed to his property, worth thousands, and was last seen in a La Porte bank in April 1907; and Andrew Hegelein, from South Dakota, also last seen in the bank, in January 1908.

Andrew Hegelein turned out to be the last of the disappearing suitors, because a few weeks after his disappearance, his brother, A.K. Hegelein, wrote to Gunness to inquire about him. She replied that he'd gone to Norway. Hegelein didn't believe her—and threatened to come to La Porte to find out what had happened to him.

LAMPHERE

We said at the start of the story that when the Gunness home burnt to the ground, killing the three children and, presumably, Belle Gunness, former employee Ray Lamphere was arrested. The reason: Lamphere had been hired in 1907 and, by all accounts, had fallen in love with Gunness. The seemingly constant coming and going of suitors enraged him, and he and Gunness fought about it. In February 1908, around the time of Hegelein's disappearance, Gunness fired Lamphere. Not only that—she went to the local sheriff and told him that Lamphere was making threats against her. The day before the house fire, she went to a lawyer and made out a will, telling the lawyer that Lamphere had threatened to kill her and her children…and to burn her house down. Under the circumstances, the sheriff *had* to arrest Lamphere—but the focus of the investigation would soon turn elsewhere.

THE WOMAN IN THE BASEMENT

Lamphere denied any involvement with either the arson or the murders. Few people believed him…but there were serious questions about the body of Belle Gunness. Doctors who inspected the remains said they belonged to a woman about 5'3" (they had to account for the missing head, of course) who weighed about 150 pounds. Gunness was much larger than that. And several neighbors who knew Gunness well viewed the remains—and said it wasn't her. Then A. K. Hegelein showed up looking for his brother. He told the police his story and insisted that a search be

---

made of Gunness's property. The search began on May 3. Two days later, five bodies, carefully dismembered and wrapped in oilcloth, were discovered buried around the farm.

BUT WAIT! THERE'S MORE!

The first body was determined to be that of Gunness's daughter Jennie, who, according to Belle, had been in school in California since 1906. The second body was Andrew Hegelein. The third was an unidentified man; the fourth and fifth were unidentified eight-year-old girls.

Neighbors told investigators that they had often seen Gunness digging in her hog pen, so they dug up that area—and found body after body after body. Included in the group: suitors John Moo, Ole Budsburg, and Henry Gurhold. In the end the remains of more than 25 bodies (some reports say as many as 49) were found, many of them unidentifiable.

Belle Gunness had obviously lured the men to her farm and killed them for their money. People in La Porte began to believe that if she could do that, she could fake her own death, and that the body found after the fire was yet another of her victims. It was beginning to look like A. K. Hegelein's threat to come look for his brother made Gunness panic and come up with her bloody plan. But then a problem arose: On May 16 a part of a jawbone and a section of dentures were found in the ruins of the house. Gunness's dentist, Ira Norton, inspected them—and said the dental work on the teeth belonged to Belle Gunness.

THE AFTERMATH

After a long investigation the body of the woman in the fire was officially declared to be that of Belle Gunness, and was buried as such. Ray Lamphere was tried for arson and murder—but because of all the lingering questions surrounding the case, he was convicted only of arson. He received a 20-year prison sentence and died less than a year later of tuberculosis. While in prison he reportedly confessed to a prison minister that he had helped Gunness bury some of her victims— and that the woman in the basement was *not* her. Gunness had hired a woman from Chicago as a housekeeper just days before the fire, he said, and drugged her, killed her, decapitated her, dressed her in Belle's clothes, and put her in the basement. He helped Gunness start the fire, he said, and was then supposed to escape with her, but she

double-crossed him and left on her own. However, none of his story could be substantiated.

People reported seeing Belle Gunness at dozens of locations across the U.S. over the following decades. None of those sightings were ever confirmed. Then, in 1931, a woman named Esther Carlson was arrested for the poisoning murder of her husband in Los Angeles…and she reportedly looked a lot like Belle Gunness. Carlson died awaiting trial, but some La Porte residents made the trip to the Los Angeles morgue and viewed the body. They said that they believed it was Gunness.

UPDATE

In 2008 Andrea Simmons, an attorney and graduate student at the University of Indianapolis in Indiana, led a team of forensic biologists to the graveyard where Belle Gunness was buried. With permission from Gunness's descendants, they dug up the grave with the intent of extracting DNA from the corpse and comparing it to the DNA of living relatives. Results were hoped for by April 28, 2008, the 100th anniversary of the fire at the Gunness farm, but they were, unfortunately, inconclusive. Attempts are ongoing, and someday, possibly soon, the mystery of Belle Gunness, one of the most diabolical serial killers in history, might finally be solved.

*   *   *

TWO ILLEGAL WORD ORIGINS

• In 1849 a man named William Thompson would walk up to strangers in New York City and, after making friends with them, ask, "Have you confidence in me to trust me with your watch until tomorrow?" If they said yes, Thompson would gratefully borrow the watch…and then keep it. When he was caught, the prosecutors referred to him as a "confidence man." That didn't fit on headlines, so newspapers shortened it to "con man."

• Another trickster in 1840s New York was Alec Hoag. He used prostitutes to lure men into hotel rooms. When the men's clothes were on the floor, Hoag lifted money from the pockets via a hole in the wall. He was known for his ability to stay one step ahead of the police…and brag about it all over the city. The nickname the cops gave to Hoag survives as a slang term used to describe an intelligent, cocky person: "smart alec."

That's teetotaling: In the 1820s, a temperance movement tried to ban coffee and nearly succeeded.

REAL TOYS OF THE CIA

*Uncle John loves those clever spy gadgets in the James
Bond movies devised by Q. It turns out that some of
them are real. Here are a few actual spy tools.*

IT LOOKS LIKE: A cigarette
BUT IT'S REALLY: A .22-caliber gun
DESCRIPTION: This brand of cigarette packs a powerful puff.
Intended as an escape tool, the weapon only carries a single round, but
with good aim it can inflict a lethal wound from close range. To fire the
cigarette, the operator must twist the filtered end counterclockwise, then
squeeze the same end between the thumb and forefinger. Warning: Don't
shoot the weapon in front of your face or body—it has a nasty recoil.

IT LOOKS LIKE: A pencil
BUT IT'S REALLY: A .22-caliber pistol
DESCRIPTION: Like the cigarette gun, this camouflaged .22 comes pre-
loaded with a single shot. The weapon is fired in the same manner as the
cigarette: simply turn the pencil's eraser counterclockwise and squeeze.
The only difference between the weapons
is that the pencil has a greater firing distance—up to 30 feet.

IT LOOKS LIKE: A belt buckle
BUT IT'S REALLY: A hacksaw
DESCRIPTION: Fitted inside a hollow belt buckle is a miniature hacksaw.
When the buckle is opened, a small amount of pressure is released from
the saw's frame, exerting tension on the blade. This makes the saw a more
efficient cutting machine, keeping the blade taut when sawing through,
for example, handcuffs. The belt buckle saw will cut through anything
from steel to concrete in about 15 minutes and will tear through rope and
nylon. Don't wear belts? Buckles can be put on coats and luggage, too.

IT LOOKS LIKE: Eyeglasses
BUT IT'S REALLY: A dagger
DESCRIPTION: Concealed in the temple arms of these CIA glasses are

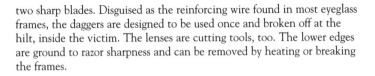

two sharp blades. Disguised as the reinforcing wire found in most eyeglass frames, the daggers are designed to be used once and broken off at the hilt, inside the victim. The lenses are cutting tools, too. The lower edges are ground to razor sharpness and can be removed by heating or breaking the frames.

IT LOOKS LIKE: A felt-tip marker
BUT IT'S REALLY: A blister-causing weapon
DESCRIPTION: Don't mistake this pen for your Sharpie, and be careful: you wouldn't want it leaking in your pocket. A little over three inches long, the marker distributes an ointment that creates blisters on the skin. In order to activate the applicator, press the tip down on a surface for one minute—then simply apply a thin coating of the colorless oil over any area, such as a keyboard or door handle. The ointment will penetrate clothing and even shoes, and will cause temporary blindness if it comes in contact with the eyes. Blisters will cover the skin wherever contact is made within 24 hours and will last for about a week.

IT LOOKS LIKE: Dentures
BUT IT'S REALLY: A concealment device (and much more)
DESCRIPTION: What could possibly fit inside a dental plate? A lot more than you'd think. Items such as a cutting wire or a compass can be placed in a small concealment tube and hidden under a false tooth. A rubber-coated poison pill can be carried in the same manner. The poison can either be ingested to avoid capture or poured into an enemy's food and utilized as a weapon. Radio transceivers can be placed in dental plates, with audio being transmitted through bone conduction. The CIA has even created a dental plate that alters the sound of one's voice. If all of these gadgets prove ineffective, then the dental plate itself can be removed and its sharp scalloped edge used for digging, cutting, or engaging in hand-to-hand combat.

*　　　*　　　*

James Bond: "They always said, 'The pen is mightier than the sword.'"
Q: "Thanks to me, they were right."

—Goldeneye

About 200 thefts of nuclear material are reported each year. Most of it is never recovered.

WHODUNIT?

*A young woman is murdered on her wedding night. Her lover is
charged with the crime, and the people and newspapers of New
York convict him before the trial even begins. Here's a murder
mystery that's ripped from the headlines...of 1799.*

A SENSATIONAL MURDER

On the evening of December 22, 1799, Gulielma "Elma" Sands got dressed up and left her home—a boarding house at 208 Greenwich Avenue, owned by Elias and Catherine Ring. She was never seen alive again. According to Catherine Ring, Elma's cousin, the young woman was planning to get married that night. Instead, 11 days later, her body was pulled out of the Manhattan Well, which stood near the intersections of Greene and Spring Streets in what is now SoHo, just a short carriage ride from the boarding house.

Elma's tragic death was the talk of New York. It was the city's first big murder mystery, and the press and public speculated over who might have killed her. Soon, suspicion fell on a young carpenter named Levi Weeks, who worked for his brother Ezra Weeks, a prominent, wealthy builder. Levi lived in the same boarding house as Elma and had been courting her for some time; the two were said to be lovers, a scandalous situation in the 18th century. After Catherine Ring claimed that Levi was the man Elma had planned to elope with on the night she disappeared, an inquest was held—and Levi Weeks was indicted for murder.

The newspapers, of course, weighed in with their own version of the story, speculating that Levi had seduced an innocent girl and murdered her because he didn't want to get married. Then fellow boarder Richard Croucher publicly declared that Weeks had an accomplice in New Jersey who'd confessed to the murder. By the time the trial began in 1800, the public already considered Weeks a guilty man. Elma's sympathizers packed the courtroom, and those who couldn't get in milled around outside, yelling, "Crucify him!"

LEVI'S LAWYERS

The U.S. legal system was only 11 years old when the Levi Weeks trial

---

Jesse James once wrote a press release about a train robbery, which he handed to the engineer.

began, and the idea that anyone accused of murder deserved more than torture or a quick hanging was still new. Trials ran all day—sometimes until well after midnight. Requests for breaks from exhausted lawyers on either side were frowned upon and often denied. Fortunately for Levi, his wealthy brother Ezra rounded up the most brilliant lawyers of the day— Alexander Hamilton, Aaron Burr, and Henry Brockholst Livingston—to defend him.

Hamilton, America's first Secretary of the Treasury, was one of the Founding Fathers and had been a trusted advisor to President George Washington. Burr was a hero of the Revolutionary War and former New York Senator who would go on to become the third vice president of the United States. Livingston was one of the nation's most prominent attorneys, and in 1802, he would become a justice on the U.S. Supreme Court.

LOOKING BAD FOR LEVI

The trial began at 10 a.m. on March 31, 1800. *New York Evening Post* editor William Coleman wrote a transcript of the proceedings, making the Weeks spectacle America's first recorded murder trial. After the jury was chosen, the prosecutor presented his case: Weeks had come to live at the Greenwich boarding house in July 1799 and seduced Elma Sands. He became secretly engaged to her sometime in the fall, promising to elope with her on December 22. On that evening, however, Weeks actually took his fiancée to the Manhattan Well, where he killed her. To back up his argument, the prosecutor presented testimony from a long string of witnesses.

Boarders at the Rings' home testified that Levi had been in Elma's room overnight several times, and that they appeared to be lovers. Catherine Ring testified that on December 22, Elma believed she was eloping with Weeks, and the two had exited the house within a short time of one another—Catherine heard them talking on the porch before they left. More witnesses said they'd seen a horse and sleigh near the crime scene that resembled one belonging to Levi's brother Ezra. There was even testimony from a witness who'd seen Levi measuring the Manhattan Well about a week before Elma disappeared. A medical expert testified that Elma's body showed signs of being badly beaten and strangled, and Levi was said to have returned to the boarding house looking "pale and nervous" the night Elma disappeared.

By the time the prosecution rested, things didn't look good for Levi.

Hello Kitty has appeared on more than 15,000 different products, including an AR-15 assault rifle.

Many in the courtroom believed that even the great triad of Hamilton, Burr, and Livingston wouldn't be able to save his life.

THE DEFENSE TO THE RESCUE

Hamilton and Burr did most of the defense work for the trial. Burr gave a stirring speech, asking the jury to set aside their anger toward Weeks and portraying the carpenter as "an injured and innocent young man" who'd never treated Elma badly. Then the defense brought in its own string of witnesses.

First, the defense established that Levi had an alibi—several people had seen him at Ezra's house on the evening of December 22, placing him far from the Manhattan Well area at the time Elma disappeared. Other witnesses asserted that Ezra's horse and sleigh never left the barn. Character witnesses spoke of Levi's "goodness." Defense medical experts declared that the marks on Elma's body could have come from her autopsy rather than from a deadly beating. (The autopsy had been carried out to determine whether Elma was pregnant; she wasn't.)

The defense also brought in boarders from the Rings' house on Greenwich Street. But these people contradicted the prosecution's version of Elma as a happy innocent girl until Levi seduced her. They claimed that Elma used a drug called laudanum—a powerful opiate— and that she'd talked of killing herself with an overdose. One man, who lived in the room next to Elma, said Levi Weeks wasn't her lover at all. According to him, Elias Ring, the owner of the boarding house, sometimes spent the night with Elma when his wife was away. Levi's defense team painted the Ring boarding house as a place of sexual intrigue—a kind of 18th-century Peyton Place with Elma as a key player. And as for the prosecution's star witness, boarder Richard Croucher, the defense showed that he hated Weeks and implied that he might have lied on the witness stand.

A VERDICT AND A CURSE

The trial of Levi Weeks lasted two days—longer than most criminal trials of the time. It broke for recess at 1:00 a.m. the first night, after some jurors nodded off. The next night, it ended after 2 a.m. At that point, the judge bluntly informed the jury that the prosecution's collection of circumstantial evidence was a flimsy basis for conviction. Five minutes later, the jury returned its verdict: not guilty.

Elvis once volunteered to be an FBI drug informant. (His services were refused.)

As the defense team congratulated each other, it's said that a furious Catherine Ring—whose dead cousin, marriage, and boarding house had all been dragged through the mud—cursed Alexander Hamilton. She supposedly shouted, "If thee dies a natural death, I shall think there is no justice in heaven!" And eerily, her curse came true five years later, when Hamilton and Burr, by then bitter political enemies, met on the dueling grounds at Weehawken, New Jersey, and Burr shot and killed Hamilton. Burr was eventually acquitted of murder, but his political career was over.

As for Levi Weeks, most New Yorkers disagreed with the jury's verdict and the young carpenter was run out of town. Sentiments eventually began to change when, less than a year after the trial, Richard Croucher was found guilty of raping a young girl in the Ring boarding house. Levi finally settled in Natchez, Mississippi, where he became a successful architect, married, and had a family.

Today, the Manhattan Well where Elma Sands met her end still exists—it's in the basement of Manhattan Bistro in Soho. From time to time, employees say, an eerie vapor rises in the kitchen, and Elma's ghost causes glasses and wine bottles to go flying.

*　　*　　*

WORST DRUG-SNIFFING DOG

"Falco," at the County Sheriff's Office, Knoxville, Tennessee

In August 2000, David and Pamela Stonebreaker were driving through Knoxville in their recreational vehicle when sheriff's deputies pulled them over for running a red light. The cops were suspicious and called for backup: a drug-sniffer named Falco. The dog sniffed outside the vehicle and signaled "positive," so deputies immediately searched the inside of the RV…and found more than a *quarter ton* of marijuana.

But in court, the Stonebreakers' attorney challenged the search—the dog couldn't be trusted. It turned out that between 1998 and 2000 Falco had signaled "positive" 225 times and the cops found drugs only 80 times. In other words, the dog was wrong nearly 70% of the time. Falco, the defense argued, was too incompetent to justify searching vehicles based on his "word" alone. The judge agreed and the Stonebreakers (their real name) went free.

Losing face: In ancient China, criminals caught robbing travelers had their noses cut off.

WHAT'S THE NUMBER FOR 911?

We have a lot of respect for 911 call-takers—not only must they remain calm for people in life-and-death situations, they have to try to make sense of callers like these folks.

Dispatcher: "Nine-one-one, what's the nature of your emergency, please?"
Caller: "I'm trying to reach nine-eleven, but my phone doesn't have an eleven on it."
Dispatcher: "This is nine-eleven."
Caller: "I thought you just said it was nine-one-one."
Dispatcher: "Yes, ma'am. Nine-one-one and nine-eleven are the same thing."
Caller: "Honey, I may be old, but I'm not stupid."

Dispatcher: "Nine-one-one. Please state your emergency."
Caller: "Yeah, okay. Bill got hurt."
Dispatcher: "Who is Bill?"
Caller: "Just some dude I know. We were tossing the Nerf around, and the TV fell and cut up his leg."
Dispatcher: "We'll send someone right over."
Caller (to someone in the room): "Get the keg outta here, dude!"

Dispatcher: "Nine-one-one. What's the nature of your emergency?"
Caller: "My wife is pregnant, and her contractions are only two minutes apart!"
Dispatcher: "Is this her first child?"
Caller: "No, you idiot! This is her husband!"

Dispatcher: "Nine-one-one."
Caller: "Yeah, I'm having trouble breathing. I'm all out of breath. Damn…I think I'm going to pass out."
Dispatcher: "Sir, where are you calling from?"
Caller: "I'm at a pay phone. North and Foster. Damn…"
Dispatcher: "Sir, an ambulance is on the way. Are you an asthmatic?"
Caller: "No…"
Dispatcher: "What were you doing before you started having trouble breathing?"
Caller: "Running from the police."

Crime slang: "Getting a Valentine" in convict lingo means to receive a one-year jail sentence.

SMILE: YOU'RE ON BAIT CAR!

*If you're a fan of YouTube, but you're tired of sorting through
millions of uploaded videos for something fresh, interesting,
and (of course) odd, here's a suggestion: Type "bait car"
in the search window, press return, and enjoy the ride.*

CAR TROUBLE

In the winter of 2001, police in Vancouver, British Columbia, were battling a ring of thieves who were stealing as many as five Japanese sports cars per week from the parking lots of local golf courses, then stripping the cars to sell the parts. Auto theft is a difficult crime to fight: Stolen cars change hands so quickly that even if you catch someone driving one, it's difficult to prove that they know it's stolen, let alone prove they're the one who stole it. You have to catch car thieves in the act, and that's not easy because they tend to break into cars when there are no witnesses around. And because car theft is a property crime, not a violent crime like kidnapping, assault, or murder, there's a limit to how much time and money police agencies can spend fighting it, especially when the odds of winning a conviction are so low. How low? Fewer than 15% of all car thefts end with the thief being jailed.

CANDID CAMERA

The Vancouver police department couldn't spare enough officers to stake out every golf course in the city. If they were going to catch the crooks they'd have to find another way. Phil Ens, a Vancouver police officer assigned to auto-theft detail, had heard about a program in Minneapolis, Minnesota, where police were using "bait cars"—cars wired with hidden audio and video equipment and GPS tracking devices, then left where thieves were likely to steal them. Police could track a car using its GPS signal, then shut off the car's engine by remote control as they moved in to make the arrest. The video evidence was then used to convict the thieves and send them to prison. The approach was effective: Auto thefts were down in Minneapolis, and prosecutors were winning convictions against

---

Leavenworth Prison's walls are 40 feet high and go 40 feet below the ground.

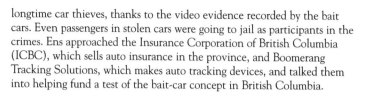

longtime car thieves, thanks to the video evidence recorded by the bait cars. Even passengers in stolen cars were going to jail as participants in the crimes. Ens approached the Insurance Corporation of British Columbia (ICBC), which sells auto insurance in the province, and Boomerang Tracking Solutions, which makes auto tracking devices, and talked them into helping fund a test of the bait-car concept in British Columbia.

GONE IN 2,700 SECONDS

Boomerang sent Ens an Acura Integra loaded with GPS tracking equipment and the remote-control device that allows police to shut off the engine. Ens added a hidden camera, a microphone, and a VCR. Then the police department placed the car in the parking lot of a local golf course...and made their first bait-car arrest just 45 minutes later.

ICBC was sold on the program—they decided to back it in a big way, donating recovered stolen cars to be wired up as bait cars and spending more than $500,000 a year to make them bait-car-ready. The provincial government of British Columbia agreed to pick up the rest of the tab, with the program to be administered by an interagency task force called the Integrated Municipal Provincial Auto Crime Team (IMPACT).

The program is still going strong today, and IMPACT continues to develop new and creative ways to put this powerful new crime-fighting tool to use. They have studied which cars are likely to be stolen in which parts of town, and plant the bait cars accordingly. They make the cars even more attractive targets by baiting them with a wallet, a purse, a cell phone, or even an open bag of potato chips left in plain view. Because car thieves commonly abandon stolen cars in the neighborhoods where they live (it's easier than walking home), if police can figure out where a particular car thief lives, they'll plant his favorite model of bait car right down the street from his house. Why stop at committed car thieves? Sometimes IMPACT even leaves bait cars unlocked with the keys in the ignition and the engine running to tempt opportunists who might not otherwise bother to break into a vehicle.

NOW SHOWING

Most of the time, police agencies keep their crime-fighting method secret to prevent criminals from figuring out ways around them. But IMPACT takes the opposite approach: They hope that by publicizing the bait-car

---

The TV show CSI caused a surge of college applications for courses in forensic science.

program as much as possible, they can convince criminals (and wannabes) that auto theft is not an easy, low-risk crime—that it's actually a crime in which arrest is almost inevitable, the charges will stick, and the penalty will be months or even years in jail. They want the crooks to believe that bait cars are *everywhere*.

What makes this interesting for the rest of us is that IMPACT has set up a Web site (www.baitcar.com) where they post actual bait-car video clips for you to watch and enjoy. The clips are making their way to other popular sites like Google Video and YouTube, too. They're worth a look: When you watch the grainy hidden-camera footage, it almost feels as like you're there in person to witness the thrill of victory as punks break into cars and speed off on a joyride, followed by the agony of defeat as they are arrested by police a short time later.

CAT AND MOUSE

Vancouver's program is working: Since it was instituted in 2002, car thefts have dropped more than 15%, with 6,000 fewer cars being stolen each year. ICBC is saving nearly $15 million a year through reduced payments to auto-theft victims. The publicity campaign and especially the bait car footage are credited with much of the success: As the bait cars themselves pull incorrigible car thieves off the streets, the footage of them being caught and taken to jail is causing less-committed thieves to lose heart and prompting at-risk, "entry-level" youth to reconsider whether they really want to begin stealing cars in the first place. "Auto theft went down right away because of word-of-mouth among the thieves," Ens told the *Vancouver Province* in 2005. "It created a level of paranoia and the advertising kept it in their conscience."

WATCH, LAUGH...AND LEARN

Are you ready to have a few laughs at the expense of ethically challenged Canadian punks? Here are the titles of some classic bait-car footage to look for. (*Warning!* Bait-car footage contains coarse language and is *not* suitable for children.)

• **I Was Caught By a Bait Car!** A mini-documentary featuring bait-car footage and a later interview with the 22-year-old car thief, who describes what it is like to be caught red-handed stealing a bait car ("I knew it was a #*&$ bait car! They bait-carred my @*&!" he says as the

---

Half of all crimes are committed by people under the age of 18.

police shut off his engine by remote control), and what it's like for a reformed car thief to view his own bait-car footage for the very first time ("I look like a retard!").

• **The Prayer.** Watch as a 19-year-old car thief and his 21-year-old accomplice steal a car, do donuts in an open field and then, with the driver's hands folded into a steeple on the steering wheel, pray aloud that the car coming up behind them is not a police car. "Please don't be a cop! Pray it's not a cop! Pray, pray, pray, just pray!" (Their prayers went unanswered.)

• **I Hope This Isn't Another %$&* Bait Car, Man!** (a.k.a. The Nose Picker). Who says car thieves have to be men? View footage of British Columbia's first-ever arrest of a *female* car thief. Watch as she and her accomplice pick up a male associate, then tag along as he picks a winner and disposes of the "evidence" in disgusting fashion moments before the police arrive on the scene.

• **If My Mom Calls.** Three punk kids steal a bait car just one day after one of them has been released from custody (perhaps for stealing another car?). Listen as their fear increases with the dawning realization that they are indeed driving a bait car, that arrest is only moments away…and that Mom is going to be really, really mad when she finds out.

• **High-Speed Escape.** Rare footage of crooks stealing *two* bait vehicles at the same time. After the bait *car* program became successful, the Vancouver police department expanded to bait motorcycles, bait ATVs, bait snowmobiles, and even bait Jet Skis. These dopes stole a bait ATV and threw it onto the back of a stolen pickup truck…which turned out to be a bait car, too.

• **So Much for Going Home.** The only thing funnier than watching these four kids count the patrol cars as they close in behind them—"Oh yeah, there's one, two, there's three! Yeah, it's a bait car, dude!"—is listening to them being arrested by a cop with a Scottish accent thicker than *The Simpsons'* Groundskeeper Willie.

* * *

"All I wanted was to be what I became to be." —**John Gotti**

First female police chief in America: Dolly Spencer of Milford, Ohio, in 1914.

HARD-BOILED HAMMETT, PART II

*On page 197 we introduced you to Dashiell Hammett,
the man who invented private detective Sam Spade.
Here's a sordid tale of fame, drinking, and politics.*

MEAN STREETS

After Hammett's highly successful run with *Black Mask*, he published his first full novel, *Red Harvest*, in 1929. Drawing on his strike-breaking experience with Pinkertons, Hammett used his Continental Op character to narrate the tale of a corrupt and lawless Montana mining town in the aftermath of a violent labor clash. Just a few months later, Hammett and the Continental Op were back with *The Dain Curse*. Without stopping for a rest, he then banged out *The Maltese Falcon* in time for a spring 1930 release.

Considered his finest novel, *The Maltese Falcon* introduced Sam Spade, who became one of America's best-known fictional heroes during the tough times of the Great Depression. In a decade that saw a high rise in crime—especially in the nation's cities—readers looked up to Spade. He was tough but full of integrity and got results from playing by his own rules. Spade's world was violent, unsympathetic, and full of irony and black humor. Readers ate it up. Sam Spade went on to star in radio dramas, comic books, and on film. Three different movies were made of *The Maltese Falcon*; the classic 1941 Humphrey Bogart version was the third.

EASY STREET

The 1930s was a good decade for Hammett. He was rich and famous (and single), hopping back and forth between Manhattan and Los Angeles to attend star-studded parties with the likes of Harpo Marx, Jean Harlow, F. Scott Fitzgerald, and William Faulkner. Hammett drank and partied for days at a time. But he was also writing. He would work on movie scripts, first at Paramount and later at MGM—where he was paid $2,000 per week. In 1934 he published his fifth and final novel, *The Thin Man*, which spawned a series of films starring William Powell and Myrna

Loy. He wrote script stories for three *The Thin Man* sequels but found writing for Hollywood less rewarding than writing novels. So he worked as little as he could get away with and drank heavily. Result: Hammett garnered an "unreliable" reputation among the film studios. His earlier impressive productivity soon fizzled into nothing. He wanted to get away from detective fiction and write more serious novels, but could never bring himself to do it. "I quit writing because I was repeating myself," he later explained. "It is the beginning of the end when you notice that you have style."

Perhaps Hammett could have written the Great American Novel had he not become such a raging alcoholic. His daughter Jo Hammett recounts in her biography, *A Daughter Remembers*, that the drinking "turned my father maudlin, sarcastic, and mean." He lost focus, starting many projects and finishing none of them.

But with a steady stream of royalties coming in, he didn't have to work, so in the 1940s Hammett became involved in leftist politics. Still stung from his strike-breaking days in Montana, Hammett became a civil rights activist and staunch opponent of Nazi Germany. Despite his age—he was in his 40s—he reenlisted to serve in World War II. They shipped him off to the Aleutian Islands in Alaska, where he spent nearly three years editing a newspaper for the troops and helping train young writers to be good news correspondents. Hammett said later that this was the last happy time of his life.

LEFT OUT

When he returned home, Hammett found himself ostracized from the industry that made him famous. Moving further to the fringe, he became vice-chairman of the leftist Civil Rights Congress in 1948, an organization that the FBI called "subversive." He also quit drinking that year, but the damage had been done—his immune system was shot, making him continuously sick with a hacking cough that was as unpleasant for Hammett as it was for those around him.

Downtrodden and out of the public eye, in 1951 Hammett was ordered to turn over a list of names of contributors to the Civil Rights Congress. But he refused. Following in the footsteps of the Continental Op and Sam Spade, he remained loyal and didn't "rat them out." Taking the Fifth, Hammett was charged with contempt of court and thrown into federal prison for five months. When he got out, he was informed by the IRS that he owed hundreds of thousands of dollars in back taxes. They garnished all his income from new publications or productions of his previous work. His days of being the toast of Tinseltown now seemed like ancient history. Hammett was broke and alone, and his health was deteriorating. He took a job in New York teaching creative writing just to pay the bills.

THE LAST CHAPTER

In 1953—at the height of the United States' anti-Communist era—Hammett was called before Senator Joseph McCarthy's House Un-American Activities Committee. McCarthy aide Roy Cohn repeatedly asked Hammett if he was a Communist. Hammett repeatedly said no. "Were you a Communist when you wrote these books?" "No." "Has any of the money you made from these books financed any Communist organizations?" "Not to my knowledge." Without an admission or evidence, McCarthy could do nothing to Hammett, but the damage had been done.

Financially in ruin, Hammett had a major heart attack in 1955. He was unable to care for himself, and was taken in by a longtime friend and confidant, writer Lillian Hellman. She moved him into her Park Avenue apartment where she saw to his needs while he edited her plays. Hammett contracted lung cancer and died in 1961 at the age of 67.

EPILOGUE

"He very much wanted to be remembered as an American writer," wrote his daughter Jo Hammett. "He was always very proud of his heritage, and it shows in his treatment of the language. Few people have written American speech as well as he did."

But more than just an American writer, Dashiell Hammett wanted to be remembered as a true American. As a veteran of two World Wars, he requested that he be buried at Arlington National Cemetery. FBI Director J. Edgar Hoover objected but was overruled. Hammett's headstone, located in Section 12 of the cemetery, simply reads:

Samuel D. Hammett
Sergeant, U.S. Army
1894–1961

America's 5,000 or so prisons and jails employ more than 400,000 people.

CLASSIC HAMMETT

Dashiell Hammett's style has inspired so many writers,
actors, and filmmakers that it's nice to go to the source
himself to read some of his grittiest crime prose.

Poisonville is an ugly city of forty thousand people, set in an ugly notch between two ugly mountains that had been all dirtied up by mining. Spread over this was a grimy sky that looked as if it had come out of smelters' stacks.

—**Red Harvest**

On Spade's desk a limp cigarette smoldered in a brass tray filled with the remains of limp cigarettes. Ragged grey flakes of cigarette-ash dotted the yellow top of the desk and the green blotter and the papers that were there. A buff-curtained window, eight or ten inches open, let in from the court a current of air faintly scented with ammonia. The ashes on the desk twitched and crawled in the current.

—**The Maltese Falcon**

Out of the moving automobile a man stepped. Miraculously he kept his feet, stumbling, sliding, until an arm crooked around an iron awning-post jerked him into an abrupt halt. He was a large man in bleached khaki, tall, broad, and thick-armed; his grey eyes were bloodshot; face and clothing were powdered heavily with dust. One of his hands clutched a thick, black stick, the other swept off his hat, and he bowed with exaggerated lowness before the girl's angry gaze.

The bow completed, he tossed his hat carelessly into the street, and grinned grotesquely through the dirt that masked his face, a grin that accented the heaviness of a begrimed and hair-roughened jaw.

"I beg y'r par'on," he said. "'F I hadn't been careful I believe I'd a'most hit you. 'S unreli'ble, tha' wagon. Borr'ed it from an engi—eng'neer. Don't ever borrow one from eng'neer. They're unreli'ble."

The girl looked at the place where he stood as if no one stood there, as if, in fact, no one had ever stood there, turned her small back on him, and walked very precisely down the street.

—**Nightmare Town**

The Monopoly character locked behind bars: Jake the Jailbird. (Policeman: Officer Edgar Mallory.)

I was leaning against the bar in a speakeasy on Fifty-second Street, waiting for Nora to finish her Christmas shopping, when a girl got up from the table where she had been sitting with three other people and came over to see me. She was small and blonde, and whether you looked at her face or at her body in powder-blue sports clothes, the result was satisfactory. "Aren't you Nick Charles?" she asked.

I said: "Yes."

She held out her hand. "I'm Dorothy Wynant. You don't remember me, but you ought to remember my father, Clyde Wynant. You—"

"Sure," I said, "and I remember you now, but you were only a kid of eleven or twelve then, weren't you?"

"Yes, that was eight years ago. Listen: remember those stories you told me? Were they true?"

"Probably not. How is your father?"

—The Thin Man

"Don Wilson's gone to sit at the right hand of God, if God doesn't mind looking at bullet holes."

"Who shot him?" I asked.

The grey man scratched the back of his neck and said: "Somebody with a gun."

—Red Harvest

"You ought to have known I'd do it." My voice sounded harsh and savage and like a stranger's in my ear. "Didn't I steal a crutch from a cripple?"

—The Continental Op, "The Gutting of Couffignal"

"Do you think he'll play ball with you after he's re-elected?"

Madvig was not worried. "I can handle him."

"Maybe, but don't forget he's never been licked by anything in his life."

Madvig nodded in complete agreement. "Sure, that's one of the best reasons I know for throwing in with him."

"No it isn't, Paul," Ned Beaumont said earnestly. "It's the very worst. Think that over even if it hurts your head. How far has this dizzy blond daughter of his got her hooks into you?"

—The Glass Key

Pretty Boy Floyd's first robbery: At age 18 he stole $3.50 in pennies from a local post office.

KILLER KARAOKE

"And now, the end is near…" is the opening line of the song "My Way." Alas, in some karaoke bars in the Philippines, that's not just a lyric but an eerily accurate prediction.

HE DID IT HIS WAY

In 1968 Frank Sinatra invited 27-year-old singer/songwriter Paul Anka to dinner, where Sinatra revealed that he was thinking of retiring from the music business. He asked Anka to write a farewell song for him. Anka already had a tune—he liked the melody of a song called "Comme d'Habitude" ("As Usual") that he'd heard while vacationing on the French Riviera. He did not like the self-pitying French lyrics about living in a loveless relationship, however, so he got the composers' permission to write new English lyrics for it.

Anka began the lyrics that very night. As he worked, he tried to make it a song about Sinatra's life, written from Sinatra's point of view, heavy with swaggering bravado. He finished at 5:00 a.m. and flew out to Las Vegas to sing it to Sinatra. The song: "My Way." It became the archetypal later-Sinatra song, so much so that Sinatra didn't retire. It became one of the most popular, most recorded songs of all time, and a staple of karaoke bars around the world. But in one country, the Philippines, the song has taken a dark turn.

ALL YOU NEED IS DEATH

The "My Way Killings" is what Philippine newspapers call them. Nobody really knows how many people have been killed during a karaoke performance of the song, but in early 2010, the *New York Times* reported that there have been "at least a half-dozen" deaths in recent years. (The *Asia Times* estimates that the number is in the dozens.) Some of the cases include:

• A singer in a San Mateo bar who ignored a heckler who complained that the guy was singing out of tune. Midway through the song, the heckler pulled out a .38-caliber pistol and shot the performer in the chest, killing him instantly.

• Faced by hecklers, another singer took the initiative and shot two audience members, killing one.

• A "Sinatra-loving crowd" reportedly rushed the stage en masse and beat a singer to death for his poor performance of "My Way." The situation so spooked employees and patrons that many karaoke bars removed the song from their machines, and families banned it from their sing-along gatherings.

As an inexpensive form of entertainment in a relatively poor country, karaoke has become an important part of Philippine culture. It's hard to escape the sound of somebody singing along to synthesized music—you can hear it in bars and nightclubs, at family gatherings, even on the street or in malls, courtesy of coin-operated kiosks. And apparently singers take their performances seriously, taking offense at audience inattention or heckling; hard-core audiences can get ugly when someone steps up to the mike unprepared or out of tune.

MY WAY OR THE HIGHWAY

But what puts "My Way" into its own category of karaoke danger? Observers suggest two possible reasons:

1. It's sung too often. On any given night, a bar-hopper in the Philippines would likely hear "My Way" performed several times, enough to drive a music lover to despair even if it was sung well. When sung badly…well, get ready to duck.

2. Because of its arrogant lyrics. The lyrics brag about being a tough guy who follows his own course, implying that anybody who doesn't is a loser. Perhaps Sinatra could get away with it, but when a taxi driver sings those lyrics, some listeners just want to pop the guy, or at least put him in his place.

THE END IS NEAR

In a hot, crowded bar, in a desperate society with millions of illegal handguns, it's easy for irritation to boil up into murderous rage. Many Manila karaoke bars have now banned the singing of "My Way" to protect patrons from alcohol-fueled fights. (Even Sinatra grew to hate it. After performing it in 1984 at London's Albert Hall, he was heard muttering, "I can't stand that song.") Although "My Way" is one of the most played at funerals and is even quoted on gravestones, Sinatra chose another of his songs as his epitaph: "The Best Is Yet to Come."

Mugging someone on a subway in Britain can get you life in prison.

THE LAST PAGE

FELLOW BATHROOM READERS:
  The fight for good bathroom reading should never be taken loosely—
we must do our duty and sit firmly for what we believe in, even
while the rest of the world is taking potshots at us.

  We'll be brief. Now that we've proven we're not simply a flush-in-the-
pan, we invite you to take the plunge: Sit Down and Be Counted! Log
on to *www.bathroomreader.com* and earn a permanent spot on the BRI
honor roll!

If you like reading our books...
VISIT THE BRI'S WEB SITE!
www.bathroomreader.com

- Visit "The Throne Room"—a great place to read!
  - Receive our irregular newsletters via e-mail
    - Order additional *Bathroom Readers*
      - Read our blog

Go with the Flow...

Well, we're out of space, and when you've gotta go, you've gotta go.
Tanks for all your support. Hope to hear from you soon.

Meanwhile, remember...

Keep on flushin'!